THE AMERICAN REVOLUTION
AND
THE BRITISH EMPIRE

THE
AMERICAN REVOLUTION
AND
THE BRITISH EMPIRE

THE SIR GEORGE WATSON LECTURES FOR 1928,
DELIVERED BEFORE THE UNIVERSITY OF LONDON
IN THE WINTER OF 1928-9

BY

R. COUPLAND

NEW YORK / RUSSELL & RUSSELL

1965

FIRST PUBLISHED IN 1930

REISSUED, 1965, BY RUSSELL & RUSSELL

BY ARRANGEMENT WITH LONGMANS, GREEN & CO., LTD., LONDON

L.C. CATALOG CARD NO: 65—18801

PRINTED IN THE UNITED STATES OF AMERICA

PREFACE.

THE text of these lectures has been expanded and re-arranged since their delivery, and divided into eight parts instead of six; but the substance is unaltered.

The author's warm thanks are due to Mr. C. R. M. F. Cruttwell for reading the proofs of the whole book, and to Professors W. P. M. Kennedy, Chester Martin, and G. M. Wrong for reading Lecture VII in typescript. He has greatly benefited from their criticisms and suggestions, but none of them, of course, must be saddled with any of his opinions.

The author would also like to take this opportunity of thanking the Provost and Fellows of University College for their courtesy at the time the lectures were delivered.

R. C.

WOOTTON HILL,
July, 1930.

v

CONTENTS.

APPENDIX.

I.

ENGLAND IN DEFEAT.

ON Sunday, 15 August, 1779, a fleet of over forty warships came to anchor in Falmouth Bay. The spectacle occasioned no surprise among the inhabitants of the Cornish coast. It was known that the British fleet under Admiral Hardy was cruising somewhere in the Channel; and in due course a boat put out from St. Keverne with a couple of local seamen at the oars and a stock of fresh provisions on board with which they intended—though it was Sunday and they were Cornishmen of Wesley's time—to do a little business on the ships. ' A young lady,' so the story goes, ' daughter of a merchant there, out of curiosity, went in the boat.' There must have been a haze on the water, for only when they reached the flagship did they discover, to their amazement and alarm, that it was not Sir Charles Hardy's but the Spanish Admiral's ! ' The Spaniards treated them very civilly,' the tale continues, ' the officers paying for such vegetables, etc., as they wanted and the sailors made free with the remainder.' One of the two seamen, an elderly man, was detained to serve as pilot. ' They desired the young man to bring some vegetables to them off

Plymouth, where they said they should be the next day, but this he declined.' The story ends there; but, since some one survived to tell it, we may assume that the second seaman was allowed to escort the curious young lady back to her father. What happened to the ancient is unknown.[1]

That is rather a startling little story to those, at any rate, who do not know how nearly England was invaded in 1779 and how it was the enemy's own fault that Falmouth and Plymouth were not occupied. It will never, unfortunately, be forgotten that England fought a war with the purpose of suppressing the American Revolution. What has been at least half-forgotten is the magnitude of England's failure and of the blow it dealt to her power, her pride, and her prestige. It is not unnatural. Our defeat in the War of American Independence stands as the most damaging and humiliating defeat in all our records; and it is a deep-rooted habit of the mind to try in self-protection to avoid dwelling on painful memories and to thrust them consciously or subconsciously into the background. The school text-books from which most Englishmen acquire their only knowledge of history are not more myopic than those of other countries. Our national chauvinism has never gone so far as to deny or to conceal reverses—after the event,

---

[1] The story is reported in a letter from Dr. Farr, of Plymouth, to James Harris, M.P. (afterwards first Earl of Malmesbury), 22, viii, 1779. Dr. Farr had it from Mr. Fox, a Falmouth merchant. *Letters of the first Earl of Malmesbury* (London, 1860), i, 428.

at any rate. But does any Englishman, did any of us at school or college, really appreciate the facts of 1775 to 1783 ? Pupils and teachers alike, did we not unwittingly avert our eyes a little ? The disastrous conflict with our kinsmen lay sandwiched between the triumphant conflicts with Louis XIV and Napoleon—an incongruous, illogical, detestable interlude in the glorious drama of England's championship of freedom. How could we linger morbidly over Saratoga and York Town ? Inevitably, humanly, we hurried on from Quiberon Bay and the heights of Abraham to Trafalgar and Waterloo.

But, since it is the object of this course of lectures to discuss the effects of the American Revolution on the subsequent development of the British Empire, it is necessary, at the very outset, to drag those painful memories out of the backs of our minds and to consider, more closely perhaps than has been customary, the main facts of that unpleasant experience and especially the impression it made on contemporary Englishmen.

The main facts are these. For the first three years of the war, from 1775 to 1778, the British, with a population (excluding Ireland) of about eight millions, were pitted only against the Americans, with a population (excluding slaves) of between two and three millions. The British troops were regular soldiers, aided after a time by German mercenaries ; but they were the invaders of a vast, little-known, mainly trackless country. The American troops were merely militia ; but they were defending their own homes. The character of the fighting throughout was desultory and spasmodic : it almost ceased in the rigours of winter : and for those first three years it was indecisive. On the one side, Carleton repelled the invasion of Canada, and Howe carried out a successful campaign in New York and Pennsylvania. On the other side, Washington captured the garrison of Trenton, and Schuyler compelled the surrender of Burgoyne and over 5000 men at Saratoga. This last great blow was not in itself by any means irreparable ; but it convinced the French Government that the day it had eagerly awaited for fifteen years had come. In 1778 France allied herself with the Americans, and from that moment the whole character of the war was changed. Without the French gold, already secretly provided but now openly assured them, the Americans could hardly have continued fighting for lack of coin and credit. The French fleet, the second strongest in the world, at once endangered that mastery of the Atlantic without which England on her side would be paralysed. And when, in 1779, Spain, the third naval Power, joined France, England, though she still continued to fight with vacillating fortunes in America, was standing at bay in Europe, in greater danger than she had ever been since the reign of Elizabeth. In the course of that black summer she lost the command even of her own narrow seas. For nearly two months the combined French and Spanish fleets, numbering at least sixty ships of the line with their attendant frigates, cruised unmolested in the Channel. The English admiral, with only thirty-eight ships of the line at his command, could not venture a battle in open water. The capture of Plymouth, before which the armada of Bourbon autocracy rode at its ease, was daily expected. And at Havre and St. Malo, French armies, 50,000 strong with 400 transports ready, were waiting to descend on English soil. When, at the end of September, the combined fleets returned to port, it was only their feeble and divided leadership, their poor equipment, the spread of sickness among their seamen, and the approach of autumn gales that had saved England from invasion.[1] And invasion—on a minute scale, it is true, but none the less humiliating—was actually achieved on other coasts. In 1778 that daring Scottish sailor, smuggler, and slave-trader, Paul Jones, who had espoused the American cause, made one landing at Whitehaven, where he seized the forts and destroyed the shipping, and another on the opposite side of Solway Firth where he looted Lord Selkirk's mansion, and then sailed off to Belfast Lough where he captured some fishing vessels and a British sloop. In 1779, with

[1] A full account, based on naval records, is given by Capt. W. M. James, *The British Navy in Adversity* (London, 1926), chap. xii. It seems probable that the Commander-in-Chief, d'Orvilliers, would have achieved a landing if (1) the Spanish fleet had not been late in joining up with the French, and (2) the plan of invasion had not been suddenly changed at Paris when d'Orvilliers was actually anchored in sight of Plymouth.

five ships, he first haunted the coast of Kerry, ' making frequent descents ' ; next, snatched some prizes off Scotland and threatened Leith Roads and the mouth of the Humber ; and, last, intercepted a British merchant-fleet from the Baltic off Yorkshire, and fought a desperate and successful action with its convoy. So much for the proud traditions of the ' sceptred isle,' the ' moat defensive,' and the ' triumphant sea ' ! In 1780, the Dutch, the last remaining sea-power of importance, joined in the continental league for the downfall of England, while Russia, Sweden, and Denmark, followed presently by Prussia and all the other maritime States, even Portugal, even Turkey, constituted the ' Armed Neutrality ' to prevent the seizure of neutral shipping by British cruisers.

Meantime, of course, the loss or at least the interruption of the command of the sea had seriously affected the outposts of the British Empire and its lines of communication. The French quickly mopped up all the British trading posts on the West African coast. Masters for a time of the Caribbean, they seized several of the British Islands in the West Indies, including Tobago, rich in cotton. Spain reconquered West Florida and captured the Bahamas. At the beginning of 1782, in all those waters, only Jamaica, Barbadoes, and Antigua remained in British hands. The position in the Mediterranean was no less alarming. The two key-strongholds, Minorca and Gibraltar, were long and closely besieged. Minorca fell at last in February, 1782, and nothing less than Elliott's magnificent three years' defence could have saved Gibraltar. And, if the outposts of the imperial structure could be thus captured or invested, the losses to British shipping, strung out along the open lines between them, were inevitably heavy. 'After the European Powers took part in the conflict,' to quote the eloquent historian of the Revolution whose loss we have lately mourned on both sides of the Atlantic, ' the annual average of our losses by capture rose to nearly to six hundred ships ; and, before the war ended, almost exactly three thousand British merchantmen had fallen into the hands of an enemy.' [1] The most striking and costly of those losses was the capture in 1780 off the Spanish coast of the great annual trading-fleet of nearly sixty ships, bound for the East and West Indies, carrying hundreds of officials, soldiers, and civil passengers, and a huge cargo of merchandise and military and naval supplies. About the same time fourteen ships of the ' Quebec Fleet ' were taken off Newfoundland. Such losses as these not only weakened the fighting-line overseas : Warren Hastings, for example, struggling against odds to maintain the British position in India, was in desperate need of those intercepted cargoes. They also, of course, dealt a serious blow to trade and industry at home. There were patches of that artificial

[1] Sir G. O. Trevelyan, *The American Revolution* (London, 1921), v, 158.

prosperity which feeds on war-contracts, but the economic complexion of England as a whole deepened steadily from grey to black. The merchant princes of the City had never known such humiliating anxiety. The safe arrival of any of the ships in which their wealth was invested was a matter for exuberant rejoicing. Their loss was never a surprise. Old-established firms went bankrupt. Rich men were ruined. Leaders of society sank into obscurity. And the whole class of their subordinates inevitably suffered with them. Unemployment rapidly increased. There was more suffering among the poor than anyone alive had known. And naturally this gloomy picture was reflected in the public finances. The cost of the fighting services rose year by year to over twenty millions. Despite increased taxation the National Debt was doubled before the end of the war, when it stood, funded and unfunded, not far short of £250,000,000. The ' three per cents.' fell from 89 to 57. No financial expert could deny that the country was sliding fast towards bankruptcy.

Such was the situation when the long, disjointed, vacillating warfare in America came at last to an end. On 19 October, 1781, Cornwallis surrendered at York Town with ' the last remains,' as Chatham had called them, ' of the all-conquering forces of Great Britain ' ;[1] and York Town, unlike Saratoga,

---

[1] Chatham to Shelburne, 18 Dec., 1777, in Lord Fitzmaurice, *Life of William, Earl of Shelburne* (London, 1912), ii, 9.

was decisive. It was clear, even to George III, that America could not now be conquered by invasion. It was clear, secondly, to the great majority of his subjects, that American Independence must now be conceded. It was clear, thirdly, to every one that this removal of the *casus belli* would clear the road to peace. It was clear, fourthly, to almost every one that England needed peace on virtually any terms. And then, at this eleventh hour, the tide turned. By the Battle of the Saints in the spring of 1782 Rodney went far to restore to England the command of the sea. In the following autumn the long and elaborately prepared attack on Gibraltar was beaten off with heavy loss and the fortress finally relieved. It was enough, not indeed to make peace less necessary, but to make it purchasable at a lower price; and the treaties concluded in 1783 must be judged, at this length of time, at least as favourable as England, so near the end of her resources, could expect. But they were none the less mortifying. Most of the captured islands in the West Indies were restored; but Tobago was ceded and St. Lucia given back to France. East as well as West Florida passed to Spain. In West Africa, Gambia was retained, but Senegal and Goree relinquished. The French recovered their forts and trading posts in India. In these and similar minor features, the Peace of 1783 was in sufficiently glaring contrast with the Peace of 1763. But, of course, all the rest of it together was not half as disastrous or half as humiliating as the loss of the thirteen American Colonies. Previous wars, and very notably the last, had increased, in strength and size, the body of the British Empire. This war had torn so great a limb away from it as almost, it seemed, to destroy it altogether.[1]

Those, barely stated, are the facts. Let us now consider the nature of the impression which they made on Englishmen's minds. Let us try to stand in the shoes of those ancestors of ours and look through their eyes at what was happening around them. And we will begin with an Englishman who, to the great profit not merely of historians but of all students of human nature, left behind him in his innumerable letters a more detailed revelation of himself than anyone else in his day.

Throughout those anxious years Horace Walpole was living his customary life in his terrible toy-castle at Strawberry Hill in the rural parish of Twickenham, with his gout and his bric-a-brac and his tea-tray and the dogs and the cats and the gold-fish and the squirrels, outwardly as vivacious and nimble-witted and cynically cheerful as of old despite his sixty years, but inwardly—it is obvious again and again—more deeply concerned about bigger matters than his friendships and his comforts and his tastes than he had ever been before. It is not only the bad news of the fighting on land or sea that moves

[1] The British Empire had lost at least a quarter of its white population : see L. C. A. Knowles, *Economic Development of the Overseas Empire*, 1763-1914 (London, 1924), ii.

him : he sees himself at Twickenham the effects of the war on the welfare of the nation. ' Distress is already felt,' he writes in 1778 ; ' one hears of nothing but of the want of money ; one sees it every hour. I sit in my blue window and miss nine in ten of the carriages that used to pass before it. Houses sell for nothing which, two years ago, nabobs would have given lacks of diamonds for.' Three years later, on a visit to London, ' the distress of the public . . . is visible even in this extravagant and thoughtless city. The number of houses to be let in every street, whoever runs may read.' Indeed, the letters of the war period are the most serious of the whole collection. The self-conscious author still turns his polished phrases. He can make his witticisms and his puns about the misfortunes of the nation ; but, none the less, he feels them. An hereditary and tenacious Whig, he can regard what he calls the ' flagrancy of a civil war ' in America from a very different angle from that of the supporters of the Court ; but, none the less, he is conscious of its humiliations. And at times, especially when his English pride is wounded to the quick on the sore point of sea-power, the patriot flames through the poseur and the partisan. As early as the spring of 1778, convinced that France was on the brink of war, he had formed the gloomiest opinions. ' There are no grounds for confidence anywhere. We shall moulder piecemeal into our insignificant islandhood.' ' The term *Great Britain* will be a jest,' he writes

that summer ; and, on the news of the French in-
tervention, ' To be ruined by France ! ' he cries ;
' there the Englishman in me feels again. . . . It
is difficult to be very tranquil when the navy of
England is at stake.' In 1779, when Spain, too,
enters the arena, the tone of pessimism hardens. ' I
do but look on and lament the fall of England.'
' They [the Government] have hurried us, and then
blundered us, into a civil war, a French war, a
Spanish war. America is lost ; Jamaica, the West
Indian islands, Gibraltar, and Port Mahon, are
scarce to be saved ; Ireland is in great danger from
invasion or provocation.' ' I see no way by which
we can escape happily out of this crisis. . . . So
adieu, England ! it will be more or less a province
or kind of province to France.' ' At present '—the
date is now 23 August—' the combined fleets are
gone or blown from Plymouth, and the bells at
Richmond rang last night as if they were gone to
the bottom. . . . Yet it is below a man to rail when
England totters to its foundations. Disgraced it is
for ever ! ' At the end of 1779, he allows himself
one of his characteristic flippancies. ' All the good
news I know is that the devil of a winter is come
in that will send armies and navies to bed. . . . I
am heartily glad that we shall keep Jamaica and the
East Indies another year, that one may have time to
lay in a stock of tea and sugar for the rest of one's
days.' But the rupture with Holland at the New
Year provides one of the most serious—and finest

—passages he ever wrote. ' Is it possible that we should not sink in this ocean of troubles ? . . . In vain that selfish uncomfortable question occurs : " What is it to thee, poor skeleton, what is the future fate of thy country ? The churchyard at Houghton will not be narrower than it is." Still the love of that country, of its liberty and prosperity, will be uppermost, and grief for its fall.' And so the old patriot's heart goes on sinking and sinking till, after York Town, in a letter to Lord Strafford who had often deplored his lack of an heir, it touches bottom. ' You must be happy *now* not to have a son, who would live to grovel in the dregs of England.' [1]

Black pessimism, then, was the product of the American war in one intelligent Englishman's mind at any rate. But, it may be asked, was Horace Walpole typical ? This endless talk of ruin and desolation, these ' good-byes ' to England, that last appalling groan—is any of it really sincere ? Or, if sincere, is it not a bit hysterical, a bit morbid, the sort of thing one would expect from a neurotic invalid ? Did any other Englishman think or talk like that ? Yes. Far greater Englishmen than Walpole used almost the same language. At the

[1] *Letters of Horace Walpole*, ed. Mrs. Paget Toynbee (London 1904), x, 269 ; xii, 113 ; x, 238, 205, 272, 284, 386, 432, 445 ; xi, 15, 53, 92, 105. See also x, 240 (on losing ' the throne of Neptune ') ; xii, 59 (' viceroys of the Channel . . . during their pleasure,' i.e. of France and Spain) ; xii, 141 (' Nothing will be left of England but the vestiges of its grandeur ') ; and other similar passages.

beginning of 1778 the Countess of Chatham described what was passing in her husband's mind in a letter to one of his friends. ' He sees,' she wrote, ' the distractions and ruin impending over us, and fears that nothing is left for the zeal of the best intentioned, however called upon, but to do their duty and fall with a falling country.'[1] That may probably be taken as a not unfaithful reproduction of the burden of Chatham's talk in those days of his despondency. Three months later, the last words of the last speech he made in Parliament were these : ' If we must fall, let us fall like men.'[2]   Nor was that the first, though certainly the most impressive, nor by any means the last occasion on which the House of Lords was warned of impending ruin. ' The moment,' Shelburne had declared a few weeks earlier, ' that the independence of America is agreed to by our Government, the sun of Great Britain is set, and we shall no longer be a powerful or respectable people.'[3]   Listen, too, to the greatest of all

[1] Countess of Chatham to Thomas Coutts, Hayes, 14 Jan., 1778, in E. H. Coleridge, *Life of T. Coutts* (London, 1920), i, 98.

[2] B. Williams, *Life of William Pitt* (London, 1913), ii, 330.

[3] Fitzmaurice, *op. cit.*, ii, 14.   As early as Sept., 1777, Shelburne wrote to Dr. Richard Price, ' What will become of England ? ' (Massachusetts Historical Society, 2nd series, xvii, 313).   In June, 1780, he spoke in the House of Lords of the retention of the American colonies as being ' necessary to the power and independence of Great Britain ' and of their final separation as ' fatal ' (Fitzmaurice, *op. cit.*, ii, 81).   At the opening of the Session after York Town, he said that the King ' had seen his empire from a pitch of glory and splendour perfectly astonishing

Irishmen. Writing to his friend, Richard Campion, in that dreadful August when the enemies' fleets ' domineer in our seas and anchor in our havens,' ' I am low and dejected at times,' Burke confesses, ' in a way not to be described.' And again : ' I cannot look our present situation steadily in the face ; and everything in prospect appears to me so very gloomy that I am willing to turn to any sort of trifling amusement which has a tendency to avert my mind from all speculation upon evils which no thoughts of mine can at all avert or lessen.'[1] Or take General Conway in 1780. ' We are turned out for the hunt,' he told the country-gentlemen in the House of Commons, ' like the stricken deer, deserted and abandoned by all the herd.'[2]

Such is the chorus of grief and shame, swelled by the voices of many lesser men, that echoes through those years. But again, perhaps, the sincerity of it all may be questioned. Those desperate complainants, it may be said, are all politicians and all Whigs. Of course they exaggerate the evils brought upon the country by a Tory Government. ' Sunset ' and ' ruin ' mean little on any party platform. . . . Well, do not two at least of those quotations strike the impartial ear with a note of deep, of painful

and dazzling tumbled down to disgrace and ruin with a degree of precipitation which no previous history could parallel.' (Fitzmaurice, *op. cit.*, ii, 83.)

[1] *Correspondence of Edmund Burke* (London, 1844), ii, 286, 302.

[2] Debate of 5 May, 1780 : *Parl. Hist.*, xxi, 573.

sincerity ? But other witnesses can be summoned
if they are needed. Call Thomas Coutts, banker.
' Nothing can be more anxious,' writes that practical and prosperous man of business in the summer
of 1778, ' than the state of people's minds here at
present—every hour in expectation of news of a
sea-battle where the force against us is superior and
on which everything seems to depend.—Though,
indeed, even with victory on our side, the ruin
hanging over us is dreadful.' Again, a year later :
' The moment our great fleet is beat, there is an
end of the Empire. How this is to be avoided I
know not. . . . The apprehensions of all sensible
thinking men are very great indeed.' In 1781, before the news of York Town, ' I fear,' he writes,
and on this theme with authority, ' I fear, if the
activity of hostile operations do not succeed to give
us a sudden overthrow, that we must fall by the
slower hands of consuming expense and its certain
consequences—national bankruptcy.' And later,
much later, even after peace has been attained :
' Nobody more than a banker feels the impending
ruin.' [1] Call, next, Nathaniel Wraxall, honest Tory

---

[1] E. H. Coleridge, *op. cit.*, i, 113, 119, 136, 171. In January,
1778, Coutts thinks that Chatham's return to office is ' essential
not only to the welfare but even to the existence of Great Britain
as a powerful nation ' (p. 99). In July, 1779, he writes of the
naval situation in the Channel : ' It is said both sides have orders
to fight—a dreadful interval. Meanwhile affairs in America look
better, and I should hope something good might be brought
about in that quarter, if our system could be altered here ; but
I fear the old system will go on and that this happy Kingdom

and faithful follower of Lord North until his ' baneful alliance ' with Fox. ' Never,' he records, ' did a deeper political gloom overspread England than in the autumn of 1779. . . . I question whether at the time of the destruction of the ships of war lying in the Medway, burnt by the Dutch, under Charles the Second ; or after the defeat of the English and Dutch fleets by the French off Beachy Head, in 1690, under William and Mary ; which constitute two of the most calamitous epochs in our history ; greater despondency, consternation and general dissatisfaction prevailed throughout the kingdom.' Again, ' We must reluctantly confess that the Navy of England at this period of the present reign had sunk to a point of depression hardly conceivable when compared with the times of Hawke, Saunders, and Boscawen.' And after reviewing all the crises of the great French War from 1793 to 1814, he declares that at none of them, not even in 1797, nor after Austerlitz, ' did a deeper despondency prevail among all ranks of society than towards the close of the American Contest.' [1] Call, third, Lord

and Constitution is devoted to destruction ' (p. 120). In November, 1780 : ' It seems determined to drive on the American War as long as there is a guinea to be found. It seems to me that we are undone people either way, so that we may as well take the spirited side ' (p. 132).

[1] Sir N. W. Wraxall, *Historical Memoirs of My Own Time* (London, 1904, reprint), 187, 189, 292. See also p. 222 : ' The calamitous era of the American War which familiarized us with disgraces and reverses.' And p. 394, *re* naval humiliation ; p. 431, *re* losses in the West Indies.

Bathurst, Chancellor in the North Government, who wrote to his chief at the end of 1777, confessing to great despondency, prophesying the French alliance, American independence, and the loss of the West Indies, and declaring himself ' for peace on any terms.' Call, fourth, Lord North himself. Though he put a bold face on it in the House of Commons, North was often profoundly anxious and depressed. Even before Saratoga he would have done almost anything ' to get out of this d——d war ' : and, shortly after, he began his rather pitiful and quite futile attempts to quit the service of his royal taskmaster.[1]   Nor is there any reason to question the famous story of how the news of York Town came to Downing Street. Wraxall (it will be remembered) tells us that he asked Lord George Germain how the First Minister took it.   ' " As he would have taken a ball in the breast," replied Lord George.   For he opened his arms, exclaiming wildly as he paced up and down the apartment for a few minutes, " O God ! it is all over ! " Words which he repeated many times, under emotions of the deepest agitation and distress.'[2]   And, lastly, call the King.   No lamentations, it is true, came from those stubborn lips.   Through all that series of disasters for which he bore so large a share of responsibility, no saying of his is recorded, no written

[1] R. Lucas, *Lord North* (London, 1913), ii, 54, 65.   Bathurst's letter, 55.

[2] Wraxall, *op. cit.*, 398.

word has survived, to suggest that he realised how low he had helped to bring his kingdom. Even the shock of York Town did not bend him as it bent his ministers. To Wraxall again we owe that unforgettable picture of the dinner-party at Lord George Germain's house on the day the black news arrived, with its sharp contrast between the despondency of host and guests and the tenor of the King's reply to Lord George's announcement of the surrender. It deserves quotation in full.

' I dined on that day at Lord George's ; and though the information, which had reached London in the course of the morning, from two different quarters, was of a nature not to admit of long concealment, yet it had not been communicated either to me, or to any individual of the Company, as it might naturally have been through the channel of common report, when I got to Pall-mall, between five and six o'clock. Lord Walsingham, who likewise dined there, was the only person present, except Lord George, acquainted with the fact. The party, nine in number, sat down to table. I thought the Master of the Horse appeared serious, though he manifested no discomposure. Before the dinner was finished, one of his servants delivered him a letter, brought back by the messenger who had been dispatched to the King. Lord George opened and perused it : then looking at Lord Walsingham, to whom he exclusively directed his observation, " The King writes," said he, " just as he always does, except that I observe he has omitted to mark the hour and the minute of his writing, with his usual precision." This remark, though calculated to awaken some interest, excited no comment ; and while the Ladies, Lord George's three daughters, remained in the room, we repressed our curiosity. But they had no sooner withdrawn, than Lord George having acquainted us, that from Paris information had just arrived of the old Count de Maurepas, First Minister, lying at the point of death ; " It would grieve me," said I, " to finish my career, however far advanced in years, were I first Minister of France, before I had witnessed the termination of this great contest between England and America." " He has survived to see that event," replied Lord George, with some agitation. Utterly unsuspicious of the fact which had happened beyond the Atlantic, I conceived him to allude to the indecisive naval action fought at the mouth of the Chesapeake, early in the preceding month of September, between Admiral Graves and Count de Grasse ; which in its results might prove most injurious to Lord Cornwallis. Under this impression, " My meaning," said I, " is, that if I were the Count de Maurepas, I should wish to live long enough to behold the final issue of the war in Virginia." " He has survived to witness it completely," answered Lord George : " The army has surrendered, and you may peruse the particulars of the Capitulation in that paper " ; taking at the same time one from his pocket, which he delivered into my hand, not without visible emotion. By his permission I read it aloud, while the company listened in profound silence. We then discussed its contents, as affecting the Ministry, the Country, and the War. It must be confessed that they were calculated to diffuse a gloom over the most convivial society, and that they opened a wide field for political speculation.

After perusing the account of Lord Cornwallis's surrender at York Town, it was impossible for all present, not to feel a lively curiosity to know how the King had received the intelligence ; as well as how he had expressed himself in his note to Lord George Germain on the first communication of so painful an event. He gratified our wish by reading it to us, observing at the same time that it did the highest honour to His Majesty's fortitude, firmness, and consistency of character. The words made an impression on my memory, which the lapse of more than thirty years has not erased ; and I shall here commemorate its tenor, as serving to show how that Prince felt and wrote, under one of the most afflicting, as well as humiliating occurrences of his reign. The Billet ran nearly to this effect : " I have received, with sentiments of the deepest concern, the communication which Lord George Germain has made me, of the unfortunate result of the operations in Virginia. I particularly lament it, on account of the consequences connected with it, and the difficulties which it may produce in carrying on the public business, or in repairing such a misfortune. But I trust that neither Lord George Germain, nor any Member of the Cabinet, will suppose that it makes the smallest alteration in those principles of my conduct, which have directed me in past time, and which will always continue to animate me under every event, in the prosecution of the present contest." Not a sentiment of despondency or of despair was to be found in the letter ; the very hand-writing of which indicated composure of mind. Whatever opinion we may entertain relative to the practicability of reducing America to obedience by force of arms at the end of 1781, we must admit that no sovereign could manifest more calmness, dignity, or self-command, than George the Third displayed in this reply.'[1]

[1] Wraxall, op. cit., 399-402. The King's note to Germain is not printed in the Correspondence ; but the tenor of his note to North, written three days later after Parliament had opened—and duly timed ' m. 40 pt. 8 A.M.'—is the same. ' Lord North's account that the Address was carried this morning by a considerable majority is very pleasing to Me, as it shows the House retains that spirit for which this Nation has always been renowned, and which alone can preserve it in its difficulties ; that some principal Members have wavered in their sentiments as to the measures to be pursued does not surprise me ; many men choose rather to despond on difficulties than see how to get out of them. . . . With the assistance of Parliament I do not doubt if measures are well concerted a good end may yet be made to this War, but if we despond certain ruin ensues.' Correspondence of King George III, 1760-1783, ed. Fortesque (London, 1928), v, 303-4.

Wraxall's tribute is deserved. George III had courage as well as obstinacy ; but, for all the stiffness of his outward bearing and however tight he shut his mind against it, the thought must sometimes have crept in that, after all, he might lose the thirteen colonies ; and his convictions as to what that would mean for England were at least as gloomy as Walpole's or Shelburne's. At the very end, when he was compelled to accept the loss—not, indeed, of his own will, but simply because his subjects could no longer be induced to carry on the American war—he blurted out the fears that haunted him. In his historic, pathetic, patriotic letter to Shelburne during the peace negotiations, ' I am unable,' he declares, ' to add anything on that subject but the most fervent prayers to Heaven to guide me so to act that Posterity may not lay the downfall of this once respectable Empire at my door ; and that, if ruin should attend the measures that may be adopted, I may not long survive.' [1]

No, the disgrace of England was not a Whig invention. Tories, however reticent in public, must have confessed it to themselves ; and foreign observers, with less than no reason for reticence, made

---

[1] *Correspondence*, vi, 129. Cf. the letters of 22 Dec., 1781, and 21 Jan., 1782, in which George III refuses to contemplate peace after York Town as involving ' the irrecoverable destruction' of the Empire, and declares that ' a separation from America . . . would annihilate the rank in which this British Empire stands among the European States.' *Ibid.*, v, 317, 334.

the most of it.   Shelburne was not far wrong when
he said in 1780 that ' we had become the contempt
and standing jest of all Europe.' [1]   The best European judge of political and military realities had
closely watched the operations of his old allies—
' ces goddam ' as he called them—in America,
criticised their blunders, and foretold at an early
stage their certain result ; and, when it was all over,
he talked of the ' abasement ' of England and the
chastening of her ' excessive pride and disdain for
the rest of Europe ' as the latest act in the world's
perpetual comedy of change.[2]   What the King of
Prussia said was echoed, gleefully enough, no doubt,
by a multitude of small fry.   Indeed a tour on the
Continent was now an unpleasant and perhaps a
salutary experience for self-satisfied Englishmen.
' Thomas Pitt,' reported one of his audience in the
House of Commons in 1780, ' drew a terrible picture
of the difference he had felt between his former
journey abroad and his last ; from what he knew
of the dissimilar situations of his country, then so
flourishing, now so fallen, and from what he heard

[1] *Parl. Hist.*, xxi, 640.
[2] Frederick to d'Alembert, 26 April, 1782 : *Oeuvres de
Frédéric le Grand* (Berlin, 1854), xxv, 222.   After Saratoga, he
prophesied the French entry into the war, the independence of
the colonies, and, ' if fortune is not too contrary,' the recovery
of Canada by France (xxv, 83, 89).   For allusions to bad strategy
at the outset of the war, see xxv, 83 : to George III and Bute,
xxvi, 401 : to the hired Hessians, xxiii, 380.   He wrote to Eliott,
in October, 1782, as ' an old companion in arms ' warmly con-
gratulating him on his defence of Gibraltar : xxiv, 359.

foreigners say of it.'[1]   And Sir Robert Murray
Keith, who took a more robust view of the situation
from the British Legation at Vienna than his friends
at home, was constantly complaining at this time
that the gloomy opinions expressed in British news-
papers had the worst possible effect in those countries which, as one of his correspondents put it, ' are
now so obliging as to pity us.'   ' What the devil is
the matter with Old England,' he asks, ' that she
has lost every grain of her old spirit ? . . . I find
it a hard matter to hold my head as high as I shall
ever wish to hold it amidst a score of foreign ministers who (upon the faith of our own representation
of our own affairs) look upon the faithless Bourbons
as the very lords of the ascendant.'[2]   But, in truth,
though a British diplomat abroad could scarcely be
expected to admit it, continental opinion was based
on more concrete evidence than jeremiads in the
Press.   Consider the effect on British prestige in
Europe of one such incident as the taking of the
Trading Fleet in 1780.

' Such a prize [records the *Annual Register*] had never
before entered the harbour of Cadiz.   An English fleet of
near sixty ships, led captive by a Spanish squadron, was
extremely flattering to a people to whom naval captures,
from such an enemy, were an unusual spectacle.   All their
ancient losses, all the insults which their coasts, and that
city and port in particular, had formerly endured, seemed

[1] *Letters of H. Walpole*, xi, 152.
[2] *Memoirs and Correspondence of Sir R. M. Keith* (London,
1849), ii, 109.

now, at one stroke, to be done away. The appearance of the numerous prisoners, consisting of all orders and denominations, and resembling more the various inhabitants of a sacked city than the ordinary crews of a fleet, seemed to render the triumph even more complete and made the sight still more singular. They consisted of 1520 seamen, including their proper officers ; of 1255 soldiers, part in the service of the Crown, and part in that of the East India Company ; of 74 land officers ; of 149 women ; and of 137 passengers of both sexes, among whom were some married and unmarried ladies of condition. The whole amounting to 2865 persons.' [1]

In such guise now, bedraggled and dusty with defeat, the arrogant victor of the Seven Years War was exhibited to Europe.

It is needless to cite more evidence. The facts, indeed, speak for themselves. How could Englishmen be anything but deeply mortified, anxious, and, at the worst moments of those bad years, veritably despondent, especially when they were confronted with the fact which must have impressed them, as it impressed all Europe, most—the loss of supremacy at sea. It was bad enough that enemy privateers should make free of the Channel and prevent Englishmen from enjoying their customary holidays on the Continent, as Dr. Burney and his daughter were prevented by ' the fears and dangers of being taken by the enemy '—fears which, as Fanny says, were soon proved to have been justified by the capture of ' the Duchess of Leicester, Lady F. Campbell, and several others ' on their way to

[1] *Annual Register*, 1781, 2-3.

Spa.[1]   But, of course, such lesser humiliations were
as nothing to the shame of August, 1779. ' In our
own seas, *we have seen*,' wrote Rockingham to
Admiral Keppel a few months later, ' and Europe
is now fully satisfied, that the fleets united of France
and Spain are superior, *at least in numbers*, and can
ride insultingly and *unmolested* even off our ports
and within our channel.'[2] Along the coasts of
Devon and Cornwall the spectacle of the French
and Spanish ships, so much at ease, so close to shore,
was unforgettable.   ' The consternation amongst all
ranks here is not to be expressed,' wrote a doctor
at a Plymouth hospital ; ' many families have already

---

[1] *Diary and Letters of Mme. D'Arblay* (London, 1905), i, 254.
Correspondence was similarly interrupted. ' I am afraid,'
writes Keith from Vienna, ' that some cursed captain of a Dun-
kirk cutter is now amusing himself and family with the perusal
of a score of my letters from my friends in England.' (*Memoirs*,
etc., ii, 89.)

[2] *Memoirs of the Marquis of Rockingham* by the Earl of Albe-
marle (London, 1852), ii, 385-6. In the same letter Rockingham
refers to the possibilities of the future in language which, even
for the leader of the Opposition, is pretty desperate. ' Some
degree of hope might also arise that even America, cruelly and
wickedly as she has been treated, might become calm and cool
enough to weigh *whether*, in good policy, for *herself*, as *an independent State*, the annihilation of England, as a great European
power, was advisable.' (*Ibid.*, 388.) The humiliation may be
forgotten now, but it was remembered vividly enough by the
next generation. Huskisson, for instance, speaking in the House
of Commons in 1826, said : ' Can we forget the period when
the combined fleet of the House of Bourbon was master of the
British Channel—when a West India convoy was obliged to
assemble at Leith and go north about in order to evade capture
by an enemy's fleet within sight of our principal sea-ports ? '
And so on. *Speeches* (London, 1831), iii, 53.

removed, and others are removing.'[1] A landing was feared at Torbay : and all up the Channel an anxious watch was kept. ' Notwithstanding the invasion,' writes Banker Coutts, with conscious English phlegm, ' I am going to a place on the sea-coast near Bright-helmstone for a few weeks.'[2] Barrister Pitt, aged twenty, was as brave a man as Coutts and as English, but he had his widowed mother to think of, and her Somersetshire home was within eighty miles of Plymouth. ' While the idea prevailed,' he writes to her, in that rotund, middle-aged style from which he could so rarely free himself, ' of a force actually landing at Plymouth, I was more particularly soli-citous because your neighbourhood to that place, though not such as to expose you at all to anything immediately very serious, might, I feared, be pro-ductive of great inconvenience and distress.'[3] ' We are all well,' wrote Burke to his friend Campion, who had offered to shelter Mrs. Burke in the event of an invasion, ' as far as we can be so in the present dreadful state of anxiety.'[4] Nor, as we have seen, was it only the south coast that suffered these alarms. Thanks to Paul Jones, there was a certain ' liveliness ' in the North Sea ; and, while Burke was awaiting

[1] Dr. Farr to James Harris, 17 Aug., 1779, *Letters of the First Earl of Malmesbury*, i, 422-3. Mrs. Harris wrote to her son from Salisbury on 22 August : ' God send the times may mend. We have an additional prayer in the churches : that is all we have to avail us.' *Ibid.*, 430.

[2] *Life of T. Coutts*, i, 121.

[3] Earl Stanhope, *Life of William Pitt* (London, 1861), i, 32.

[4] *Correspondence of Burke*, ii, 304 (29 Aug., 1779).

the worst in London, his leader, Lord Rockingham, was at Hull, warning the citizens in the Town Hall that Paul Jones might easily ' come up the Humber and lay off the town,' conferring with the mayor as to how to improve the defences, offering to ' treat the town ' to a battery of 18-pounders which had recently been forged in the neighbourhood and were lying on a ship on the river, and arranging for them to be shifted to the most effective sites on shore. ' I am very well,' he tells his marchioness, ' quite alert—up at night. . . . Don't fidget yourself.' [1]

Enough has been said to show how really black the skies were between 1779 and 1782, and that Englishmen of the day, when they talked about the ' shame ' and ' ruin ' of their country, meant nothing less than shame and ruin. It is possible now to paint into the picture, without fear of a false effect, the dash of lighter colour that the truth demands. There was something to alleviate the gloom—something which, though it did not lessen the risk of England's ruin, just took the edge off England's shame. And this was the fact that the American War was a civil war. If passionate lovers of liberty like Fox could almost welcome the news of Saratoga, their cooler-headed compatriots could find at least

---

[1] *Rockingham Memoirs*, ii, 381-3. Lord Carlisle wrote to George Selwyn from Castle Howard (24 Sept., 1779) : ' We have alarms upon our coast. One Paul Jones flings us all into consternation and terror, and will hinder Lady Carlisle's sea-bathing.' *G. Selwyn and his Contemporaries* (London, 1882), iv, 256.

a grain of consolation in the thought that it was
mainly men of British blood and bone who had
dealt this blow to British arms.   It became increas-
ingly obvious, moreover, that the American War was
also largely responsible for our reverses in Europe.
England was fighting her old enemies across the
Channel with one hand tied up across the Atlantic.
And as the fight with the foreigner went more and
more against us, so the fight with our kinsmen grew
more and more unpopular.   At the outset public
opinion had, on the whole, supported the war.   The
failure of the colonists to contribute to imperial
costs had touched English pockets.   Their rebellion
against Crown and Parliament had, as Gibbon observed,[1] touched English pride.   But the fact that
recruits for the actual fighting were almost unobtain-
able shows that there was no real war-spirit in the
mass of the people ; and, while the entry of France
and Spain into the conflict at once revived the old
antagonism towards those traditional enemies of
England, the new antagonism towards the colonists

---

[1] Gibbon's *Autobiography* (ed. Lord Sheffield : *World's Classics*
Edition, London, 1907), 197. 'The American war had once
been the favourite of the country : the pride of England was
irritated by the resistance of her colonies. . . . But the length
of a fruitless contest, the loss of armies, the accumulation of
debt and taxes, and the hostile confederacy of France, Spain,
and Holland, indisposed the public to the American war, and
the persons by whom it was conducted ; the representatives of
the people followed, at a slow distance, the changes of their
opinion ; and the ministers, who refused to bend, were broken
by the tempest.'

of England and their cause steadily waned. A few
stout Tories might agree or pretend to agree with
George III to the bitter end ; but Boswell confessed
in the spring of 1781, though he did not dare say
it in Dr. Johnson's presence, that ' almost every
man ' was now ' against the American War.' [1] Six
months later, after York Town, the great majority
of Englishmen desired to finish it on any terms,
even if, like the King, they thought the acknowledg-
ment of American independence a ' dreadful price '
to pay,[2] even if it seemed to mean the sunset of the
Empire.   By accepting complete defeat at their kinsmen's hands, they might hope to avoid complete
defeat at the hands of France and Spain. And
then, as if to confirm such hopes, came that last
happy turn in the tide of the European War. On
the news of Rodney's victory the psychological
reaction was tremendous. ' The capital and the
country,' says Wraxall, ' were thrown into a delirium
of joy.' The public exultation, he records, was
greater than anything of the kind he saw in after
years, and he lived to see ' the glorious First of
June ' and Trafalgar. ' It constituted a sort of
compensation to Great Britain for so many years
of disgrace, for so great an expenditure of blood
and treasure, and even for the loss of America
itself. The country, exhausted and humiliated,
seemed to revive in its own estimation and to re-

[1] Boswell's *Life of Johnson* (Oxford, 1909), ii, 394.
[2] *Correspondence of George III*, vi, 45.

sume once more its dignity among nations.'[1] And,
if such emotions were a little too hysterical to last,
if it was soon evident that one battle had not quite
reversed the balance of the war, none the less it
must have been gratifying for those Englishmen who
had read of the abasement at Cadiz to read now of
the arrival of the Count de Grasse—' the first commander-in-chief of a French fleet or army who has
been prisoner in England since the reign of Queen
Anne, when Marechal Tallard was taken by the
Duke of Marlborough '—how he landed with his
suite on South Sea Common at Portsmouth, where
they were met by Vice-Admiral Sir Peter Parker
and conducted in carriages to the ' George ' to par-
take of ' a most sumptuous dinner ' and how they
proceeded presently to London ' to Mrs. Nugent's
(the mother of Lady Parker) in Queen Square,
Westminster . . . from whence Count de Grasse
walked up to the Royal Hotel in Pall Mall.'[2] In
all that there was some consolation, and some, too,
even in the peace. For, if it was peace without
honour, at least it left England erect. The settlement with France and Spain implied defeat but
not disaster.

There was more—it need hardly be said—than
this little lifting of the clouds, this escape from the
worst into the merely bad, to alleviate the pessimism
of Englishmen—at least of liberal-minded English-

[1] Wraxall, *op. cit.*, 460-2.   [2] *Annual Register*, 1782, 216.

men—at the end of the war. The immediate effects of the American Revolution on England had not been external only : they had penetrated to the heart of her domestic politics. The fact that the collapse of George III's system of government was due to the ' disgraces and reverses ' of the American War is one of the most certain facts in history.

The method by which George III re-established the personal control of the King over the government of England was simple and effective. On his accession to the throne he found that political power was virtually the monopoly of the great Whig families. He devoted the first decade of his reign to the easy task of disrupting this ' Venetian oligarchy ' by widening the cracks which divided its jealous and self-seeking factions. Then, in 1770, he chose for his first minister a man of considerable ability and of such fidelity to his royal master as to be willing to execute the royal will even when his conscience as well as his intellect condemned it. For most of Lord North's colleagues he succeeded in obtaining similarly docile, if on the whole less competent men, including one or two whose only function or capacity was to spy upon the rest and report their conduct at the Palace. And by every other means he strove to prevent the ministry from becoming, save only in acceptance of the policy with which he provided them, a united or homogeneous ' Cabinet.' But, since he never challenged, except on one famous occasion, the rule that ministers must resign unless they enjoy the confidence of the House of Commons, he was obliged also to provide his ministers with a majority. To this end he created a little party of his own, notorious to history as the ' King's Friends,' by various means—by buying seats in the ' borough-market ' at Elections, by playing on the nobler loyalties or meaner snobberies of individual M.P.'s, by judicious and unambiguous gifts from the huge treasury of patronage—places, sinecures, pensions, everything from a peerage or a lord-lieutenancy or a governorship to a military commission or something less—all of which lay in his hands, and last, if need be, by cool bribes of money. It must not be supposed that the ' King's Friends ' constituted anything like a dominant party. Recent research tends to moderate the traditional view of the venality of parliamentary life in the eighteenth century.[1] Many members of the House of Commons were reasonably upright and independent men. But the ' royal ' group could be depended on to keep the balance steady in favour of its master's policy as long as it was supported by a sufficient number of those representatives of the electorate who were not amenable to ' influence.' The making and the maintenance of this solid and efficient machine of government was a very great—though, perhaps, not a very wise—achievement. Few men have realised so

[1] See L. G. Namier, *The Structure of Politics at the Accession of George III* (London, 1928). These scholarly volumes are indispensable to any serious student of the period.

fully such big political ambitions ; and George III was working practically single-handed. He made himself what none of his predecessors had ever been, not only his own Prime Minister, not only the leader of his own political party, but also its chief whip, its organiser of victory at the polls, and, on one undignified occasion, one of its local canvassers. One wonders, indeed, whether, in the high-tide of his success, he fully grasped its implications. Did he realise that by openly descending from the throne to the arena of party politics he was compelling his subjects to hold himself and his ' system ' responsible for what they did ? Did he foresee what must happen if the policy he imposed on his ministers and his ' Friends ' should lead the country into difficulties or even disasters ? Or did he, with an honest and not ignoble trust in himself and in divine right, simply rule out any such eventuality ? Yet such, of course, was the event. And at once that imposing fair-weather edifice began to shake and slide like a house of cards in a breeze.[1]

Exhausted by the tumults of the seventeenth century, placidly contented with the ' Glorious Revolution,' concerned with little else than the protection of its fruits from Jacobite reaction, the political mind of the English people in 1760 had been long quiescent ; and it is quite conceivable that George III's ' system ' would have been tolerated

[1] The facts of George III's system are clearly stated in A. M. Davies' *George III and the Constitution* (Oxford, 1921).

for at least a generation if only it had been successful. George III, after all, was only doing, and in
much the same way, what the Whig grandees had
done for as long as anybody could remember. Nor,
in any case, could public opinion be easily informed
and stimulated, much less organised, in a country
still equipped with such bad roads and with a Press
still so small and limited in scope. The nation was
certainly moved by Pitt's direct appeal to it, by his
subsequent treatment by the King, and by the
Wilkes affair ; but it was only (it has been well
said) like a man stirring in his sleep.[1] For a real
awakening, for the oncoming of one of those periodic
bursts of political interest and energy to which the
evolution of English liberties has been mainly due,
something more sharp and shocking was required—
a sponge, so to speak, of the coldest water. The
American Revolution provided it.

The first impact was in the field of political theory
rather than practical politics. The subject-matter
of the quarrel with the colonies excited a new interest in constitutional questions. Englishmen began to ask themselves, many of them for the first
time, what the powers of Parliament were and on
what they rested. There were different views,
it appeared, on the two sides of the Atlantic as to
the nature of representative government, as to

[1] G. S. Veitch, *The Genesis of Parliamentary Reform* (London,
1913), 24. The compressed narrative in the following paragraphs is mainly based on chap. iii of this valuable book.

the meaning of representation. The revolutionary
leaders were refusing to be taxed because they were
not represented, as they understood it, in the House
of Commons at Westminster. But, when one came
to think of it, were Englishmen in England much
better represented there than Englishmen in the
colonies ? Could a body of members, of whom so
large a proportion were practically elected by a few
wealthy landowners or by the King, through influence or purchase, be seriously regarded as the
representatives of the people—unless, of course, one
held the view that property, not people, should be
represented ? Were there not large and fast-growing
urban communities in England which were not
represented at all ? Some such interaction of ideas
was inevitable, and it can be seen working in the
mind of that fine philanthropist and patriot, Granville Sharp. The subject of a pamphlet he published
in 1774 was a defence of American and Irish liberties, but he called it *A Declaration of the People's
Natural Right to a share in the Legislature which is
the fundamental principle of the British Constitution
of State*.[1] He was also obliged, therefore, at least to
raise the question of the inadequate operation of
that ' fundamental principle ' in Britain itself, and
he devoted two further pamphlets, published in

[1] London, 1774. Sharp's main argument is that ' all British
subjects, whether in Great Britain, Ireland, or the Colonies, are
equally free ' (p. 2) ; and since ' Great Britain itself is only a
part of the British Empire,' the British Parliament cannot legislate for those other parts which are not represented in it. (P. 14.)

1780 and 1782, to a plea for more equal representation and more frequent Parliaments.[1] No one, indeed, can imagine that the coincidence in time between the development of the revolutionary movement in America and that of the reform movement in England was a mere coincidence in fact. It was, of course, no accident that the first of many motions in Parliament for a drastic reform of the representative system was made within twelve months of Lexington, or that *Take your Choice*, the pamphlet which won for Cartwright the title of ' The Father of Reform,' was published later in the same year.[2] And it was, of course, the disappointments and reverses of the war in America that converted Reform into a question of practical politics. The county members, the country-gentlemen, not amenable to bribes, in whose hands the fate of the King's ' system ' rested, might be little interested in theoretical discussions of representation and the rights of the people ; but, when taxation and debt began steadily to increase without being transmuted into victory,

[1] *A Circular Letter to the several Petitioning Counties, Cities, and Towns, etc.*, and *The Claims of the People of England* (by ' A Loyal Englishman ').

[2] F. D. Cartwright, *Life and Correspondence of Major Cartwright* (London, 1826), i, 82 ff. Cartwright was, of course, strongly pro-American ; but, when asked by American friends to join the revolutionary forces, he declared that, though he would never ' draw arms against the liberties of America . . . nothing could absolve a man from the duty he owed his own country, and that he would stick by the old ship as long as there was a plank of her above water.' *Ibid.*, i, 81.

they were bound to wonder how all the money was being spent. And even the Tories among them, prepared on principle to support Lord North, began to shake their heads over the manifest mismanagement of the war. They were naturally the last, those loyal Tories, to be convinced that the only way to save their country was to desert their King ; and naturally the Whigs had fewer doubts or scruples. Long before the tale of national defeat and disgrace was crowned by York Town, the Whig spokesmen of Reform had been pleading their cause in Parliament and a great body of public opinion, not all of it by any means partisan, had been organised outside it and was beating on its doors. In April, 1778, six months after Saratoga, two months after the French Alliance, the attack· on political corruption was opened by Sir Philip Jennings Clerke's motion for leave to introduce a Bill for the exclusion of contract-holders from the House of Commons. In November, 1779, two months after that black August in the Channel, Christopher Wyvill began his long campaign by canvassing the great Yorkshire landowners on the question of Reform ; and on 30 December, two hundred and nine of the ' Nobility, Gentlemen, Clergy and Freeholders of the County ' assembled at York and adopted *nem. con.* the historic petition declaring that the public money was being squandered on sinecures and pensions ' whence the Crown has acquired a great and unconstitutional influence, which, if not checked, may soon prove fatal to the liberties of this country,' and calling on the House of Commons to withhold supplies until those ' gross abuses ' had been stopped. Throughout the gloom of 1780, the year of the Armed Neutrality, the movement gathered strength both outside and inside Parliament. In February the Yorkshire petition, signed by over eight thousand freeholders, was presented, together with similar petitions from the cities of York and Bristol. Meantime, a committee appointed at the York meeting—after the precedent, conscious or unconscious, of the Correspondence Committees in America—' to carry on the necessary correspondence for effectually promoting the object of the petition and to prepare a Plan of Association ' had quickly begun to organise the movement on a wider scale. Twenty-eight other counties and at least eleven other cities and towns adopted the Yorkshire petition. In March, a convention of delegates from eighteen of these communities was held in London : and in accordance with the advice it tendered to the local committees, County Associations were promptly formed with Yorkshire in the van. While Wyvill was thus busy, Cartwright was not idle. He was mainly responsible for the foundation, in April of the same year, of the Society for Promoting Constitutional Information which was soon hard at work distributing free literature on Reform. In Parliament, meanwhile, the attack was steadily pressed. Shelburne led it in the Lords in February, and Richmond in June. In the

Commons, three days after the presentation of the petitions, Burke in one of his greatest speeches expounded his full-scale plan of Economical Reform, and on 6 April, in the course of one of the debates on it, Dunning carried by a majority of eighteen his famous resolution ' that the influence of the Crown has increased, is increasing, and ought to be diminished.'

But the ' system ' still held its ground. Its defenders, it was clear, were not to be terrorised by speeches and pamphlets. Indeed, as the agitation outside Parliament increased, they began to talk seriously of anarchy and to stiffen their backs to confront the impending revolution. No further victories were won by Dunning and his friends. And in June, as if to confirm their stubbornness, came the Gordon Riots, making an indelible impression on all who witnessed the unprecedented spectacle of London under mob-rule for four days, leaving behind the wildest rumours and suspicions of conspiracy and sedition on the part of the Government's opponents, and compelling his most unsparing critics to recognise what they owed at that crisis to the courage of the King. A fortnight later Burke's Bills were thrown out. And when in the autumn Parliament was dissolved, the gathering clouds of the dispute with Holland could not prevent the King and his faithful servants from securing a renewal of their majority. So the story of 1780 was repeated in the first half of 1781. Clerke's

and Burke's Bills were again rejected. Again the
Convention met. Again a petition was presented.
Nothing happened. . . . Then, after the summer
interval, the Yorkshire Committee made one more
effort. On 17 October they decided the terms of
a new appeal to the electorate. Taking courage
from failure, they now put Economical Reform in
the background and called for the more drastic
measures at which hitherto some of their weaker
brethren had shied, for ' some substantial reform
of Parliament.' . . . Two days later, Cornwallis
surrendered.

York Town, as North instantly recognised, was
as decisive a blow in Downing Street as it was in
America. The fall of his Government and, with
it, the King's ' system ' was now only a question
of time. His ' Friends ' might still feel bound to
earn their pay. A real devotion to his person might
keep others true to him in this his darkest hour.
But the patient loyalty of most of those independent
county members could stand the strain no longer.
The House of Commons began again to represent
the opinion of the country ; the old majority steadily
fell, till finally a motion of ' no confidence,' moved
by a Tory member, was only defeated by nine votes ;
and on 20 March, North announced his resignation.
George III knew what it meant. ' At last,' he wrote,
' the fatal day is come.' [1]   And though, it is true, the
Whig ministries of Rockingham and Shelburne

[1] *Correspondence of George III*, v, 421.

were short-lived, the first lived long enough to carry
Burke's reforms and the second to make peace
certain.   And though, again, George III presently
found in Pitt at least a refuge from Fox, though he
still asserted at times his royal will, with disastrous
success on two historic occasions, though his status
was still very different from that of Queen Victoria
and, yet more, from that of George V, none the less,
after York Town, his 'system' lay on the scrap-
heap, and after 1784 it was a Prime Minister, with
a steadily consolidating Cabinet, that ruled England.

Not slight nor transient, then, were the immediate
effects of the American Revolution on British politics.
Partly through the theoretical discussions it provoked, still more through the practical results of
the defeats and disgrace it occasioned, it was the
chief factor in the collapse of the Georgian reaction.
Nor did it only do so much to stop the drift backwards—backwards, as many anxious Whigs believed,
to something like despotism.   It started also a new
forward movement.   In the course of the same
political drama, as the outcome of the same ideas
and events, parliamentary corruption, though far
from eradicated, was robbed of half its force ; and
a current of public demand for a more truly representative House of Commons was set flowing which,
though soon to be checked and almost blocked by
the effects of another Revolution and another revolutionary war, was ultimately to reach its goal in
1832.

Thus the parting gift of the colonists, as they severed themselves from their mother-country, was twofold. With the help of the Bourbon monarchies of France and Spain, they gave her defeat and disgrace. With the help of more natural allies on her own soil, they gave her a new birth of freedom. And that was why the darkness of the closing stage of the war was lightened by something more than Rodney's victory. Free-minded Englishmen, who had felt almost as much humiliated by the mere fact of George III's ' system ' as by what had happened under it, could lift their heads and hope again. ' Let us save the constitution,' wrote poor old Horace Walpole on hearing that North's Government had fallen, ' and I shall not die brokenhearted. If England is free, and America free though disunited, the whole earth will not be in vassalage.' [1] One wise old vassal of the King of France had thought much the same. Writing not long before his death in 1781 to Richard Price, Turgot had stoutly denied that the loss of her colonies would make Britain *une nation méprisable*. If her misfortunes should lead to the suppression of corruption and the reform of the representative system, then she might gain as much as America from the Revolution. ' For you would keep your liberty ; and with it and through it your other losses would very quickly be made good.' And so,

[1] *Letters of H. Walpole*, xii, 210.

of course, thought Price himself. 'Britons themselves,' he wrote, 'will be the greatest gainers [by
the Revolution] if wise enough to improve properly
the check that has been given to the despotism of
their ministers and to catch the flame of virtuous
liberty which has saved their American brethren.'[1]
And if other patriots, with as great a love of freedom
but with cooler heads and longer sight, could scarcely
share all Price's satisfaction at the tragic schism of
the British Commonwealth, at least they could feel
that England was now herself once more and, being
herself, could hope at least to hold her own against
'the four corners of the world.' Shelburne, for
example, whose 'sunset' speech had never been
forgotten, now told his fellow-peers 'to prepare for
the rising of England's sun again.'[2] But the most
striking, the most promising comment on the close
of the war—at once a confession of downfall and
a *sursum corda*—came, appropriately, from Chat-

---

[1] R. Price, *Observations on the Importance of the American
Revolution and the Means of making it a Benefit to the World*
(London, 1785), p. 1. Turgot's letter, 105. Like other enthusi-
asts in other days, Price combined admiration for America with
contempt for Europe. On p. 6 he says : 'Perhaps I do not go
too far when I say that, next to the introduction of Christianity
among mankind, the American Revolution may prove the most
important step in the progressive course of human improvement ' :
and on p. 76 : 'Thus singularly happy, why should they [the
Americans] seek connexions with *Europe* and expose themselves
to the danger of being involved in its quarrels ? What have they
to do with its politics ? Is there anything very important to them
which they can draw from thence—excepting INFECTION ? '

[2] Speech of 10 July, 1782. *Parl. Hist.*, xxiii, 194.

ham's son. ' I feel, Sir, at this instant,' he said in the House of Commons in a debate on the Peace, ' how much I was animated in my childhood by a recital of England's victories. I was taught, Sir, by one whose memory I shall ever revere, that at the close of a war, far different indeed from this, she had dictated the terms of peace to submissive nations. That . . . was the memorable era of England's glory. But that era is past. . . . The visions of her power and pre-eminence are passed away.' And then, even while he recapitulates England's losses and admits them to be ' ruinous,' the young orator changes his tone. He emphasises the less unfavourable side of the peace conditions. He sounds a note of hope, a call to action. ' Let us examine what is left with a manly and determined courage. Let us strengthen ourselves against inveterate enemies and reconciliate our ancient friends. The misfortunes of individuals and of kingdoms that are laid open and examined with true wisdom are more than half redressed.'[1]

That is not the voice of a North or a Rockingham or a Walpole. It is the voice of young post-war England, heralding the birth of a new and better Empire from the ruins of the old.

[1] Speech of 21 Feb., 1783. *War Speeches of William Pitt the Younger* (ed. R. Coupland, Oxford, 1916), p. 5.

II.

THE OLD EMPIRE.

' THE misfortunes of individuals and of kingdoms that are laid open and examined with true wisdom are more than half redressed.' Rarely in history has faith been so speedily justified by works. A little island, less than half the size of France, with only about a third of her population, abandoned now by almost all her sons across the sea, defeated, discredited, well-nigh bankrupt, Britain in 1783 seemed to have fallen for ever from the rank of first-class Powers. Ten years later she had not merely recovered her footing ; she was about to engage in another and very different war, arising out of another and very different revolution, with strength and self-confidence so wonderfully restored that she was able to fight on, sometimes single-handed, for more than twenty years against the most powerful and best-directed system of Cæsarism the world had ever seen until, mainly through her efforts, it was ' wholly and finally destroyed.' History and literature are strewn with examples of sudden fall from high estate : but the happier tale—a *peripeteia* in reverse—is seldom told, and there can be few, if any, cases of national recovery on record so swift as this or so complete.[1]

That Britain was Great again in 1793, that her misfortunes had been distinctly more than half redressed in that short decade of peace, was mainly due to good domestic management. The precocious wisdom of the statesman whose words have just been quoted, and who, within a year of their utterance, at the age of twenty-four, was Prime Minister—and a real Prime Minister—was directed in the first instance to financial reconstruction. To dispel the shadow of bankruptcy, to revive the sense of economic security, to give free play to the unbroken commercial vigour of the country—these in Pitt's eyes were the best methods of nursing Britain back

---

[1] On the financial position in 1783, see R. Price, *The State of the Public Debts and Finances in January*, 1783 (London, 1783). He compares the expenditure on the last four years of the last three wars as follows—1745-48, £31,813,317 : 1759-62, £60,355,190 : 1779-82, £80,016,090 (p. 14) ; and blesses ' the makers of the peace ' for saving the country the cost of further fighting. ' Still, however, we are far from being safe. Much hard work remains to be done. If, before another war begins, the revenue is not reinstated, the public debts put into a *fixed* course of payment, and some progress made in reducing them, it is impossible but the *catastrophe* must come towards which we have been for some time advancing' (p. 17). On Pitt's relations with Dr. Price, see R. Thomas, *Richard Price* (Oxford, 1924), 102-6. (It should be noted that Lecky's criticism of Pitt, quoted on p. 104, refers to the period of the French War.) For Pitt's financial administration between 1784 and 1793, see Lecky, *History of England in the XVIIIth Century* (London, 1917), v, 294-326 ; J. Holland Rose, *Life of William Pitt* (London, 1912), vol. i, chap. viii.

to her natural health. It was, of course, the right treatment, and it was brilliantly successful. British character, it was soon evident, had not lost its old resilience: British business men were as keen and competent as ever. At the end of the decade the revenue showed a steady average surplus of half a million pounds, a great part of the unfunded national debt had been funded and nearly eleven millions of the funded debt cleared off, and the 3 per cents. had touched 97.

It was in this domestic field, in the national counting-house, that Pitt's genius was most at home during those years of peace. But he was bound to take an active part in foreign affairs if only for the reason that his plans of economic recuperation could not possibly be realised unless Europe were given a breathing-space from war. And for those ten years, except in Eastern Europe, there was no war. But the political field Pitt had mainly in mind when he spoke of redressing the misfortunes of his country was neither domestic nor foreign, but imperial. He was advising Englishmen to resign themselves to the inevitable schism of the Empire and to try to repair the loss by examining ' what was left.' It was not, of course, merely the acceptance of this sound advice that brought all the cardinal problems of the Empire to the front of British politics in that same post-war decade. Those problems were not created by the American Revolution ; they had existed side by side with the American problem ; and, if the latter had

not come to a head in 1775 and been solved or at
least eliminated in 1783, those others must still have
come up for settlement in those post-war years. What
the American Revolution did was to give them a new
importance, to make it more obviously and urgently
necessary than before that they should be carefully
studied and wisely handled. The result was a
series of inquiries and adjustments in one imperial
field after another, not unlike the series of inquiries
and adjustments which is being conducted in this
present post-war age.[1] But there is this difference.
The changes we are now engaged in making are
evolutionary, not revolutionary. We are not adopting new principles : we are only continuing and extending the application of old ones. But the work

[1] The relations between the self-governing nations of the
British Commonwealth were settled in principle at the Imperial
Conference of 1926, and proposals as to the legislative action
required were made by a special Conference on the operation
of Dominion Legislation and Merchant Shipping Legislation
in 1929. The question of Indian government was examined
by a Statutory Commission under Sir John Simon from 1927
to 1930, and its report, together with those of other cognate
bodies, has recently been published. Three official inquiries
were held into the East African question between 1925 and 1929,
and similar ' inquiries and adjustments ' have been, or are being
made in Ceylon, British Guiana, and elsewhere. The general
process of imperial revision since the War is also illustrated by
the holding of an Imperial Economic Conference in 1926 and
1930, and of a Colonial Conference (for ' dependent ' colonies,
etc.) in 1927 and 1930, and by the separation from the Colonial
Office of a new Dominions Office with its own Secretary of State.
For the general re-organisation of the administrative system, see
the Official Memorandum of 1929, Cmd. 3268.

required of Pitt and the British people after 1783 was more drastic.   As each field came up for review, a new light played over it, the light of new ideas and ideals, revealing the inadequacy (to say the least) of the principles on which its old system of government was based.   Perforce, therefore, they found themselves thinking out and laying down new principles and trying to apply them.   And the ultimate outcome was a revolution, not an evolution.   They initiated in each field and in one carried far along its course a process that can only be described as the transformation of the British Empire.   Nor were they working only for their day.   The new Empire they founded still endures.   Its principles—the principles we are now continuing and extending in their application—are the same principles which they established.   The Second British Empire is to-day, as it will be (we may hope) to-morrow, a natural and consistent growth from the seed that was sown in the period of the American Revolution.[1]

In subsequent lectures we will watch that process of transformation at work.   But, since we cannot understand it without first examining the nature of

[1] In naming his deservedly well-known book *The Third British Empire*, Mr. A. E. Zimmern strikingly emphasised the great advance in the development of the imperial system since 1914. But it has been an advance on old accepted lines, not a new departure ; and an unguarded use of Mr. Zimmern's phrase might falsely suggest that the Empire of to-day differs as much in principle from the pre-war Empire as the latter differed from the First British Empire of Chatham's day.

the object before it was transformed, we must now call to mind, in as summary a fashion as possible, what the structure of the British Empire was at the time of the American Revolution and what the principles on which it rested.

In 1775 the territories under British rule outside the island of Britain were divided into five distinct groups. First, Ireland—in a class by herself, the nearest of the overseas territories, but ranking with them rather than with England, Wales, and Scotland. For, as far as Ireland was concerned, the British Isles had been only a geographical expression. The suggestion of a moral or material unity which the phrase conveyed and long continued to convey was illusory. Already, by the middle of the eighteenth century, human weakness and error had so magnified the natural breadth of the Irish Channel as to separate the bulk of the Irish people from the English, Welsh, and Scots, both in their interests and in their affections, both in law and in life, even farther than the colonists on the other side of the Atlantic were separated from their kinsmen in the mother country. Secondly, British North America—including Newfoundland and the thirteen mainland colonies, almost all the product of British settlement with an almost wholly British population; the colony of Nova Scotia and the islands off the mouth of the St. Lawrence, half-British and half-French in origin and population; the great province of Quebec, stretching far inland to the upper waters of the Mississippi, the product of French settlement with (apart from the Indians) an almost wholly French population ; and the Spanish Colonies of East and West Florida, ceded like Quebec at the close of the Seven Years War. Thirdly, British India—i.e. the territories controlled by the East India Company which, in 1775, comprised, besides Bombay and its vicinity, virtually the whole of Eastern India from Bengal to Travancore. Fourthly, the West Indian group, consisting of the British West Indies together with the Bahamas and Bermudas and one or two strips of the Central American coast. The British trading-posts in West Africa may be regarded at that time almost as a part of the West Indian group, since they formed one economic system with the West Indies. The fifth and last group—the little group of strategic naval stations for the maintenance of British sea-power on the main lines of communication—stands by itself and, though (as has been seen) it figured prominently in the naval warfare of 1778 to 1783, it need not concern us further.

The ground plan of the First British Empire in 1775, though far smaller than that of the Second British Empire as it stands to-day, was still immense. It sprawled across the world. Between its component parts stretched thousands of ocean miles. And those dividing gulfs, if distance be judged by the time it takes to cover it, were vastly wider than they are now. When the student of to-day sees the

Atlantic crossed by steam or motor ships in fewer days than the weeks it took the sailing ships of 1775 and faster yet by air, still more when he finds he can actually converse across the oceans in a manner which even the most enlightened scientists of 1775 would have regarded as something like black magic, he must surely wonder how our forefathers — by what policy, on what principles, with what unifying purpose—could possibly hope and try to hold that huge imperial conglomerate together in any single frame.

The answer is simple and familiar. They hoped and tried to hold it all together with ropes of pounds, shillings, and pence. Their policy, their principle, their purpose was trade, and practically nothing else. To almost every British statesman of the period, the British Empire, West or East, was only, so to speak, a huge estate and their fellow-Britons, living or trading therein, only, so to speak, its cultivators. No foreigners were allowed to trespass there. The exploitation of the estate was the monopoly of its owner, Britain ; and to its owner, Britain, belonged its profits. The cultivators could make what they could up to, but never beyond, the point at which their interests began to conflict with the owner's. There was nothing peculiar, of course, in this imperial system. It was the common, the notorious Mercantile System. Every other colonial Power adhered to it. If the First British Empire was a mercantile Empire, so or still more ruthlessly so were the Portuguese, Spanish, French, and Dutch. Nor was the governing motive of the system in itself unnatural or unwise or, by standards of international conduct by no means yet outworn, immoral. The system offended against nature and good sense and virtue mainly because that governing motive was the only motive. Chained to that economic standpoint, unable to think about the Empire except in the familiar commercial terms, British statesmen failed to envisage its other aspects. Yet, deep-rooted in that unwieldy body, lay political and moral problems even more closely bound up with its life and welfare than the problems of profit and loss. But for these the statesmen had no eyes. Now and again, spasmodically, reluctantly, they glanced at them and blinked. They never saw them steadily nor saw them whole.

A narrow mind has its compensations. It can concentrate all its forces on its own particular end. And alongside this constricted vision of the Empire, this exclusively commercial conception of it, must be set the growing prosperity of British industry and trade and shipping in the eighteenth century, and the stronger ' sinews of war ' which prosperity provided in that century of wars. But, as Adam Smith was one day to convince his countrymen, similar or better results might have been obtained under a more enlightened system ; and in any case the economic advantages of Mercantilism, such as they were, sink almost to insignificance beside its political and moral disadvantages. In the long run, in every quarter, the net results of the narrow mind were disastrous.

They were nowhere more disastrous than in that field which we put first in our classification. In Ireland, it is true, Mercantilism was only one factor in a terrible complex. Memories of conquest and subjection, the blood-feud of Saxon and Celt, political fear and religious hate between Protestant and Catholic—these were older and more lasting causes of the long Irish tragedy. But it is essential to remember that from the seventeenth century onwards the misfortunes of Ireland were shared, though by no means in equal measure, by the Protestant and Saxon as well as by the Catholic and Celtic Irish, and that the aggrieved and insurgent Ireland with which we are dealing in these lectures is not the Ireland of O'Connell and Parnell and Collins, but the Ireland of Grattan and Flood—an Ireland in which the immigrant stock of Protestant Anglo-Irish monopolised the political life of the country almost as completely as the Spartans in Laconia and in which the original Celtic population was almost as much outside the pale of politics as the ' redskins ' of America. True, this Protestant, half-English Ireland could not altogether escape the evil consequences of the old conflict of race and faith : it was inevitably implicated in the fate of the greater Ireland to which it was tied : but its misfortunes were mainly due to that other factor, to

Mercantilism. We must not forget—it is too often forgotten—that the word ' plantation ' in its human application was first used of English settlers in Ireland ; that Englishmen planted their first ' colony,' and so termed it, on the other side of the Irish Channel long before they planted any colony on the other side of the Atlantic ; and that Irish history before the Union of 1800 and since the treaty of 1921 should be regarded not as English history nor even as British history in its narrower sense, but as Colonial or Imperial history.[1] It might have been otherwise. If the English, before it was too late, had dealt with Catholic Ireland as they dealt with Wales, or with Protestant Ireland as they dealt with Scotland, how much happier the story of the two British Isles might have been ! But on the morrow of her ' Glorious Revolution ' England made two fatal decisions. She conceded the desire of the Anglo-Irish for a ' Protestant ascendancy ' and the subjection of the Catholics. She rejected their desire to be united like the Scots in a Greater Britain.[2]

[1] This point is well brought out by L. Curtis in *The Commonwealth of Nations* (London, 1919), chap. vii, and by C. H. McIlwain, *The American Revolution, a Constitutional Interpretation* (New York, 1923), 78-80.

[2] A legislative union of England and Ireland, temporarily established by Cromwell, was asked foɪ by the Irish House of Commons in 1703 and 1707. See J. A. Froude, *The English in Ireland in the Eighteenth Century* (London, 1901 ed.), i, 319-26, 334-8. Froude quotes a Dublin pamphlet of 1704 which cited the example of Wales as proving ' that the Celtic and the Saxon temperaments were not in themselves incompatible.' For Molyneux' opinion, see Lecky, *History of Ireland*, v, 123.

Ireland was not to be incorporated on equal terms into the Commonwealth, but to remain a colony. And that meant, and was intended to mean, and under the Mercantile System could only mean, that in economics Irish interests were to be sacrificed to British and in politics the Irish colonists were to be regarded not as the equals or partners of the British in the ' mother-country ' but as their inferiors and dependents. Like the American colonists, therefore, they were expected to be content with an Executive responsible to the British Government and a Legislature subordinate to the British Parliament. But, since Ireland was so much nearer than America, the status of the Irish ' colonists ' was still more degraded that that of the American. In the first place they did not possess the same measure of representative government. The Irish caste-system was not limited to the division between Protestants and Catholics. The majority of the Protestant Irish were Presbyterians, and the members of the Established Church of Ireland, closely allied with its sister Church of England just across the narrow channel, exercised over this majority a social and political ascendancy, similar to, though not so overwhelming as that which the Protestants as a whole exercised over the Catholics. The Presbyterians were not deprived of the franchise, but, lacking social influence and the means for ' marketing ' seats in the counties and excluded by the Test Act from the corporations which elected most of

the borough members, they were practically un-
represented in their ' representative assembly,' the
Dublin House of Commons, while the House of
Lords, of course, was still more securely protected
from nonconformist intruders. In other words,
the Irish Legislature, though it was composed of
Irishmen, represented a minority of a minority of
the Irish people. Moreover, it was more explicitly
subordinate than any colonial legislature to the British
Government and Parliament. Poynings' Act of
1494 provided that no Irish Parliament could be
summoned until the measures to be submitted to it
had been approved by the King—a provision which
enabled the English Privy Council to initiate, super-
vise, reject, or amend all Irish Bills.[1] At the end

[1] Text-books have made the name of Poynings' Act more
familiar than its contents. It provided that ' No Parliament be
holden hereafter in the said land, but at such season as the King's
lieutenant and counsaill there first do certifie the King, under
the great seal of that land, the causes and considerations, and all
such acts as them seemeth should pass in the same Parliament,
and such causes, considerations, and acts affirmed by the King
and his counsail to be good and expedient for that land, and his
licence thereupon, as well in affirmation of the said causes and
acts, as to summon the said Parliament under the great seal of
England had and obtained ; that done, a Parliament to be had
and holden after the form and effect afore rehearsed ; and if
any Parliament be holden in that land hereafter, contrary to the
form and provision aforesaid, it be deemed void and of none
effect in Law.' *Statutes at Large, Ireland* (Dublin, 1786), 10
Henry VII, c. iv, p. 44. Another Act of the same year (c. xxii)
confirmed as having force in Ireland all statutes ' late made '
in England : *ibid.*, p. 56. An Act of 1556, to declare the meaning
of Poynings' Act, prescribed a similar procedure during the
course of a Parliament : 3 and 4 Philip and Mary, c. iv : *ibid.*,

of the seventeenth century and again early in the eighteenth, Irishmen began to question the superior status of the English Parliament.[1] They ventured to assert the supreme authority of the Irish Legislature over all things Irish and, in particular, over the disposition of Irish revenues : and, advancing from the legislative to the judicial field, they claimed that the Irish House of Lords was the final court of appeal for Irishmen. This was dangerous doctrine for the Mercantilist Empire, and it was sharply repudiated by those English ministers who, as Swift declared with all his Irish indignation, were ' apt from their high elevation to look down upon this Kingdom as if it had been one of their colonies of outcasts in America.'[2] In 1719 they carried through the British Parliament a short and stiff Declaratory Act ' for better securing the dependency of the Kingdom of Ireland upon the Crown of Great Britain,' which swept away the appellate jurisdiction of the Irish House of Lords, and declared that the British Parliament ' had, hath, and of right ought to have full power and authority to make laws and statutes of sufficient force and validity to bind the kingdom and people of Ireland.' Lastly, the Irish Parliament was so filthily corrupt that, as will appear in a later

---

p. 246. All these were Acts of the Irish Parliament. The Declaratory Act of 1719 was, of course, an Act of the British Parliament ; 6 George I, cap. v.

[1] For Molyneux and Swift, see pp. 90-2 below.

[2] Swift's *Works* (ed. Scott, Edinburgh, 1814), vii, 25.

lecture, it was usually an easy matter for the Executive to bribe away any tiresome opposition to its will.[1] And this Executive, for its part, was more rigidly, continually, and effectively controlled by the British Government than any Governor and Council in the colonies for the simple reason that the Viceroy in Dublin was within a few days', not a few weeks', post from his masters in London. More easily, therefore, could the Irish Government and the Irish Parliament be brought to serve the purposes of the system to which they belonged. It was the business of the one to advance, it was impossible for the other to prevent, the application of Mercantilism to the economic life of Ireland.

It was a drastic process. In the first of the Navigation Acts, which were the pillars on which the whole system rested—the Act of 1660—Irish ships, it is true, were accorded the same liberty as English ships ; but the mistake was corrected by a series of Acts between 1663 and 1696 by which Ireland was excluded from almost all trade except with England. Her exports and imports had to pass through England, and they could only be carried in English ships, manned mainly by English seamen. The results of this part of the system were bad enough. It blocked the natural development of Irish commerce. It eliminated Irish shipping. It cancelled out the economic advantages which nature had given Ireland in her geographical position and

[1] See Lecture III.

her admirable harbours. And though a great deal can be said for the Navigation Acts, at least in principle, though the common interest of the whole Empire in the maintenance of British sea-power can be pleaded in their defence, though Adam Smith himself can be cited as an apologetic witness, it is difficult to find a high political motive in refusing to Irish shipping what was conceded to that of the American colonies and in practically classing Irish ships with those of foreign countries.[1] But the results of the second part of the system were still more destructive. The deliberate deletion of Irish industries in the interests, real or unreal, of their British rivals, was at least as inexcusable as the imposition of the Penal Laws. In the middle of the seventeenth century, the mainstay of economic prosperity in Ireland was the export of livestock and, to a less extent, of meat and dairy-produce to England. In the reign of Charles II it was cut clean away by the prohibition of all those imports in the interests of English landowners. The Irish then fell back on the manufacture of wool; but no sooner had a vigorous woollen industry developed, largely in Protestant hands, than first the import of Irish woollens into England was practically prevented by high duties and then their export to any country

[1] S. Gwynn, *History of Ireland* (London, 1923), 329. See also Lecky, *History of Ireland in the Eighteenth Century*, i, 174. For the Navigation Acts, see C. M. Andrews in *Cambridge History of the British Empire*, i, 279-81, 287.

whatever prohibited altogether by an Act of the English Parliament. Something was done by way of compensation to assist and protect the Ulster linen industry against foreign competition ; but, as soon as a rival industry was established in England and Scotland, it was assisted and protected in its turn against Irish competition. And with that the Mercantilist programme was complete. Indeed no more was needed. The triple blow at pastoral, agricultural, and industrial Ireland had condemned the mass of the Irish people to poverty or exile.[1]

Make every possible excuse, not indeed for such British landowners and manufacturers as were thinking only of their own pockets, but for such British statesmen as were thinking mainly of the safety of the realm : consider their paramount desire to increase to the utmost the wealth and thereby the strength of Britain in view of her perilous conflict with France : remember their fear of a wealthy and strong Ireland as a weight for the most part on the Catholic side against the Protestant and as a threat to Britain's flank in time of war—and still this terrible Irish story remains in itself a sufficient indictment of the old imperialism. But was it then,

[1] A. E. Murray, *Commercial Relations between England and Ireland* (London, 1903) ; livestock trade, chap. iii ; woollens, chap. iv ; linen, chap. vii. Irish poverty as result of commercial restrictions in conjunction with Penal Laws, pp. 92-4. For the linen trade, see Burke's *Letters, Speeches and Tracts on Irish Affairs* (ed. Matthew Arnold, London, 1881), 113 : and Froude, *op. cit.*, i, 296 ; ii, 103, 114, 137, 176. See also pp. 101, 102 below.

it may well be asked, the inevitable or at least the natural outcome of Mercantilism ? Trade, after all, and the wealth and strength which come from trade are good things. Was there something inherently vicious in basing the unity of Empire on inter-imperial trade ? Did it necessarily imply the sacrifice of the outer parts to the centre ? Was there no one in Britain capable of conceiving a fairer scheme of economic union ? Was Mercantilism in itself bound to ruin Ireland ? To answer those questions we must leave on one side for a moment the ideas about the Empire which generally prevailed in Britain and look at Mercantilism at its best. Let us examine the very similar opinions of the greatest imperial statesman of the eighteenth century and the greatest exponent of the English political tradition. Let us consider what may be called the idealist conception of the Empire.

To Chatham and Burke the Empire was in theory or ideal a Commonwealth : the profits of its common trade were meant for the common weal : all its parts and peoples were to share therein. In their eyes, therefore, the story that has just been told, so far from being a natural or inevitable outcome of mercantile imperialism, was the very reverse— a perversion of its true nature. No one protested more vigorously than Chatham against withholding from the Protestant Irish the local liberties of British subjects.[1] No one deplored more bitterly

[1] See pp. 88, 105 below.

than Burke the trade-laws which crippled all Ireland.[1] The odd thing is that neither of them seems to have asked himself how such aberrations were to be prevented. Since economics cannot be divorced from politics, their ideal could obviously not be realised without the appropriate political machinery. Yet, no better in this than the common herd of Mercantilists, they virtually ignored the political crux. They took it for granted that their commercial commonwealth *could* be well ordered and governed—though, as regards Ireland, at any rate, it manifestly was not—by a body which represented one of its parts alone. Look, for instance, at the placid logic with which Burke dismissed the problem in 1773, in connexion, as it happened, with an Irish controversy.

'If it be true [he writes to an Anglo-Irish friend] that the several bodies which make up this complicated mass are to be preserved as one Empire, an authority sufficient to preserve that unity and by its equal weight and pressure to consolidate the various parts that compose it, must reside somewhere : that somewhere can only be in England. Possibly any one Member, distinctly taken, might decide in favour of that residence within itself ; but certainly no Member would give its voice for any other except this. So that I look upon the residence of the supreme power to be settled here ; not by force or tyranny or even by mere long usage, but by the very nature of things and the joint consent of the whole body. If all this be admitted, then without question this Country must have the sole right to the Imperial Legislation : by which I mean that law which

[1] See p. 115 below.

regulates the polity and economy of the several parts as they relate to one another and to the whole.'[1]

Q.E.D.; and the argument seemed unanswerable, at any rate till Adam Smith and the younger Pitt had answered it. So, while Chatham stood up for the rights of the Irish Parliament, he never questioned its subordination to the British; and while Burke condemned the trade-laws, he never doubted the right of the British Parliament to make them.[2] And this ' blind spot,' as it seems to us now, with our longer and even sadder experience, is more re-markable in Burke than in Chatham. An Irishman himself and able, as Chatham never was, to sym-pathise with the Catholics of his mother's race as well as with the Protestants of his father's, Burke had the deeper understanding of the Irish problem and the closer contact with it. He saw clearly enough that the real interests of the twin islands were not antagonistic but complementary, that a free and contented sister was less dangerous than a resentful serf, and that a rich Ireland was better for British trade than a poor. ' England and Ireland may flourish together,' he said. But how did he think that happy dream was to be given shape ? By following the precedent of the other three nations of the British Isles ? By political union on a basis

---

[1] Letter to Sir C. Bingham, *Works* (London, 1826 ed.), ix, 136.

[2] E.g. *Irish Letters*, iii, 319.

of equality ? When he was asked his opinion on
that issue in 1778, he evaded a direct reply. ' A
union of interest and affection,' he declared, ' is a
far better thing than any nominal union of government '—wherein he spoke the truth indeed, but ignored the fact that, whereas a political union implied
equality, his union of interest and affection was a
union of superior with dependant. And in his noble,
sincere, and futile defence of his Irish policy against
the profiteers of Bristol he confessed as much. He
had wished, he wrote, ' to unite the interests of
the two nations in a manner that would secure the
supremacy of this.' [1]

Supremacy. There lay the fatal flaw even in so
enlightened a version of Mercantilism as Burke's.
If the British Parliament had been composed of
Burkes, it might have used its power to control
the trade of the Empire for the common profit of
all its parts. It might have treated Ireland not only
fairly but generously ; and, so doing, it might have
gone far to redress the past and to create a new
atmosphere in which a national reconciliation, a
union of affections, would not have seemed a dream.
But even then, so long as it clung, as Burke clung,
to its ' supremacy,' so long as it refused to share its
imperial power, so long as it denied to the Irish,
even the Protestant Irish, political equality, the
Irish problem could not have been fully or finally
solved. As it was, of course, the problem was not even

[1] *Irish Letters*, 102-3, 106, 320.

partially or temporarily solved. It was intensified, rather, and inflamed. For the British Parliament did not consist of Burkes but of average Englishmen, Welshmen, and Scotsmen ; and, since human history gives us no right to expect a nation or a class to be altruistic or even to be a just judge in its own cause, it is surely not surprising that, confronted with a conflict, as they believed it to be, between Irish interests and their own, those average Englishmen, Welshmen, and Scotsmen, not to mention the more ignorant and inexperienced electors at their back, were incapable of rising to the heights demanded by the imperial idealism of a Chatham or a Burke.

It would seem, then, that, like too many other ideals, the idealist conception of the old commercial Empire must be dismissed as beyond the scope of practical politics. For even the greatest of the few who envisaged it were content to leave the political side of the imperial system unchanged. And, that being so, their ideal could only be realised by a revolution. The fate of Ireland *was*, if not the inevitable, at least the natural outcome of Mercantilism. And since it had made them feel, Protestants almost as much as Catholics, an alien and subject people, since it had refused them not only an equal political status with their British fellow-subjects but also an equal chance of economic prosperity, would the Irish have been to blame if throughout the eighteenth century their attitude to Britain had been—as a

matter of fact it was not—the same as the Helots'
attitude to Sparta, ἀεὶ ἐφεδρύοντες τοῖς ἀτυχήμασιν,
always lying in wait to take advantage of their conquerors' misfortunes ? And is it to be wondered at
that, when the chance came, they found or thought
to find their only remedy in Revolution ?

Of the second field, the American colonies, little
need be said here : for the main facts about the
American colonies in the eighteenth century are more
generally known than the main facts about Ireland,
though Ireland is a hundred times nearer Britain.
Suffice it, then, to say that the status of the American
colonies under the Mercantile System was much the
same as that of the Protestants in Ireland. The
measure of self-government which they enjoyed was
similarly inferior to that enjoyed by their kinsmen
in the mother-country. In most of the colonies the
Executive was composed mainly of outsiders, directly
or indirectly appointed by and responsible to the
British Government in London. In each colonial
capital, as at Dublin, there was a little Parliament;
and though there was no Poynings' Act for America,
its legislation was similarly subject to veto by the
British Government and similarly subordinate to the
authority of the Parliament at Westminster. Only
with regard to taxation, when that issue was so short-
sightedly raised in 1765, was anyone to be found
as yet in Britain who questioned this legislative
overlordship ; and when, in 1766, an attempt was

made, with scarcely longer vision, to lay the issue
to rest again, the repeal of the Stamp Act was accompanied by a Declaratory Act for America identi-
cal not only in purport but in language with the
Declaratory Act for Ireland.[1] Something will be
said in later lectures about other aspects of the
superior political status of Englishmen at home ;
the point to be stressed here is that this legislative
predominance was used, precisely as in Ireland, to
operate the Mercantile System, to keep the young
and vigorous currents of economic life in the colonies
within channels conducive to the welfare of the
mother-country. This fact has never been more
starkly stated than by the colonists' most famous
friend. ' The power of Parliament,' said the elder
Pitt in 1766, ' like the circulation of the heart, active,
vigorous, and perfect in the smallest fibre of the
arterial system, may be known in the colonies by
the prohibition of their carrying a hat to market
over the line of one province into another or by
breaking down a loom in the most distant corner
of the British Empire in America ; and if this power

---

[1] 6 Geo. III, c. 11, repealed the Stamp Act. 6 Geo. III, c. 12,
was entitled ' An Act for the better securing the dependency of
His Majesty's Dominions in America upon the Crown and Parliament of Great Britain,' and declared that the British Parliament
' had, hath, and of right ought to have full power and authority
to make laws and statutes of sufficient force and validity to bind
the colonies and people of America, subjects of the Crown of
Great Britain, in all cases whatsoever.' Compare the Act of
1719, p. 59 above.

were denied, I would not permit them to manufacture a lock of wool or a horseshoe or a hobnail.
In everything you may bind them except that of
taking money out of their pockets without their
consent.'[1]   Again that harsh assumption of ' supremacy,' to be echoed again, more melodiously, by
Burke ; but it sounds less startling on the lips of
those imperial idealists when they are speaking of
America. For in America the actual operation of
the Mercantile System was not so complete a tra-
vesty of their ideal. It was possible for the British
Parliament to pursue its old devices for enriching
Britain without ruining the American colonies as it
had ruined Ireland. Distance and their youth protected them. The development of local industries
in unchecked competition with British was not yet
essential to their prosperity. The restrictions of the
Navigation Acts were evaded by smuggling more
easily and effectively than in Ireland ; and against
them could be set the inflow of British capital, a
safer market in Britain than the unhappy Irish agri-
culturists enjoyed, and those bounties and other
aids which could safely be conceded to colonists who
were not as yet competitors. In America, moreover,
there was a livelier sense of the political benefits
conferred by the imperial connexion. The Irish—at
least the Catholic Irish—came in the end to dread a
French invasion less than the American colonists ;
and, as long as British sea-power was supreme, they

[1] Speech of 14 Jan., 1766.   B. Williams, *op. cit.*, ii, 191-2.

had much less need to dread it, since France was not contiguous with Ireland. But the protection of British arms for the American colonists by sea or land was a real weight in the balance against economic subjection as long as New France was contiguous with New England. And on this consideration (as every one knows) the tacit contract which underlay the old colonial system was mainly based. Both parties profited, or thought they profited. Both parties were more or less content—till 1765.[1]

And yet, though Mercantilism was at its best in this American field, what a bad ' best ' it was ! For, through it all, active, vigorous, and perfect in the smallest fibre of its arterial system, ran the fatal poison of inequality—an inequality which was as untenable in theory as it proved intolerable in fact. In fact it again led straight to Revolution. In theory it involved even its greatest upholders in what

[1] The view that the Mercantile System was a primary cause of the American Revolution because the colonists (at any rate before 1763) resented its restrictions or suffered grave economic injury has been untenable since the publication of the late G. L. Beer's invaluable work (see especially *British Colonial Policy*, 1754-65, New York, reprinted 1922 ; and see also for an English acceptance of his case, W. J. Ashley, *Surveys Historic and Economic* (London, 1900), 309-60). But the reaction against the older view may go too far if it overlooks the fact that the Mercantile System provided the most obvious demonstration of political inequality. As the late Professor Egerton said in his judicious *American Revolution* (Oxford, 1923), 68 : ' The *pacte coloniale* had been settled by only one of the parties concerned with the agreement.' The effect on political *morale* is most clearly stated by L. Curtis, *op. cit.*, chap. vi.

should surely have seemed a manifest contradiction. Chatham knew well enough that the American colonists possessed by right of blood the heritage of English freedom. ' The Americans are the sons, not the bastards of England.' Yet, save in the matter of ' internal ' taxation, they were to be less free than Englishmen in the mother-country. ' It is my opinion that this kingdom has no right to lay a tax upon the colonies. At the same time I assert *the authority of this kingdom over the colonies to be sovereign and supreme* in every circumstance of government and legislation whatsoever. They are the subjects of this kingdom, *equally entitled with yourselves to . . . the peculiar privileges of Englishmen ;* equally bound by its laws and *equally participating of the constitution of this free country.'* [1] How sharp the contradiction seems to-day, and how strange that the speaker did not himself detect it. Chatham, again, saw far more clearly than most of his contemporaries that the quarrel of the colonies with the mother-country was drawing them together into a great community inspired by a common purpose. It was he who spoke of ' the nation of America,'[2] and who, on the very eve of the Revolution, proposed the first, immediate, practical measure needed for the readjustment of inter-imperial relations—the establishment of a national pan-American government. Yet at the outset of his Bill he declared once

---

[1] Speech of 14 Jan., 1766 ; B. Williams, *op. cit.*, ii, 190.
[2] Speech of 20 Jan., 1775 ; *ibid.*, ii, 305.

more the right of a Parliament in which no colonist was represented ' to bind the British colonies in America in all matters touching the general weal of the whole dominion of the imperial crown of Great Britain.' [1]

The same assumption and the same contradiction are apparent in all Burke's American doctrine. ' We are bound, as much as possible, to extend the spirit and benefit of the British constitution to every part of the British dominions.' ' Deny them this participation of freedom and you break the sole bond.' But the noble phrases in which the incomparable musician played his variations on the theme of ' the spirit of the English communion ' are too familiar for quotation. And they were true—as true then as they are true now. Indeed, if George III and his ministers could have admitted them or even understood them, the Revolution might have been long delayed. None the less, Burke's imagination, immeasurably wider though it was than that of his political opponents, was as constricted as Chatham's. In America, just as in Ireland, his mind was fettered to the notion of ' supremacy.' He could not or would not see that ' the spirit of the English communion ' must some day fade and die if it were

[1] Chatham's ' Provisional Bill,' introduced on 1 Feb., 1775, recognised Congress as the legal organ of the American people and assigned to it the function of determining the grant of revenue for the alleviation of the national debt and of allocating the quota to be paid by each colony. B. Williams, *op. cit.*, ii, 309.

not embodied in corporeal equality. The practical
policy which emerged from all his magic eloquence
was purely negative and, if it had sufficed for the
day, it could not have sufficed for the morrow.
Deliberately and definitely he painted on one-half
of his canvas the colonies enjoying as much self-
government as they had enjoyed before the Stamp
Act and on the other half the Parliament of Great
Britain in her ' imperial character, in which, as
from the throne of heaven, she superintends all
the several inferior legislatures, and guides and con-
trols them all, without annihilating any ' ; and then,
with a strange complacency, he regarded the incongruous picture as a ' sufficient ' reconciliation of
' subordination and liberty '—for ever and ever.[1]

Even in Chatham's and Burke's eyes, then, the
sons of England in America were subordinate to
their brothers in the homeland ; and for all their
high and genuine talk of an equal heritage in theory
they denied them equality in practice. In practice
the average Englishman's idea of the imperial relation held the field—-the idea of privileged manufacturers and protected producers and customers—
and that was not enough to keep alive ' the spirit
of the English communion,' to maintain that sense
of common ideals and duties by which alone political
societies can live and last and which was needed in
special measure by a society assaying the tremendous

[1] *Works* (World's Classics ed.), ii, 126, 235, 149.

task of bridging the Atlantic. In fact, when Burke was speaking, there was little notion of communion left. Quite naturally, the general attitude on the British side had become an attitude of smug superiority. Quite naturally, when colonial visitors came to England, they found themselves treated as something less than country-cousins and had to confess it piqued their pride ' to hear us called " *our* Colonies, *our* Plantations," with such airs as if our property and persons were absolutely theirs, like the villains in the old feudal system.' [1] Nor was such snobbery the worst evil of a false imperialism. It tempted every Englishman to feel himself better and bigger for being some other body's master—a ' disposition ' which, when the Revolution came, explained, to Burke's mind at any rate, the enthusiasm of ' many men in very humble life ' for the American war. ' *Our* subjects in America ; *our* colonies ; *our* dependants. . . . This siren song of ambition has charmed ears that one would have thought were never organised to that sort of music.' [2] And on

---

[1] Judge Curwen, a loyalist, in England in 1776, quoted by Sir G. O. Trevelyan, *op. cit.*, iii, 241. Cf. the colonial pamphlet of 1765, quoted by G. B. Hertz, *The Old Colonial System* (Manchester, 1905), 91, complaining of Englishmen speaking of the colonies as their property. The development of a new colonial status in the Second British Empire and its gradual recognition by public opinion in the mother-country could be amusingly illustrated if it were possible to define all that Englishmen in the xixth and early xxth centuries implied when they said ' our Colonies ' or ' our Dominions.'

[2] *Irish Letters*, 174.

the other side of the Atlantic what could have been better calculated than Mercantilism to narrow the political horizon, to smother any notions of imperial solidarity or purpose, to degrade the high associations of blood and language and tradition to the level of the counter ? ' I state to you,' said Chatham to his fellow-Englishmen, ' the importance of America ; it is a double market : a market of consumption and a market of supply.'[1]   In what other sort of language could Americans be expected to state the importance of England ?   How could they construe the ties of Empire except as terms in a commercial contract ?   And what was to happen to the contract when the most important item on one side of the bargain was cut out, when, as the result of the Seven Years War and the annexation of French Canada, the colonists no longer needed, or thought they no longer needed, the protection of the mother-country against France ?   Those foreign observers who declared that Britain's triumph in 1763 would soon be followed by the loss of her colonies were not indulging in frivolous or fantastic prophecy.   They were putting two and two together.[2]

[1] Quoted by G. M. Trevelyan, *History of England* (London, 1926), 444.

[2] Peter Kalm, the Swede, before the Seven Years War, doubted for this reason whether Britain really intended to conquer Canada (G. L. Beer, *British Colonial Policy*, 1754-65, 170).   Montcalm (or Roubaud) during the war ; *ibid.*, 172.   Vergennes in 1763 ; Egerton, *American Revolution*, 129.

When we pass from Ireland and America to the third and fourth groups, the scene grows darker. And naturally so. For, when mercantile imperialism crossed the line between European colonies in the true sense of the words and European trading settlements in countries peopled by coloured races, the effects of its onesidedness were bound to be still more marked and still more vicious. To concentrate on commerce only, to neglect the political and moral issues, was folly in America and worse than folly in Ireland : in India it was a crime. Not, of course, a deliberate crime, nor even, perhaps, inexcusable. For a long time after the first establishment of English trade in India the danger in the situation was only latent. The East India Company, bent solely on trade, desired no territorial conquests in India, no political power beyond the control of their three or four trading townships on the coast, so long as the natives of India could maintain the peace, order, and security which trade required. With rare and brief interruptions this policy was maintained for a century and a half. The Company prospered under it, was content with it, got used to it. And then, in the middle of the eighteenth century, the whole scene in India was suddenly transformed. Through various causes—the collapse of the Mogul Empire, the spread of internal strife and anarchy, the growth of French rivalry and intrigue—the Company, striving now to maintain not only its trade but its very foothold on Indian soil, was forced from commerce into politics ; and in a few years' time, mainly through the genius of Clive, its directors and agents were confronted with the astonishing and rather disquieting fact that they, a body of respectable business men, had become, without at all intending or desiring it, the political masters of a gigantic area in Eastern India. They must not be blamed too hardly because they failed to adjust themselves at once to such a drastic change of character. Nor could public opinion in England, knowing and caring nothing about India except as a source of legitimate commercial profit, be expected closely to examine or clearly to understand the new situation. And so the Company, unchecked, almost unnoticed, attempted what seemed the easiest course. It ignored the change ; it carried on ; it pretended still to be only a trading concern ; and in order to maintain the pretence it refused to accept any responsibility for the government of the territories of which it was now *de facto* sovereign or for the welfare of the countless Indians who were now *de facto* its subjects. Opinion at home followed suit. Government and Parliament continued to imagine that they were not concerned with the affairs of a private company in India beyond seeing that its commercial status was properly adjusted to the general structure of mercantile imperialism. One man, indeed, was partly at least aware of what the changed position in India involved—the man who had done most to bring it about. In his famous letter to Pitt in 1759,

Clive admitted that the ' sovereignty ' not only over Bengal but over all the dominions of the titular Mogul Emperor, while it was easily within its grasp, ' may possibly be an object too extensive for a mercantile Company.'

' I have therefore presumed, Sir, to represent this matter to you, and submit it to your consideration, whether the execution of a design, that may hereafter be still carried to greater lengths, be worthy of the Government's taking it into hand. I flatter myself I have made it pretty clear to you, that there will be little or no difficulty in obtaining the absolute possession of these rich kingdoms : and that with the Mogul's own consent on condition of paying him less than a fifth of the revenues thereof. Now I leave you to judge, whether an income yearly of two millions sterling, with the possession of three provinces abounding in the most valuable productions of nature and of art, be an object deserving the public attention ; and whether it be worth the nation's while to take the proper measures to secure such an acquisition—an acquisition which, under the management of so able and disinterested a minister, would prove a source of immense wealth to the kingdom, and might in time be appropriated in part as a fund towards diminishing the heavy load of debt under which we at present labour. Add to these advantages the influence we shall thereby acquire over the several European nations engaged in the commerce here, which these could no longer carry on but through our indulgence, and under such limitations as we should think fit to prescribe. It is well worthy consideration, that this project may be brought about without draining the mother country, as has been too much the case with our possessions in America.' [1]

That letter is one of the most significant documents in the history of the First British Empire. It

[1] R. Muir, *The Making of British India* (Manchester, 1917), 63.

betrays Clive's limitations in insight or imagination just as Pitt's are betrayed by his speech about horseshoes and hobnails. Neither of the two Englishmen, who were, in practical affairs at least, the greatest of their day, could free their eyes from the blinkers of Mercantilism. As Pitt saw nothing wrong in the political subjection of Ireland or the American colonies, so Clive saw no other argument, at least he stated none, for British rule in India than the fact that it was a more paying proposition than British rule in America. It reveals—and this should make us careful of our censure—how universal, how profound, how inspissated was the mercantilist obsession.

Whatever his principles, Clive's policy, of course, was right. In the situation into which she had drifted, the only salvation for India lay in the assumption by the British Government and Parliament of responsibility for her administration ; and it was unfortunate for India and for the good name of Britain that Clive's arguments, inadequate as they were, left Pitt unconvinced. Disaster and dishonour followed. Already, at the price of an enormous ' war-indemnity ' and of ' presents ' to Clive and his subordinates scarcely less enormous, an Indian puppet-prince had been installed on the throne of Bengal. His was to be the responsibility, but not his the power. If any Indian doubted that no force in Eastern India could be matched against the victors of Plassey and Chinsurah and Wandewash,

he doubted no longer after Buxar. And so, while
Mir Jafar or Mir Kasim were allowed to play at
ruling within the limits of their masters' interests,
the real rulers were those masters. Sooner or later,
directly or indirectly, the things that were done
were the things which the English officials and
officers and clerks, and even their Indian subordinates and go-betweens and hangers-on, wanted done.
There is no call for wonder, still less for scorn or
anger, at the inevitable result. Power without responsibility—the most wickedly dangerous thing
known to politics—sets too severe a strain on the
virtue of ordinary men at any time or place ; and
those men, remember, had been born and bred, like
Clive and Pitt, in the atmosphere of Mercantilism
and were now exposed to all the insidious attacks
which life in the tropics among a weaker people
makes on white men's characters. So came the one,
the only, black decade in the chronicles of British
rule in India—the five years before and the five
years after the brief interval of Clive's second governorship in Bengal from 1765 to 1767. It need
not be described here. We have read our Burke—
not, it may be hoped, without due discrimination.
It is enough to quote what Clive, who was not an
ordinary man, thought about it himself. ' I shall
only say,' he reported, ' that such a scene of anarchy,
confusion, bribery, corruption, and extortion was
never seen or heard of in any country but Bengal ;
nor such and so many fortunes acquired in so

unjust and rapacious a manner.'[1]　With that we may drop the curtain over the Indian section of the First British Empire.

And raise it over the fourth and last section—to disclose, unhappily, the worst picture of the set. It can be described in four words, the words which linked the West Indies and West Africa in one economic system—Slavery and the Slave Trade. And it can be very briefly explained. The indigenous population of the West Indies was neither numerous nor strong enough to provide the manual labour needed for their economic development. Their climate prevented Europeans from providing it.　From the outset, therefore, the English planters were confronted with a labour problem. They solved it, like all other European settlers in the tropics in that period, by buying slaves.　The importers, the slave-traders, obtained the slaves in West Africa by purchase from native chiefs for arms or powder or alcohol or simply by force or fraud.　The results were twofold.　First, the institution of Slavery was taken, as it were, from the scrap heap of earlier civilisations, refurbished, rehabilitated, and established firmly and on a great scale within the British

---

[1] R. Muir, *op. cit.*, 76.　See also the statements of Becker, one of the Company's officials, in 1769, and those of Warren Hastings in 1774 and 1782, quoted by P. E. Roberts in *Cambridge History of India*, v, 198, 207-8.　Chatham said in 1773 : ' India teems with impurities so rank as to smell to earth and heaven.' B. Williams, *op. cit.*, ii, 293.

Empire. When the time came, as it was bound to come, for its abolition, there were not far less than a million slaves in white men's ownership on British soil. Secondly, the sea-going peoples of Europe were engaged for over a century in inflicting on the peoples of Central Africa the greatest wrong recorded in the annals of mankind. Not only were several million Africans stolen from their homes and shipped oversea in conditions of atrocious cruelty, but the barbarism of those who remained in Africa was made more barbarous by the operations of the Trade. And in this lucrative and loathsome business England, as a natural result of her growing preponderance over France and other maritime Powers in overseas and colonial commerce, acquired the largest share.[1]

Of all the examples so far cited of the power of Mercantilism over men's minds this is surely the most striking. The evils of Slavery, for which a little could be said in palliation, the worse evils of the Slave Trade, for which nothing could be said at all, were tolerated by our forefathers, who were presumably, on the whole, as well-meaning and good-natured as we are, simply because they regarded them as essential parts of the economic system of the Empire; and even when the inhumanity of it all was forced on their attention, they still for many years excused it on the plea of

[1] The methods and results of the Slave Trade are described in R. Coupland's *Wilberforce* (Oxford, 1923), 71-4, etc.

economic ' necessity.' As late as 1783 Lord North, a kind-hearted man, expressed his regret that ' it would be found impossible to abolish the Slave Trade . . . for it was a trade which had, in some measure, become necessary to almost every nation in Europe ';[1] and the House of Commons tacitly agreed with him.

Such was the old imperialism, such the system which gave body and soul to the British Empire in 1775 and still held together those remains of it which the younger Pitt asked his countrymen to examine in 1783. We are now in a position to consider what came of his request.

[1] Coupland, *op. cit.*, 85.

III.

THE IRISH REVOLUTION : FIRST PHASE.

' A VOICE from America shouted to Liberty, the echo of it caught your people as it passed along the Atlantic, and they renewed the voice till it reverberated here.' [1] Those words were spoken in Ireland, and in no part of the British Empire were the effects of the American Revolution more immediate, more direct, or more far-reaching. Even British politics were less violently affected than Irish. Even the downfall of George III's system was not, at first sight at least, so great a matter as what occurred in Ireland. And the reason is plain. The Irish (it has been seen) were relegated to the same inferior or dependent status in the Empire as the American colonists. Their grievances, which were indeed far more substantial, were due to similar causes, and the burden of them was aggravated in a similar manner by the course of British policy after 1763. When, therefore, the issue—fundamentally one and the same issue—came to a head in the

---

[1] Henry Flood in the Irish House of Commons, 14 June, 1782. *History of the Proceedings and Debates of the House of Commons of Ireland* (Dublin, 1784), i, 427.

colonies, Irish sentiment was bound to be deeply stirred. Inevitably the Irish movement for freedom and equality was associated in its direction and in its fortunes with the American, and, mainly as a result of events in America and their reaction on events in Europe, it culminated like the American in a revolution.

For many years before 1763 the two movements had followed a parallel course ; but the Irish had started earlier than the American and developed more variously and vigorously, though with even less results. For since the American colonies (as we observed in the second lecture) did not suffer as Ireland suffered from the economics of mercantile imperialism, their spokesmen had little provocation or desire—till after 1763—to question the basis of its politics. Practically ignoring the deeper issues of imperial power, they concentrated, not without success, on levelling up their local system of colonial self-government to conform with its English model. Their main efforts were directed to increasing the power of the legislature and the judiciary as against the Executive—without (it may be noted in passing) attaining the constitutional harmony attained in England by making the Executive responsible to the legislature.[1] Thus the British Septennial Act of 1716 was copied by New York in 1743 and by Virginia in 1762. South

[1] See p. 314 below.

Carolina and New Hampshire, more radical, achieved Triennial Acts in 1721 and 1728, but similar Bills in New Jersey were vetoed.[1] The colonists were less successful in their efforts to obtain the same independence for their judges as that which had been guaranteed in England by the Act of Settlement in 1701. Bills for making the tenure of judicial office 'during good behaviour' instead of 'during pleasure' were carried by the Assemblies in Pennsylvania in 1759, in North Carolina in 1760, and in New York in 1761 ; but they were all vetoed or disallowed ; and the unredressed grievance survived to figure in the comminatory clauses of the Declaration of Independence.[2] Now these measures, naturally, were also to be found in the programme of Irish patriots. In 1761 the heads of a Septennial Bill were passed by the House of Commons, under unusual pressure from the constituencies, but they were rejected by the British Government.[3] The claim for judicial independence likewise was often aired, but in the air it remained.[4] In Ireland, however, these were relatively minor issues. So much nearer than America to Britain, she was subjected to intrusions by the British Executive into her own

[1] E. B. Greene, *The Provincial Governor* (Cambridge, Mass., 1898), chap. viii. The charters of Pennsylvania and Massachusetts required annual elections. South Carolina changed to annual dissolution in 1745 and biennial in 1747.

[2] E. B. Greene, *op. cit.*, chap. vii.

[3] Lecky, *op. cit.*, ii, 73-7.

[4] For a statement of the case, see *Irish Debates for* 1763-64 (ed. Caldwell, London, 1766), i, 292-6.

local field of self-government which, had they been practicable and practised in America, would have provoked a far earlier Revolution. It was not only that the Viceroy and his ministers were under the more direct and continuous control of the Government in London than any colonial Governor and Council, and more able by corruption to impose the will of London on their Parliament. In accordance with the British interpretation of Poynings' Act Irish Bills, including Money Bills, were customarily rejected, amended, and sometimes or in some degree initiated by the British Government. In other words the Irish Parliament could enact a Bill in the precise form in which it came or came back to it from London or not at all. From the morrow of the Revolution settlement onwards—the first occasion was in 1698—the Dublin Commons had protested, especially with regard to Money Bills, and once at least they had refused for a time to vote supplies dictated from across the Channel. And though such opposition could never long resist the gilded blandishments of ' Dublin Castle,' this violation of the basic right of self-taxation remained a burning question with the small but growing body of Irish politicians who formed, about the middle of the century, the first ' patriots ' party.[1] Ireland, more-

---

[1] See p. 58 above. Chatham, as might be expected, supported the Irish claim concerning Money Bills in the teeth of Bedford and a majority of his colleagues in 1759-60. B. Williams, *op. cit.*, ii, 46. See also p. 105 below.

over, even in peace-time, was not permitted to control, though she was expected to provide, her own defences. Every American colony had its militia, but not Ireland. The only troops in Ireland consisted of a standing army of 12,000 men, recruited solely from Irish Protestants and maintained solely from Irish revenues, yet an integral part of the British army and at least as effectively under British control as the integral part of the British army which is stationed in India to-day. It was created by an English Act of Parliament in 1698 and governed by the annual British Mutiny Acts. It lay beyond the pale of Irish legislation. Naturally, therefore, another and a prominent plank in the patriots' platform was an Irish Mutiny Act.[1]

The Irish movement, then, before the end of the Seven Years War, though necessarily similar in character, operated along more varied lines of grievance and agitation than the American. But the most notable difference between them has yet to be stated. In Ireland all those other issues were subordinate to one great issue—the Trade Laws and the power which enacted them. Americans might have no substantial reason before 1765 to question the ' supremacy ' of the Imperial Parliament. To Irishmen it was the author of their ruin.

[1] The English Act (10 Will. III, c. 1) provided for the disbandment of all troops then in Ireland excepting 12,000 which were to be ' maintained at the sole charge of the kingdom of Ireland.'

And it was with a direct assault on that central citadel of the whole imperial structure that the Irish movement had actually begun. As early as 1692, when the English Parliament was in the midst of its ruthless work, William Molyneux, a distinguished Irish philosopher and mathematician and a friend of Locke, published a booklet, replete with historical and legal learning, moderate, even loyalist in sentiment, but emphatically declaring that the Irish Parliament was by right the sole and supreme legislative authority in Ireland. Repudiating the idea ' that Ireland is to be looked upon as a colony from England ' as ' the most extravagant of all the objections raised against us,' Molyneux argued that the claim that Ireland should be ' bound by acts of parliament made in England ' was contrary to the rights of mankind, to the principle of consent, to the English common law, to the statute law of England and Ireland, to concessions and charters given to Ireland, to the rights of the Crown in Ireland, and to the precedents of earlier times.[1] Some twenty years later a doughtier champion of Ireland entered the lists. In 1720 Dean Swift of St. Patrick's, chafing at Britain's commercial tyranny, set an historic precedent by urging the Irish to wear nothing but cloth of their own manufacture. ' Let a firm resolution be taken by male and female never to appear with one single shred that comes from

[1] W. Molyneux, *The Case of Ireland being bound by Acts of Parliament made in England stated* (reprint, Dublin, 1782), 52-60.

England, and let all the people say, AMEN.'[1] The light-hearted tone of this short pamphlet concealed the almost savage hatred of injustice that simmered in Swift's heart; but after the astounding scandal of ' Wood's Half-pence,'[2] it boiled up and over in a stream of scalding irony and ridicule. Nor was the Dublin draper (in whose character Swift wrote his famous series of open letters) content to excoriate the wretched Wood: in language that was to be echoed in the coming days of Revolution on both sides of the Atlantic, he laid bare the roots of the evil—British supremacy, Irish subjection. ' Were not the people of Ireland born as free as those of England ? Is not their parliament as fair a representative of the people as that of England ? . . . Are not they subjects of the same king ? Does not the same sun shine upon them ? And have they not the same God for their protector ? Am I a freeman in England, and do I become a slave in six hours by crossing the channel ? ' And recalling

---

[1] *A Proposal for the Universal Use of Irish Manufacture*, etc. Swift's *Works* (ed. Scott, Edinburgh, 1814), vii, 19.

[2] A patent was granted in England to the Duchess of Kendal, George I's mistress, for coining copper halfpence for use in Ireland. The coins were to be of less than half the market-value of the metal and of lower intrinsic value than those in use in England. To magnify the profits the amount of halfpence coined was to exceed in money-value a quarter of the estimated total of all coins then current in Ireland. The Duchess sold the patent to Wood, an English ironmaster. No Irish authority was consulted in the matter. See Lecky, *History of Ireland in the Eighteenth Century* (London, 1919), i, 451, and other authorities.

and approving the arguments of ' the famous Mr. Molyneux,' he declared that ' freedom consists in a people's being governed by laws made with their own consent, and slavery in the contrary.' [1] Swift, of course, was not a party politician, but Charles Lucas, the crippled and soured Dublin chemist who was the next to preach Swift's doctrine, was the founder of a new and vigorous nationalist party. In 1747 he began in his *Citizen's Journal* a long series of vituperative attacks on the existing order. In 1761, glorified in his followers' eyes by Government persecution and a brief exile in the Isle of Man, he was elected M.P. for Dublin. And, while he played his part in the minor controversies mentioned above, his first, his shrillest, his most obstinate demand was for the repudiation of British ' supremacy ' and the recognition of the right of the Irish Parliament to an independent and equal status.[2]

Before 1763, then, the Irish movement had gone farther and deeper than the American. But after 1763 the American movement, galvanised by the Stamp Act and its sequel, not only caught up the Irish but took the lead and swept ahead to its climax and conclusion. In this last period, therefore, the two movements become more closely assimilated and interlinked.

[1] *The Drapier's Letters ; Works*, vii, 140, 182, 229.
[2] Lecky, *op. cit.*, i, 211, 461.   Froude, *op. cit.*, i, 677-80. *D.N.B.*, *s.n.*

Note, in the first place, that Ireland had been at
least as loyal to the Empire in the war as the American colonies. Her share of its burdens, indeed, had
been relatively far greater. The Irish House of
Commons—' the most willing that ever sat,' it was
said—had voted a war-credit of half a million sterling and provided—for this at any rate was permitted it—for an increase of five battalions in the
army in Ireland. Pitt, it is true, grumbled at the
shortage of fresh recruits and scoffed at Ulster's
tender devotion to its ' looms and manufactures.' [1]
But it must be remembered that the Irish troops
available at the outset of the war, from which Pitt
took large drafts for the fighting in America, had
numbered no less than 12,000, that these had been
recruited from the Protestant Irish only, and that
the corresponding figure for the standing army in
Britain had been only 17,000.[2] The Catholic Irish,
for their part, had begged in vain to be allowed to
serve ; and the leaders of their faith had been out-
spokenly loyal, although the King's enemies were

[1] B. Williams, op. cit., ii, 43-5. Froude, op. cit., i, 696.
[2] Lecky (op. cit., ii, 68) holds that Ireland supported England
' to the utmost of her small abilities.' Burke stated in 1785
that 24,000 Irishmen were provided for the Irish Army and
33,000 sent abroad ' to fill up regiments in the British service '
(Parl. Hist., xxv, 651, quoted by Lecky, op. cit., ii, 342). In
1779 it was reckoned that no less than 100,000 Irishmen had
seen military or naval service in the war (ibid., ii, 221, note 2).
Froude expresses, with some violence, a very different view
(op. cit., i, 696 ; ii, 38).

the two great Catholic Powers of Europe.[1]   By the
end of the war Pitt had become a national hero in
Ireland as in America; at Cork as at Dedham,
New York, and Charleston a statue was erected to
the organiser of imperial victory.[2]   In Ireland, as in
America, it was not the winning of that victory that
strained and cracked the structure of the old imperial system but the subsequent burden of paying
for it and safeguarding its fruits.

The attempt of the British statesmen of the time,
the last upholders of the Old Empire, to solve their
fiscal and military problem is writ large in history.
Everybody knows how the Grenville Government,
by stiffening up the administration of the Trade
Laws and the collection of the duties they imposed
and by the Stamp Act, tried to obtain from the
American colonies a contribution towards the increase in the British standing army which was required mainly for their own defence.   It is not so
well known that Ireland came within the scope of
those new imperial designs.   About the time of the
Stamp Act, Grenville himself proposed to enlarge
the Irish section of the army, ' so that Ireland might
bear *a part of the public burden of the country* and
have a sufficient number for her own defence.'[3]

---

[1] Lecky, *op. cit.*, ii, 69.   Froude, *op. cit.*, ii, 17-20.   A plan
was mooted for enrolling seven Irish Catholic regiments for
service with the allied Portuguese army.

[2] B. Williams, *op. cit.*, ii, 206.

[3] Cavendish, *Debates of House of Commons* (London, 1841),
i, 555.   Grenville explained that the army in Ireland had fallen

The proposal lapsed, but only for a time. When the futility of the Grenville policy in America had been recognised, when the Rockingham Government had repealed the Stamp Act, its successor, the Government which bore the name and little else than the name of Chatham, determined to get from Ireland what could not be got from America. It was a far easier task. Taxation by an external authority was not the novelty in Ireland that it was in America. The British Parliament, it is true, had never exercised, though doubtless under the Declaratory Act of 1719 it could assert, the right to tax Ireland directly over the head of the Irish Parliament by such a measure as the Stamp Act:[1] but Irish measures of supply had figured from time to time among those amended and even initiated by the British Government under Poynings' Act,[2] and the Irish Government had always been required by its masters in London to raise Irish money for other than Irish needs.[3] And in the last resort it could

to 5000, but it is clear from the context that he proposed to increase it above the 12,000 to which the Act of 1698 had limited it.

[1] The right was expressly asserted by Rigby and other members of the House of Commons in 1775. Lecky, *op. cit.*, ii, 157: cf. p. 138 below.

[2] See p. 88 above. Grenville had no doubt about the right ' to transmit a money bill ' to the Irish Parliament. Cavendish, *Debates*, i, 554.

[3] Among other charges the Irish Exchequer maintained sundry sinecure posts held by Englishmen. The most notorious case is that of C. J. Fox, who inherited the Clerkship of the Pells from his brother in 1774 and was compensated for resigning it

be raised in Ireland as it could never have been raised in America by the old-established method of bribing with places and pensions the requisite quota of the local legislature. So though Ireland had been brought to dire poverty through the selfish commercialism of Britain, though her national debt had continued to increase even after the war, though her expenditure already exceeded her revenue, the Irish were required to make good the backwardness of their more prosperous fellow-subjects beyond the Atlantic. In 1767, a few months after Charles Townshend had laid his notorious petty taxes on America for other purposes, his colleagues appointed his elder brother, Lord Townshend, Viceroy in Ireland, with instructions to put through a measure for augmenting the standing army maintained by that country, from 12,000 to over 15,000 men.[1]

As to the object of this ' augmentation ' there was no doubt at all. It was certainly not for the better maintenance of law and order in Ireland which was then passing through one of her many periods of agrarian disturbance,[2] nor for her external defence. For those purposes it was deemed sufficient to maintain the statutory force of 12,000 up to strength,

with £30,000 and an Irish pension of £1700 a year for thirty-one years. Fox gave up the pension in 1776, probably because it was incompatible with a seat in the English Parliament. Lecky, *op. cit.*, ii, 148.

[1] Lecky, *op. cit.*, ii, 85-7.

[2] Froude (*op. cit.*, ii, 68 ff.) gives this as the purpose of the augmentation and strangely states no other.

and for those purposes it was decided, in accordance
with a strong Irish appeal, to insert in the preliminary
British Act of Parliament a clause guaranteeing that
those 12,000 should be permanently stationed in
Ireland. But the main intent of this British Act
was to get rid of the limitation to 12,000 imposed
by the Act of 1698 ; and its preamble, accordingly,
stated as the only reason for this measure of repeal
—' whereas the public service of these kingdoms
doth require that some part of the troops kept in
the establishment of Ireland should be employed
towards the necessary defence of his Majesty's
garrisons and plantations abroad.'[1] There was no
concealment, then, nor misunderstanding. As a
member of the Irish Commons said a few years
later, the ' augmentation ' was ' avowedly to make
a contribution to the support of the whole Empire.'[2]
Quite plainly, quite frankly, the Augmentation
Scheme was the Irish edition of the Stamp Act.
It followed that Act's repeal. It openly sought to
succeed where it had failed. It emphasised the
dangerous contrast between well-to-do recusants in
America and submissive paupers in Ireland. And
how gross and clear was its inequity ! The American

[1] 8 Geo. III, c. 13. The words ' some part ' to ' abroad '
were repeated in the King's Message to the Irish Parliament.
Lecky, *op. cit.*, ii, 94. The exact ' augmentation ' above 12,000
was 3235. It is perhaps worth noting that the Stamp Act
had been intended to provide the cost of one-third of the 10,000
men to be stationed in America, i.e. of about 3330.

[2] Sir H. Langrishe in 1783. *Debates of Irish H. of C.*, ii, 78.

colonists had never maintained a standing army at
all, while Irish taxpayers had kept thousands of men
for seventy years. In the recent war, moreover,
Irish blood had been shed quite as freely as American
to safeguard those colonies from the French danger.
And now, in peace, it was still mainly for the defence
of those colonies and not at all for that of Ireland
that the additional 3000 Irishmen were demanded.
Unfair enough, surely, in itself : but put the Trade
Laws in the scales and what then ! Ireland was to
bear the burden of defending colonies with which
she was prohibited from trading ! Already, in 1763,
a speaker in the Dublin House of Commons had
complained that peace had brought to Ireland no
benefit but the cessation of war and that Irish lives,
ill spared from a half-peopled country, had purchased conquests 'from which this part of the
British dominion can reap no advantage adequate
to the cost. . . . We have bled to fertilize another
soil.'[1] A just complaint, and nothing could have
been better designed to confirm and intensify it than
the Augmentation Scheme.

It was obvious, indeed, to Shelburne, the Secretary of State concerned, and his colleagues as well
as to the Viceroy that the Scheme was unlikely to
be popular in Ireland. It was decided, therefore,
to gild the pill. Irish patriots were to be persuaded
to swallow the 'augmentation' by concessions on
the old issue of local Irish liberties—concessions, be

[1] Caldwell's *Debates*, ii, 612-3.

it noted, that were still firmly denied to the American colonists. In 1762 the Governor of New Jersey was removed from office for permitting judges to receive commissions ' during good behaviour.'[1] Yet in 1767 Lord Townshend in his speech from the throne in Dublin announced the King's intention of granting this long-desired reform. On this point, however, he had exceeded his instructions : he had been expected only to ventilate the question, as also those of an Irish militia and a Habeas Corpus Act, in private ; and, when the Irish Parliament transmitted its Judicature Bill to London, it was returned with amendments subjecting the judges to control by the British Government and Parliament, and thereupon thrown out in Dublin.[2] The second concession was more wholehearted. Although in that same year a general instruction was dispatched to all the colonial Governors, directing them to withhold their assent from any Bill limiting the duration of legislative assemblies, the Irish Parliament was actually encouraged to draft a Septennial Bill which in due course was returned from London, amended only into an Octennial Bill, and in that form was triumphantly enacted as an Irish statute.[3] The Augmentation Bill itself, moreover, was not only to be enacted by the Irish Parliament, but the insertion of clauses was permitted which would give to the Irish Act a measure of that control over the Army

[1] Greene, op. cit., 136.   [2] Lecky, op. cit., ii, 81-2.
[3] Greene, op. cit., 157. Lecky, op. cit., ii, 90-1.

in Ireland which had hitherto been exercised by English law alone. Meantime, of course, the Viceroy, tactfully ignoring a refusal of the Irish Commons to accept a Money Bill imposed from London, was busy with the usual process of canvassing supporters. It was, therefore, with an illusory appearance of harmony that the Augmentation Act finally went through in 1769. And then, as if to expose the illusion, Townshend promptly prorogued his Parliament and kept it unassembled for fourteen months.[1]

The British Government had obtained from Ireland what it had failed to obtain from America. Provision had been made for upwards of 3000 new regulars for colonial defence. But for that little gain British ministers had paid a big price. They had not only aggravated once more in the hearts of the ' patriot ' Irish minority the sense of their political and economic subjection. They had for the first time definitely linked their cause with that of the American colonists. Who, indeed, could miss the connexion between the Stamp and Augmentation Acts ? And, if Lucas himself, accepting defeat for the moment, was content to cast a silent vote against the Bill, another member of the House at an earlier stage had blurted out a dangerous half-truth. ' The Augmentation,' exclaimed Pery, ' was intended to enable Britain to keep more troops in

[1] Lecky, *op. cit.*, ii, 101-4.

America in order to crush the spirit of her colonies.'[1]
Those words, it may be said, proclaimed the definite
and conscious conjunction of the American and
Irish movements.

The active interaction of ideas and aims which
now developed between Ireland and America was
not by any means one-sided. So far, indeed, Ireland had had little to learn from American experience. It had been hers, rather, to teach. And her
lesson was now being steadily driven home by the
thousands of ruined and exasperated Irish farmers
and linen-weavers who were pouring into the colonies in increasing volume. It is reckoned that
20,000 were driven into exile by the destruction of
the wool-industry, that thousands more fled like the
English founders of New England from Episcopalian
ascendancy, and that the decline of the linen trade
and agrarian evictions reinforced the outward stream
until it was flowing between 1772 and 1774 at the
rate of 10,000 a year. In vain Townshend pleaded
that bounties given to Manchester for linen might
be given also to Belfast. In vain the Dublin Commons protested against new duties laid on Irish
sail-cloth. It was not till 1774 that the British
Parliament, moved at last by the information that
at least one-third of the Ulster linen-manufacturers
were out of work or had gone to America ' taking
their machines with them,' consented to help the

---

[1] Fitzmaurice, *Life of Shelburne*, i, 357. Lucas, *ibid.*, 358.

Irish trade as it had long helped the British.[1] And then it was too late. Those tens of thousands had taken more than their machines across the sea. Nearly all Protestants, mostly from the North, stubborn, independent folk, they had clung as passionately to their political doctrines as to those of their Church, and they had not left them behind in their deserted homes. In a more congenial air, at a greater distance from Britain, among kinsmen whose rightful liberties, it seemed, had been violated by the same imperial tyrant, and with the bitterness of involuntary exile still fresh in their hearts, they must have preached those doctrines with a knowledge and a zest that cannot have been quite without result. History has recognised the vigorous part played later on the battlefield by those enemies which Mercantilism had made so recklessly for Britain. But what of the part they played, before it came to fighting, at town-meetings, in debating-clubs, at corners of the village street ? How many of the arguments that led to Revolution were taken from the Irish armoury of Molyneux and Swift and Lucas ? Observe that in 1766, Benjamin Franklin drew the parallel between the colonies and Ireland in the course of his examination in the House of Commons. ' The colonies,' he said, ' have assemblies of their own which are their parliaments, and they are in that respect in the same situation as

[1] Lecky, *op. cit.*, ii, 153.   Froude, *op. cit.*, i, 435 ; ii, 103. 114, 137, 176.   *Parl. Hist.*, xvii (1771-74), 1144-58.

Ireland. When money is to be raised for the crown upon the subject in Ireland or in the colonies, the assent is given in the parliament of Ireland or in the assemblies of the colonies.'[1] Observe, too, that in 1768 Dickinson devoted the tenth of his ' Farmer's Letters ' to the wrongs of Ireland and bade his countrymen ' grow wise by the misfortunes of others.'[2] Note also that by 1770 American and Irish leaders were in personal contact : for in that year a letter was sent by the Town of Boston to C. Lucas, Esq., with information of the famous ' massacre,'[3] and in the next year, Benjamin Franklin was in Dublin conversing with the ' patriots.' And when the American leaders began to concentrate on the legal issue, when they framed their case for legislative independence, when Samuel Adams in 1772 set the British Parliament's claim to legislate ' for the colonists in all cases whatsoever ' at the head of his ' List of Infringements and Violations of Rights,' and when finally, in 1774, the fourth resolution of the Continental Congress flatly denied the British doctrine of legislative ' supremacy,'[4] must we not suppose that Irish influence and instruction took a share in directing the currents of American resentment on to the issue which had hitherto been neglected in America but had been

[1] *Parl. Hist.*, xvi, 156.
[2] S. E. Morison, *Sources and Documents illustrating the American Revolution* (Oxford, 1923), 51-3.
[3] McIlwain, *op. cit.*, 36, note 1.
[4] Morison, *op. cit.*, 91, 120.

the great outstanding issue in Ireland since the eighteenth century began ? [1]

But whatever help was given by the Irish movement to the American, it was more than repaid. Example is better than precept ; and in the matter of the Stamp Act, the colonists had not merely questioned but defied—and successfully defied—the authority of the British Parliament. It was a direct encouragement to their fellow-subjects in Ireland to do likewise. Was not their status of dependency virtually the same ? Were not the results of it in their case far more grievous ? And, as if some evil spirit was now pulling all the strings of British policy, it so happened that, just at this critical time when the long American dispute over the Townshend duties was drawing to a head, the Irish were given yet further proofs of British domination and the motives that inspired it. In 1773 the Irish Government was finding it more than usually difficult to wring an adequate revenue from the impoverished country. Taking another leaf from Grenville's American book, it had so tightened up the excise administration as, in Grattan's words, to ' trench upon the subject's birth-right.' [2]   Soldiers were act-

[1] This thesis is forcibly argued by McIlwain, *op. cit.* For the views of Jefferson, Wilson, and John Adams on legislative independence, see also R. G. Adams, *Political Ideas of the American Revolution* (Durham, N.C., 1922). McIlwain's case that the colonial claim was justified in law is controverted by R. L. Schuyler in *Parliament and the British Empire* (New York, 1930).

[2] *Speeches of Henry Grattan* (London, 1822), i, 3.

ually employed as tax-collectors. But still more money was needed ; and it is not surprising that the new Viceroy, Lord Harcourt, was tempted to permit the Irish Parliament to lay its hands on an old-standing, solid, certain, but hitherto sacrosanct source of revenue. A measure was drafted to lay a tax of 10 per cent. on the rents of landlords who lived less than six months of a year in Ireland. As Adam Smith afterwards declared, it was an equitable tax, since the absentees contributed virtually nothing to the Government which kept their estates secure.[1] Lord North was willing to allow it. Chatham, true to his doctrine as to the powers of local legislatures over internal taxation, accepted it on principle. ' The fitness or justness,' he said, ' of the tax in question I shall not consider if the Commons of Ireland send it here.'[2]   He carried Shelburne with him ; but Rockingham and some of his Whig associates who were large proprietors of Irish land denounced the tax as an outrage, and the greatest Irishman of the day composed for them a persuasive but disingenuous plea that the tax was at once a violation of British ' supremacy ' and a menace to the real interests of Ireland. City companies owning Irish estates joined in the attack ; and it seemed as if public opinion throughout the country was on the point of becoming quite inflamed by this new appeal to British selfishness

[1] *Wealth of Nations* (ed. 1904), ii, 339.
[2] Fitzmaurice, *Life of Shelburne*, i, 456-9.

when North instructed Harcourt to withdraw the
tax—an order which he obeyed by securing ' by
most dexterous management ' a majority against it
in the Irish Commons.[1] But, if they showed themselves in this matter more generous to Ireland than
the Whigs, the Tories were no less determined to
keep the Irish in their place. In that same year
the North Government insisted once more on modi-
fying the normal Money Bills transmitted from
Dublin, and, by some malicious chance, they chose
to make a slight alteration with regard to the duties
on tea—a few months before the ' Boston tea-
party.'[2] In the same spirit, in 1774, they rejected,
as often before, the heads of a Habeas Corpus Bill,
and this time they ordered the Irish Government

[1] This story, so damaging to Whig reputations, is fully told
by Lecky, op. cit., ii, 119-32. Rockingham was particularly
indignant. ' I doubt,' he wrote to Lord Bessborough, ' whether
a minister who should advise the King to tax absentees from
Ireland for living here might not be impeachable '—his own
italics. (Rockingham Memoirs, ii, 228.) It is pleasant to find
Sir George Savile more moderate. ' In truth,' he wrote to
Rockingham, ' I cannot quite so much wonder at the measure
being adopted in Ireland. Perhaps it may be unjust, but I
would not undertake to prove it so.' (Ibid., ii, 231.) The
Duke of Richmond could also see the Irish side of the case.
(Ibid., ii, 230.) Burke's arguments are in his Correspondence
(i, 434-45), and his Letter to Sir C. Bingham (Works, 1826, ed.
ix, 134-47). His main case was (1) that laws which interfered
with the liberties of any British subjects as to residence should
only be enacted by the British Parliament, and (2) that the tax
would tend to prevent eminent Irishmen from serving the interests of Ireland in the British Parliament.

[2] Froude, op. cit., ii, 175.

'to transmit the Bill no more.' It was 'irreconcilable with the idea of a dependency.' It was 'a solecism in politics to make the constitution of a colony the same as that of the mother-country.'[1] Old ideas, old policies, but with a new significance in 1773 and 1774. It was as if British politicians, Whig and Tory alike, were deliberately asking the Irish ' colonists ' to identify their cause with that of the American. And that, of course, was what the Americans, on their side, were now asking. Benjamin Franklin, whose courteous reception in the House of Commons at Dublin in 1771 was in notable contrast with the treatment he received on a more famous occasion in 1774 before the Privy Council in Whitehall, had already made the most of the obvious point in his conversations with the ' patriots.' ' I found them,' he recorded, ' disposed to be friends of America, in which I endeavoured to confirm them with the expectation that our growing weight might in time be thrown into their scale, and by joining our interests with theirs, a more equitable treatment from this nation [Britain] might be obtained for themselves as well as for us.'[2] And, when at last the long wrangle in New England ended in open rupture, the American Congress drew up, together with its addresses to the people of England and to the people of Canada, an address to the people of Ireland asking for their sympathy and support. But neither

[1] Froude, op. cit., ii, 178-9.
[2] Franklin's Works, vii, 557, cited by Lecky, op. cit., ii, 159.

British provocations nor American appeals were
needed. When the issue of ' supremacy ' and ' dependence ' was first raised by Grenville, the Irish
leaders were instantly aware that Irishmen and
Americans had a common cause. They saw in the
Stamp Act a more dangerous threat to their own
liberties than any casual interference with their own
Money Bills. They realised the significance of the
fact that the Declaratory Act of 1766 was a copy of
the Declaratory Act of 1719. The existing modes of
their political subjection, the existing tyranny of the
Trade Laws—those things were intolerable enough :
but, if once the British Parliament made good its
claim ' to bind the colonies in all cases whatsoever,'
then for Ireland, it seemed, if not for the colonies,
the last hope of liberty and justice was gone. And
so, from first to last, they gave to the Americans that
passion of sympathy which can only be given to
those who are fighting the same battle by those who
hope to share in the same victory or fear to share
in the same defeat.

' Ireland,' said Chatham a few months before the
American War began, ' they have to a man . . .
joined as it is with the cause of the colonies, and
placed at their head.' [1] The words were intended
as a warning to British obstinacy, and they were
prophetic rather than accurate in 1775. The
' patriots,' it is true, were a stronger party than

[1] Speech of 20 Jan., 1775. Thackeray, *Life of Chatham*
(London, 1827), ii, 286.

they had ever been. Grattan and Flood, younger and abler men than Lucas, had succeeded to its leadership. A young and vigorous Press supported it. But it was still a minority party ; and its view of what the distant fighting meant or might mean for Ireland was not yet shared by the mass of Irishmen. The results of a vigorous recruiting campaign in the course of that summer showed that the Protestants were so far no less willing to serve the King in this war than in others ; and the Catholic leaders, seizing one more opportunity of demonstrating their ill-rewarded loyalty, affirmed their ' abhorrence of the unnatural rebellion.' [1]   The Irish Parliament, moreover, was still just tractable.   The ' patriots,' indeed, were vocal.   ' If America were beaten,' said Denis Daly, ' thirty thousand English swords would impose the Irish taxes.'   ' England meant,' said Hussey Burgh, ' to reduce her dependencies to slavery.' [2]   But the majority of the Commons voted a warlike address in support of George III's ' just rights,' though more than half its members were significantly absent : and, despite the strong line it had taken on the point in connexion with the Augmentation Scheme, it reluctantly agreed to permit the removal to the war-area of 4000 out of the 12,000 troops in Ireland, though not without a promise that the troops on service should be paid by the British treasury to the great relief of Irish

[1] Lecky, *op. cit.*, ii, 165,   [2] Froude, *op. cit.*, ii, 193.

finances.[1] So far, so good ; but the Viceroy's hold
on the House of Commons at Dublin was slipping
—as one day George III's hold was to slip at Westminster. In March, 1776, so nervous was the Government that it decided to dissolve Parliament ;
and, in order to secure a safer majority in the next,
it exceeded all its previous records of corruption.
Not only was nearly £10,000 added to annual
charges for the provision of new pensions, but
eighteen Irish gentlemen became Irish peers, and
seven barons and five viscounts moved one step
farther up (or down) the slope of honour.[2]

Meantime, the ' patriots ' had been gaining
ground. The tide of opposition to the American
War was rising fast in Ulster. The Viceroy described ' the Presbyterians in the North ' as ' in their
hearts Americans ' and ' gaining strength every day.'
' If they are not rebels, it is hard to find a name for
them.'[3] And Harcourt's language was not unjustifiable when, besides ' The Glorious and Immortal
Memory of King William ' and the other traditional
Whig toasts honoured at electioneering banquets in
1776, the Ulstermen drained their glasses also to
' May the Tyranny and Persecution which the
Fathers fled from in Europe never be imposed on
the Sons.'[4] As the war dragged on, this opposi-

---

[1] Lecky, op. cit., ii, 162-4.   Froude, op. cit., ii, 193-6.
[2] Lecky, op. cit., ii, 167.   [3] Ibid., 163, 165.
[4] J. R. Fisher, The End of the Irish Parliament (London, 1911),
109.

tion stiffened.   It became clearer every month that
the Americans were making a good fight of it ; and
every month the fresh hardships, caused directly by
the war, pressed more hardly on all Ireland.   The
linen industry was still further depressed by the interruption of trade ; and the embargo, which the
British Government, without consulting the Irish
Parliament, laid on all export of provisions from
Ireland for three years, thrust farmers and peasants
still deeper into destitution.   Nor was Ireland by
any means secure from still worse evils.   If France
should decide that her time had come to reverse
the decision of the Seven Years War, could British
sea-power guarantee the safety of the Irish coast ?
In every way—it seemed more and more obvious—
Ireland was helpless unless, like the Americans, she
helped herself.   The American Revolution was not
four years old when the Irish Revolution came to
birth.

In 1778—the year in which France came into the
war, the year after Saratoga—three great events in
Irish history occurred.   The first was the beginning
of the breakdown of the Penal Code.   Among edu-
cated Englishmen, though not yet by any means
among the London mob, the principle of religious
toleration had been steadily gaining ground since
the fiasco of '45.   In the Quebec Act of 1774 Lord
North and his colleagues had gone so far, for political purposes, as virtually to establish the Roman

Church in Canada, and George III, not yet en-
tangled in the implications of his Coronation Oath,
had signed it. Some slight relief was given in this
same year (1778) to the Catholics in England.[1] And
even in Ireland, under pressure of war, the old
hard doctrine of ascendancy began to soften. When
more Irish recruits were needed than the Protestants could or would provide, Catholics were un-
obtrusively admitted for the first time into the army.
When, again, on the one hand, the opposition of the
Irish Protestants grew more and more alarming and
when, on the other hand, Catholic France joined
the Americans and Catholic Spain was evidently intending to follow suit, it seemed politic to reward
and reinforce the support which the Irish Catholics
had so far given to Government. In the summer
of 1778, accordingly, a Bill was passed in Ireland
and accepted in England relieving them at last from
those provisions of the infamous Code which had
proved in practice most injurious—the prohibition
of the leasing or inheriting of land.[2] Admirable in
itself, on grounds of common humanity long over-
due, this concession was not by any means intended
to advance the progress of Irish nationalism. In

[1] The Catholic Relief Act of 1778, which provoked 'No
Popery' riots in Edinburgh and Glasgow in 1779, and the
'Gordon Riots' in London in 1780.

[2] Lecky, op. cit., ii, 209-17. For an interesting account of
Burke's conversation with Lord North on the Catholic Relief
Bill and also on the Irish Presbyterians, see his Irish Letters,
279-87.

fact, however, it did advance it. ' The Irish Protestant,' said Grattan, ' can never be free till the
Irish Catholic has ceased to be a slave ';[1] and to
raise the Catholic but one step towards an equal
footing with the Protestant was to bring Ireland so
much nearer to the sense of national unity, to the
strength and weight of a national will, without which
her hopes of freedom might well prove unattainable.
' You are now,' wrote Burke, ' beginning to have a
country.'[2]

The second event of 1778 was the formation of
the Irish volunteers. It was definitely expected in
official quarters and widely believed throughout the
country that the French alliance with the Americans
at the beginning of that year would quickly result
in an attempted invasion of Ireland, probably on
the North coast. It was in April, 1778, that Paul
Jones revealed the weakness of its defence at sea
by sailing into Carrickfergus Bay and forcing the
sloop *Drake* to strike the British flag : and throughout the summer privateers, flying French or American
colours, haunted the Irish coast from Bray Head to
Cape Clear. The regular troops in Ireland, reduced
by drafts to America, were insufficient to prevent
invasion. And, though at last, again under war-
pressure, the British Government had allowed the
enactment of an Irish Militia Bill, the Irish Government had not the money to put it into force. So

[1] Quoted by Lecky, *op. cit.*, ii, 209.   [2] *Ibid.*, 217.

Ulster was defenceless unless she defended herself.[1] She had done it before. The failure of the French landing near Carrickfergus in 1760 had been mainly due to the swift and spontaneous mobilisation of the peasantry. And she was ready to do it again. For Ulster sympathy with the Americans had nothing to do with Ulster hatred of France, deep-rooted in memories of James II and the Boyne. The whole province leapt to arms. The leading gentry controlled the organisation ; muskets and uniforms were purchased ; officers were elected ; and old soldiers were appointed to train the recruits. The movement was soon spreading fast along the coast and into the interior. Catholics were not yet admitted to the ranks ; but, none the less, they subscribed liberally to the funds. By the end of the year a new Irish army was camped on Irish soil, several thousand strong, and as well-armed, as well-disciplined, and as resolute as Washington's army in America.[2]

In the same year the fates that presided over the First British Empire decreed that the realities of Ireland's status should be more forcibly driven home than they had ever been before into the hearts and minds of Irishmen then living. As the direct result of the stranglehold on the Irish export-trade, stiffened, as has been seen, by the war, a large part of the Irish people were now in desperate poverty, many thousands on the edge of starvation. Every

[1] Lecky, *op. cit.*, ii, 218-20.   Froude, *op. cit.*, ii, 236-7.
[2] Lecky, *op. cit.*, ii, 222-37.

one in Ireland knew, and every one who had studied
the question in Britain agreed, that the only remedy
was to admit Ireland to a share in such freedom of
trade as Britain enjoyed. In the spring of 1778 the
Viceroy, now Lord Buckingham, informed Lord
North that an enlargement of trade was a sheer
necessity to enable Ireland to bear ' the many drains
to which it was annually subject, particularly to
Great Britain '; [1] and North, with more than his
usual courage, decided that the sacred Trade Laws
must at last be violated. A series of Bills were introduced in Parliament permitting Ireland, with the
one important exception of wool and woollens, to
export her products to all British colonies and, with
the one exception of tobacco, to import their products direct ; permitting also the export of glass to
any country except Britain, and of cotton yarn, sail-
cloth, and cordage into Britain itself.[2] The occasion
lifted Burke to the heights. Reckless of the effect
on his Bristol constituents, he passionately supported, with voice and pen, this breaking, at long
last, of the ' cruel, oppressive, and unnatural ' chains
which Mercantilism had bound on Ireland ; [3] and
the British Parliament, using its ' supremacy ' for
once in accordance with Burke's imperial idealism,
passed the Bills through their initial stages with

[1] Lecky, op. cit., ii, 177.
[2] Parl. Hist., xix (1778), 1100-26.
[3] Parl. Hist., xix, 1119-23. Letters to Bristol, Irish Letters,
97-115.

little debate. . . . Instantly, in every industrial centre in Britain except London, there was uproar. ' Petitions, public meetings, instructions to members were all resorted to, and almost the whole commercial class in England protested against any measure allowing the Irish to participate in the most limited degree in British trade, or even to dispose of their own commodities in foreign markets.' [1] What a spectacle for gods and men ! What a picture of the lengths to which undiluted commercialism can carry its votaries ! But there it was ; and it is not surprising that North's courage flickered out. He cut down his concessions—down almost to vanishing point. Irish-built ships were now to be regarded as British-built and entitled to receive bounties on fishing. The meagre export trade allowed was to bear the same taxation as was levied on similar goods in Britain. Irish yarn might enter Britain free. These concessions had, indeed, a value—the value of a precedent : they were the first breach opened in the walls of Mercantilism encircling the Irish coast. But as a means of saving Ireland from starvation they were worthless.[2]

[1] Lecky, *op. cit.*, ii, 178.

[2] Looking back in 1780, Burke made the best of a bad job. ' I was in hopes,' he wrote, ' that one concession would lead to another ; and that the people of England, discovering by a progressive experience that none of the concessions actually made were followed by the consequences they had dreaded, their fears from what they were yet to yield would considerably diminish. But that to which I attached myself most particularly was to

This new exhibition of the selfishness of British business was weighed and judged by a different Ireland from that of the days when her agricultural prosperity was deliberately destroyed—an Ireland with an army of her own and with her eyes upon America. Higher than ever now burned the sympathy of the North with the fathers who had fled from tyranny ; stronger than ever now was its determination to free the sons who had stayed. ' It concerns me greatly to mention,' wrote the Viceroy, ' that the discontent of this kingdom seems increasing, fomented, I apprehend, by French and American emissaries.'[1] If there were any agents from France, he need not have troubled about them ; for on that point, as will appear, there was no parallel between the Irish and American Revolutions. And, if there were any American agents, their activities were superfluous. Liverpool, Manchester, Glasgow, and Bristol had provided all the revolutionary propaganda that was required ; and the address signed by Benjamin Franklin, which was circulated throughout Ireland in November, 1778, expounding the identity of American and Irish interests, was but adding fuel to a fire that did not need it. But that is not to say that the American Revolution had no effect, at this critical time, on developments in Ireland. It had a

---

fix *the principle* of a free trade in all the ports of these islands, as founded in justice and beneficial to the whole.' *Irish Letters*, 297.

[1] Lecky, *op. cit.*, ii, 226.

profound effect, but not so much through the now
familiar notion of the identity between American
and Irish interests as in the new and startling demonstration of the difference between American and
Irish fortunes. Six weeks before the discussion of
the Irish Trade Bills began, North had stupefied his
followers in the House of Commons by his sudden
announcement of the Government's intention to
yield to the American colonists all and more than all
they had demanded at the outbreak of the war ;
thereupon, the ' Renunciation Act,' promising never
again to tax the colonies for revenue and to apply
to colonial purposes any proceeds from duties laid
for the regulation of trade, and the Acts repealing
the Massachusetts Constitution Act and the tea-
duty were passed in quick succession ; and very
soon a Royal Commission was on its way across the
Atlantic with statutory powers to negotiate with
Congress for a treaty of peace. The Commissioners
carried minute instructions as to the concessions
they might make to secure agreement. No standing army would be quartered in the colonies. They
would not be required to make any contribution to
Britain for their defence. They might elect their
own Governors subject to the approval of the Crown.
Their judges might be given tenure ' during good
behaviour.' All Acts of Parliament since 1763, in so
far as they dealt with the colonies, might be sus-
pended, and even the Declaratory Act might be
superseded by a new statement of ' the respective

rights of Great Britain and America.' As to the regulation of commerce, ' It is impossible to foresee,' ran the royal command, ' the particular demands which may be made on you in behalf of particular branches of trade. This only we direct you to observe in general, *that no check should be given to any of them.*' And so on, almost to the last limit of surrender and humiliation.[1] A few months later, while the British cities were battering the House of Commons with petitions against the Irish Bills, the Commissioners, going further yet, beyond their brief indeed, were offering complete legislative freedom to the colonial Assemblies. As every one knows, this bid for reconciliation came too late. The Americans had made their final choice. But the failure of Britain's offer detracted nothing from the lesson which the making of it taught Ireland. On its political side the programme of concession included some things such as legislative independence for which Ireland had pleaded long before the colonies, and other things such as an elective Executive or freedom from a standing-army for which Ireland had never dared to plead at all. Nor was there anything now offered to America which had yet been granted to Ireland. The change in judicial commissions, for example, had been again refused as lately as 1776 and was to be refused once more

[1] The Instructions (12 April, 1778) are printed in full in Morison, *Sources and Documents of the American Revolution, etc.*, 186-203.

in 1780.[1] But the difference on the economic side
was still more glaring. No ' check ' was to be given
to American demands as to laws of trade, though
the colonies had suffered little, if anything, from
them in the past, while, at the same moment, the
Irish appeal against the trade-laws which had ruined
her was being vehemently rejected. Even in Britain
the contrast between the British treatment of the
Irish and the Americans was evident enough to
anyone who had eyes to see—' the first,' as Townshend declared in a bitter speech in the House of
Lords, ' loyal, affectionate, patient under the greatest
miseries and oppressions : the latter factious, re-
bellious, ungrateful, in the midst of plenty, and
after receiving a series of accumulated favours . . .
leagued with an inveterate and ambitious enemy
for our total destruction.' And what, he went on,
was our answer to their respective demands ? To
America, ' You shall be free.' To Ireland, ' Break
your chains if you can, or perish.'[2] It was an ex-
Viceroy of Ireland speaking : but, except for the
hard hits at the Americans, it might well have been
an Irish ' patriot.' Who in Ireland could fail to
recognise the contrast—and its lesson ? In the spring
of 1779, just a year after the discussion of the Trade
Bills had begun, the first active step was taken in
the Irish Revolution.

[1] Froude, op. cit., ii, 200, 269.
[2] Parl. Hist., xx (1778-80), 673. The obvious contrast was
pointed out, with more sympathy towards the Americans, by
Burke (ibid., 1209), and by Grattan (p. 126 below).

It was the step which Swift had, half-humorously, recommended to his countrymen sixty years before ; but the Americans had made it into a practical and immediate precedent by adopting it as their first method of opposition to the Townshend duties. It was obviously in direct imitation of this American example that in April, 1779, a great meeting at Dublin unanimously adopted a ' non-importation agreement,' pledging all present to abstain from buying British goods which could be made in Ireland. ' It is now too publicly known to be disguised any longer,' wrote Walpole in May, ' that Ireland has much the air of Americanising.'[1] It had indeed ! Just as the lead of Massachusetts had been followed by the other colonies, so now all Ireland followed Dublin. ' Non-importation ' became everywhere the social or domestic counterpart of the Volunteer Movement, a field in which the women, from the grandees of local society downwards, could work beside their husbands. And when they had finished for the day and sat down to dinner, ' in every Protestant or Dissenter's house '—so Shelburne reported from his estate in Kerry—the regular toast was ' Success to the Americans.'[2] Throughout that summer of 1779 the two interwoven movements proceeded swiftly and steadily. It was, remember, the black summer in the English Channel ; Dublin and Belfast were as much exposed to French attack

[1] *Letters of Horace Walpole*, x, 408.
[2] Fitzmaurice, *op. cit.*, ii, 40.

as Falmouth and Plymouth ; and an invasion of Ireland now seemed almost certain. The Government issued instructions telling the people what to do in the event of a French landing ; and, much as it disliked the Volunteers, it distributed among them 16,000 stand of militia arms. By the autumn the numbers enrolled had risen to over 40,000.[1]

They were the masters of Ireland's destiny, those 40,000 Irishmen. With a war in America and a war in Europe on its hands, the British Government and its instruments in Ireland were quite powerless to withstand them. And for that reason they were able to achieve their Revolution by only a show and not a use of force. When the Dublin Parliament met in October and the House of Commons carried, without dividing, an amendment to the address demanding free trade as Ireland's one salvation, the road by which the speaker carried it to the Castle was lined on either side by the local Volunteers who presented arms as he passed. And when on King William's birthday the Volunteers paraded round his monument on College Green, it was decked with defiant inscriptions, and beside it stood two guns, placarded with ' Free Trade—or this.' Encircled by such guardians or warders, the Irish Parliament was able at last to resist the various influences by means of which the Government at every previous crisis had ultimately got its way. The Com-

---

[1] Lecky, *op. cit.*, ii, 234-5.

mons refused to vote supplies for more than six months ; resolutions thanking the Volunteers for their exertions on behalf of Ireland were enthusiastically carried ; and—a more substantial token—a Bill was passed through both Houses to make the great Presbyterian majority of those soldiers into full citizens. The abolition of the sacramental tests for dissenters, which had hitherto barred them from part of their civic rights, was the obvious concomitant of the relief given to the Catholics in the previous year ; and, though the British Government was, not unnaturally, less inclined to favour militant Protestants than submissive Catholics, it bowed to the inevitable, and in March, 1780, it allowed the Bill to become law.[1] But already it had made a greater surrender. ' Free trade—or this ! ' There was no escape from the dilemma thrust in Britain's face by those guns on Dublin Green ; and though this Irish revolt was at least as radical a challenge to the old imperialism as the American, and though George III and his ministers were engaged in attempting to suppress that American revolt—or rather *because* they were so engaged—they chose, they were obliged to choose, Free Trade. It was not an easy choice, this surrender to a threat of force. It cannot have been easy for George III who, about a year before, had told Lord North with reference to Ireland that ' experience had convinced him that England gained nothing by granting indulgence to

[1] Lecky, *op. cit.*, ii, 240-1.

her dependencies.'[1]   And it was made no easier by
Burke's exultant taunts.   Why not treat Ireland, he
asked the Government across the floor of the Commons, as you treated America ?   ' Why not, like
ill-fated Boston, shut up the port of Dublin, burn
Cork, reduce Waterford to ashes ? . . . The answer
is plain and direct. You dare not.'[2]   It was true. Not
even the King's courage was equal to a repetition of
the American mistake.   Nor was the greed even of
British industry quite so short-sighted. ' No town
in England,' to quote Burke again, ' presumed to
have a prejudice or dared to mutter a petition.'[3]
And so, in the winter of 1779-80 a series of Bills
were enacted by the British Parliament which gave
to Ireland nearly the same freedom of trade as that
enjoyed by Britain.   The Irish section of the great
imperial system of commerce, which had stood,
compact and coherent, for a century, was almost
clean cut out.[4]

At this point the similarity between the American
and Irish Revolutions and the reaction of the one
upon the other become still more strikingly apparent.
If British statesmen had been wise enough in 1766
not only to abandon the attempt to raise revenue
from the American colonists, but also to concede
that in all their domestic affairs they should be
subject to the authority of no other laws than those
laid down by their own elected representatives—if

[1] Fitzmaurice, *op. cit.*, ii, 40.   [2] *Parl. Hist.*, xx, 1207-8.
[3] *Irish Letters*, 130.   [4] 20 George III, c. 6, 10, 18.

they had abstained from the Declaratory Act no less than from the Townshend duties—then the American Revolution might have been long postponed. But they only realised that nothing less than this could satisfy their fellow-subjects overseas when it was too late. In Ireland, similarly, the supreme political issue could not be evaded. Freedom from commercial subjection was the first demand, for Irishmen were starving. But behind it lay the old resolve to repudiate the legislative authority of Britain in every Irish field, to have done with Poynings' Act and all it implied, to tear up the Act of 1719 as the Americans had torn up the Act of 1766, and so to restore to the ancient Irish Parliament the free status it had once enjoyed. On the very morrow of the commercial concessions, therefore, the wider demand was made. On 19 April, 1780, in a speech which the orator himself and many of his audience regarded as the finest in his career, Grattan asked the Irish Commons to ' deny the claim of the British Parliament to make law for Ireland.' The grant of free trade, he declared at the outset of his argument, like the repeal of the Stamp Act, was only a mitigation of an authority still reserved.

' England thought it expedient to repeal that law. Happy had it been for mankind if, when she withdrew the exercise, she had not reserved the right ! To that reservation she owes the loss of her American empire.' The free trade, similarly, is regarded ' as a trade *de facto*, not *de jure*, a licence to trade under the Parliament of England, not a free trade under the charters of Ireland, as a tribute to her strength ; to maintain which she must continue in a state of armed preparation, dreading the approach of a general peace, and attributing all she holds dear to the calamitous condition of the British interest in every quarter of the globe. . . . England now smarts under the lesson of the American war. The doctrine of imperial legislature she now feels to be pernicious ; the revenues and monopolies attached to it she has found to be untenable ; she has lost the power to enforce it ; her enemies are a host, pouring upon her from all quarters of the earth ; her armies are dispersed ; the sea is not hers ; she has no minister, no ally, no admiral, none in whom she long confides, and no general whom she has not disgraced. The balance of her fate is in the hands of Ireland. You are not only her last connexion. You are the only nation in Europe that is not her enemy.' ' Will Great Britain [he continued], a wise and magnanimous country, thus tutored by experience and wasted by war, the French navy riding her channel, send an army to Ireland to levy no tax, to enforce no law, to answer no end whatsoever except to spoliate the charters of Ireland and enforce a barren oppression ? What ! has England lost thirteen provinces, has she reconciled herself to this loss, and will she not be reconciled to the liberty of Ireland ? Take notice that the very constitution which I move you to declare, Great Britain herself offered to America. . . . In 1778 a Commission went out with powers to cede to the thirteen provinces of America, totally and radically, the legislative authority claimed over her by the British Parliament.[1] . . . Has England offered this to the resistance of America, and will you refuse it to the loyalty of Ireland ? '

And so, harping on the American example, re-iterating the stinging truth that Ireland, as long as

[1] One of several rhetorical overstatements in this speech : see p. 119 above.

the Act of 1719 stood unrepealed, was only a ' plantation,' ' a colony without the benefit of a charter,' her legislature only ' a provincial synod without the privileges of a parliament,' the orator moved on to that inspired climax in which he portrayed the rebuilding of the Empire on the traditional basis of British freedom, and foretold—how long before its day !—the attainment, as part of this new imperial system, of a perfect union between the sister British Isles.

' There is no policy left for Great Britain [he said] but to cherish the remains of her empire and do justice to a country that is determined to do justice to herself. . . . She must go back to freedom, which, as it is the foundation of her constitution, so is it the main pillar of her empire. It is not merely the connexion of the Crown, it is a constitutional annexation, an alliance of liberty, which is the true meaning and mystery of the sisterhood, and will make both countries one arm and one soul, replenishing from time to time in their immortal connexion the vital spirit of law and liberty from the lamp of each other's light. Thus combined by the ties of common interest, equal trade and equal liberty, the constitution of both countries may become immortal, a new and milder empire may arise from the errors of the old, and the British nation assume once more her natural station—the head of mankind.'[1]

Finally, Grattan moved ' That the King's most excellent majesty and the Lords and Commons of Ireland are the only power competent to make laws to bind Ireland.'   At half-past six in the morning of 20 April, 1780, this motion was defeated by 133

[1] *Speeches*, i, 39-53.

votes to 99. The corrupt old Parliament, still representing only a minority of a minority of the Irish people, was still too submissive or too venal or too cowardly to follow Grattan's lead. But, in the cleaner air outside, the real representatives of Ireland—the Protestant Volunteers and their now fast-growing sympathisers among the Catholics—were with Grattan to a man. Reckon their silent vote, and the scene of 20 April, 1780, may be not improperly regarded as the reproduction at Dublin of the scene at Philadelphia on 4 July, 1776. It was the Irish Declaration of Independence.

IV.

THE IRISH REVOLUTION : SECOND PHASE.

THERE was, of course, an important distinction between the American and Irish Declarations of Independence. Each was made by a people in arms, but one of those peoples was at war with Britain and the other not. Each asserted the right to freedom, but one meant freedom within the British Empire and the other freedom outside it. But too much must not be made of this distinction. It had arisen from circumstances rather than from principles. Three thousand miles away from Britain, the Americans had been able, in peace-time, to prepare the way for revolution. They could agitate, organise, arm. Their legislatures, representative and not amenable to British bribes, could advance instead of retarding the popular cause. Divided as they were by provincial jealousies, they were to prove themselves capable of acting as a united nation. And, when all else failed, it might seem temerarious, but by no means desperate, to go to war. It was otherwise, of course, in Ireland, so close to Britain, so deeply disunited, her political activities concentrated in a Parliament that was both unrepresentative and corrupt. Agitation, organisation, arming on any revolutionary scale could and would have been crushed—in peace time—as easily as any local rising of Whiteboys or Oakboys or Steelboys. A war with Britain was unthinkable—in peace time. Naturally, therefore, the American movement, once it became revolutionary, had quickly and far outstripped the Irish; and, so doing, it had given Ireland not only the lead but her chance of following it. After 1775 all the impossibilities of peace had become swiftly and easily possible; and by 1780 the old positions had been readjusted. Ireland, in a sense, had shown herself stronger than America. She had got the first instalment of her freedom without fighting. And she had got it herself without accepting the help, which America had been obliged to accept, of self-seeking Bourbon despotism. The French minister, Vergennes, had been forced to confess to his allies at Madrid in 1779, that French or Spanish agents would have little chance of raising a rebellion even among their fellow-Catholics in Ireland; and indeed, in the course of that year, several Catholic gentry in the South and West had promised the Viceroy that, in the event of an invasion by ' the French or any other enemy,' they would march at the head of their tenantry to repel it.[1]   It was still possible, in fact, in 1780, for Irish ' patriots ' to sympathise with America and not with her allies : they could still, like the Americans at an earlier stage, demand more freedom as

[1] Lecky, *op. cit.*, ii, 231-3.

subjects of George III. Irish 'loyalists,' indeed, went further. They denounced the bare thought that ' the standard of rebellion ' could be raised in Ireland as it had been in the colonies. ' If ever such a damned insinuation was made,' said one of them, ' it must have arisen from the infamous practice of likening this country to America.'[1] The likeness, nevertheless, was there : and it was greater than the difference. For the likeness was in principles, the difference only in circumstances, and it would have disappeared if the British Government had acted in Ireland in 1780 as it had acted in America in 1774. Those 40,000 Protestants would have resisted. Those guns on Dublin Green would have spoken otherwise than by placard. Nor, if once it had come to fighting, could Ireland have refused the help of France and Spain. As it was, in the summer of 1780 and all through 1781 fighting was still a possibility. Free Trade had been won without it, but what of the second, the greater, the older demand ? What was to result from the Irish Declaration of Independence ? In November, 1780, King William's statue spoke again. This time the placard asked ' that the virtuous resistance of America might prove a lesson to the British Ministry.'[2] Not quite so threatening as the text on the cannon, but none the less a threat. And behind it stood the whole of the Irish movement and its army.

[1] *Debates of Irish Commons*, i, 117.
[2] Froude, *op. cit.*, ii, 291.

But to this demand, it seemed, Britain could not yield. To Whigs as much as to Tories, to Burke and Fox as to George III and North, the legislative supremacy of the British Parliament was (as we have seen) the first article of the imperial faith. It might perhaps have been surrendered to America, but only as the last inexorable price of a re-united Empire. It could not be surrendered to Ireland under any less compulsion. And so, concession and repression being both ruled out, George III and his ministers did the only thing left for them to do. They played for time—time for something to turn up, some happy change at last in the course of the war in America, some decisive British victory in European waters, something to set them free to deal with those Volunteers. And up to a point they were successful. The Declaration of Independence was ignored; and, in accordance with his instructions,[1] the Viceroy, now Lord Carlisle, took shrewd advantage of the vacillating temper of the Irish Commons to prevent that major issue coming to a head. Even on the old minor issues the old opposition was stubbornly maintained. A Habeas Corpus Act was still withheld. Commissions ' during good behaviour ' for judges were still denounced as ' dangerous and improper.' Acts

---

[1] Lord Hillsborough, in charge of Irish affairs, had instructed the Viceroy (March, 1780) ' to prevent, if possible, any propositions for innovations upon or alterations in the constitution being transmitted.' Lecky, *op. cit.*, ii, 249.

were still passed at Westminster naming Ireland as within their operation. The only concession was the allowance of an Irish Mutiny Bill, emasculated by the excision of the vital clause which limited its duration, but, none the less, a tactical gain to the ' patriots ' in that it tacitly denied the application of the British Mutiny Act to Ireland.[1] And that, it may be said, was the sole result of the Declaration in eighteen months. In October, 1781, the Act of 1719 was still on the British statute-book. . . . Yet time, as we know, was against the old *régime*. Every month the military resources of Britain had become more and more exhausted by the unending war. Every month the numbers of the Irish Volunteers had mounted—as high at last, it was alleged, as 80,000.[2] And, in the end, time, which in any case was useless to the Government unless it brought victory in America, brought York Town.

Once more, in another field, York Town was decisive. From the day the news arrived in Dublin, Carlisle's secret dispatches to his chiefs in London began to press with increasing urgency for a policy of concession. ' The independence of Irish legislation is become the creed of the kingdom,' he wrote on 29 December.[3] And one concession at any rate was quickly made—the allowance of an Irish Habeas Corpus Act. But the tide was now rising so fast

[1] Froude, *op. cit.*, ii, 314, 379. Lecky, *op. cit.*, ii, 254-9, 278. For Acts naming Ireland, see Grattan's complaint, *Irish Commons Debates*, i, 128.

[2] Lecky, *op. cit.*, ii, 268.   [3] *Ibid.*, 277.

that surrenders on the minor issues were useless. Two months after York Town was known, the delegates of the Volunteers assembled in Dungannon church, and, together with a statement of the remaining lesser grievances—the judges' commissions, the unlimited Mutiny Act—denied outright ' the claim of any body of men, other than the King, Lords and Commons of Ireland, to make laws to bind this kingdom.' They took, furthermore, a second and a long step towards national unity by affirming the principle of religious toleration and approving the relaxation of the Penal Laws.[1] A few days later, Grattan moved in the House of Commons his second declaration of Irish Independence. Once again he dwelt on the analogy between American and Irish freedom. ' Look to America ! ' he cried. ' When Philadelphia . . . sends forth her ambassadors to the different kings in Europe and manifests to the world her independency and power, do you imagine you will persuade Ireland to be satisfied with an English Parliament making laws for her, satisfied with a refusal to her loyalty of those privileges which

[1] Lecky, *op. cit.*, ii, 282-5. The measure of concession to the Catholics must not be exaggerated. Most of the Irish Protestant leaders still adhered to the ' Protestant Ascendancy ' and regarded the political enfranchisement of the Catholics as out of the question. See, for example, Flood's speech in the Commons five days after Dungannon ; *Irish Commons Debates*, ii, 255, and for the Protestant attitude in general, C. L. Falkiner's scholarly essay, ' The Grattan Parliament and Ulster,' in *Studies in Irish History* (London, 1902).

were offered to the arms of America ? . . . . Are the American enemies to be free, and these loyal subjects slaves ? ' Again the motion was defeated. But a Government majority at Dublin was useless without a Government majority at Westminster ; and within a month the defences of the old *régime* in Britain and in Ireland collapsed together. On 16 April, when Grattan, having passed to the House through lines of Volunteers, moved his third Declaration of Independence, he began his speech with the famous passage : ' I am now to address a free people. Ages have passed away, and this is the first moment in which you could be distinguished by that appellation. . . . I found Ireland on her knees ; I watched over her with an eternal solicitude ; I have traced her progress from injuries to arms and from arms to liberty. Spirit of Swift ! Spirit of Molyneux ! Your genius has prevailed. Ireland is now a nation.' [1] Time was to prove the tragic inadequacy of Grattan's conceptions of freedom and nationhood ; but, construed as he meant them, those

---

[1] *Speeches*, i, 123. The ' Declaration ' was in the form of a Resolution passed by both Houses for an Address to the King declaring ' that his subjects of Ireland are a free people ; that the Crown of Ireland is an imperial Crown, inseparably annexed to the Crown of Great Britain, on which connection the interests and happiness of both nations essentially depend ; but that the Kingdom of Ireland is a distinct Kingdom, with a parliament of her own, the sole legislature thereof : that there is no body of men competent to make laws to bind this nation except the King, Lords and Commons of Ireland ' ; and protesting against the Act of 1719, the operation of Poynings' Law, and the inadequacy of the Irish Mutiny Act. Printed in *Parl. Hist.*, xxiii, 17-20.

romantic invocations were a legitimate anticipation
of the immediate sequel. North's Government was
out and Rockingham's was in ; and so, this time,
not a single vote was cast at Dublin against the
Declaration. Eight days earlier, indeed, William
Eden, Carlisle's chief secretary, had appeared in
his place at Westminster to tell the House of Commons ' that they might as well strive to make the
Thames flow up Highgate Hill as to attempt to
legislate for Ireland.'[1] And eight days later, Carlisle's Whig successor, Portland, wrote to Shelburne
recommending a general surrender. ' It is no longer
the Parliament of Ireland that is to be managed or
attended to. It is the whole of this country. . . .
They know and feel their strength and are equally
sensible of your situation and resources.' If peace
should come to-morrow, he went on, they would
not fear a ' second experiment ' in coercion by
Britain after the ' fatal consequences ' of the first.
Refuse their demands, and ' there would be an end
of all government.'[2] Grattan added his private
ultimatum to Fox. ' The powers, legislative and
jurisdictive, are become impracticable. We have
rendered them so ourselves, and all we ask of England is that she will withdraw a barren claim that
we may shake hands with her.'[3] And so the last
act was quickly played. On 17 May, Shelburne and
Fox informed their respective Houses that the Irish

[1] *Parl. Hist.*, xxii, 1244.   [2] Lecky, *op. cit.*, ii, 303-4.
          [3] *Ibid.*, 306.

claims were to be fully met, and in due course the requisite Bills were enacted, one by the British Parliament to repeal the Act of 1719,[1] the rest by the Irish Parliament to repeal the greater part of Poynings' Act, to limit the duration of the Mutiny Act to two years, and to establish the independence and final authority of the Irish judges.[2]

It was enough for Grattan. ' Great Britain,' he said, in moving a grateful address to the Crown on 27 May, ' gives up *in toto* every claim to authority over Ireland,' and the address itself declared ' that no constitutional question between the two nations will any longer exist which can interrupt their harmony; and that Great Britain, as she has approved of our firmness, so may she rely on our affection.'[3] It was quite enough for Burke who congratulated Ireland on achieving her replica of the ' Glorious Revolution ' of 1688, though he was still clinging in his heart to his ideal of imperial legislation for imperial purposes.[4] But it was not enough for Flood who had seized his chance to contest the leadership of the Irish ' patriots ' with Grattan. The repeal of the Declaratory Act, he argued, was merely negative; it did not annul

[1] 22 George III, c. 53.

[2] 21 and 22 George III, c. 43, 47-50.

[3] *Speeches*, i, 132-4. An address to the Viceroy, moved later by Grattan, asserted that ' the sole and exclusive right of legislation, *external as well as internal*, in the Irish Parliament ' had been ' unequivocally acknowledged ' by Britain. Froude, *op. cit.*, ii, 380.

[4] Lecky, *op. cit.*, ii, 317-18 : and p. 145 below.

Britain's claim to legislate for Ireland ; that claim might one day be revived unless it were for ever renounced by a further British statute. Once more the deadly comparison was drawn between the Peace Commission's surrender to the Americans in 1778 and the precise concessions now made to Ireland. ' A simple repeal is good enough for Ireland whilst an express and a final renunciation was offered to America.'[1] In vain Grattan pleaded for leaving well alone, for trusting Britain. Nationalism, once it has tasted power, is not easily appeased ; and just at that time, as it happened, there were one or two occurrences in England which, though trivial in themselves, were sufficient to create or to intensify suspicion. A couple of English peers distinguished themselves, the one by announcing his opinion —the same as Flood's—that ' simple repeal ' was inadequate, the other by moving for leave to introduce a Bill to declare the right of the British Parliament to control the external trade of Ireland.[2] Next, by sheer ' oversight ' apparently, ' the word Ireland had slipped in ' to two trade laws enacted at Westminster.[3] Last, the British Court of King's Bench decided, as it was bound to do, an Irish appeal which had been lodged before the new

[1] *Irish Commons Debates*, i, 421-9.
[2] Lords Beauchamp and Abingdon : *Parl. Hist.*, xxiii, 30-31, 147-52, 334-7. Beauchamp maintained the Irish case and the wisdom of conceding it. For an illustration of Abingdon's mentality, see Coupland, *Wilberforce* (Oxford, 1923), 214.
[3] *Parl. Hist.*, xxiii, 336. Lecky, *op. cit.*, ii, 324.

Acts had been passed.[1] These trifles did their work. The majority of the 'patriots,' including the Volunteers, swung over from Grattan to Flood; and Temple, the third Viceroy in a year, accepted their case. 'England,' he wrote, 'is obliged by every tie of natural faith to complete a contract which is clearly incomplete.'[2] It was a Shelburne Ministry now, for Rockingham was dead; but it followed its predecessor's example. Though peace was now at hand, though Britain was free, had she wished, to concentrate what power she had left on Ireland, the old policy of repression was everywhere —as a result of York Town—at a discount; and, in January, 1783, on the morrow of the signing of the peace preliminaries which acknowledged the independence of the American colonies, an Act was passed 'for removing and preventing all doubts which have arisen or might arise concerning the exclusive rights of the parliament and courts of Ireland.' It declared that 'the right claim by the people of Ireland to be bound only by laws enacted by his Majesty and the parliament of that kingdom in all cases whatever and to have all actions and suits at law or in equity, which may be instituted in that kingdom, decided by his Majesty's courts therein finally and without appeal from thence shall be, and it is hereby declared to be, established

[1] Lecky, *op cit.*, ii, 324.
[2] 20 Nov., 1782. Froude, *op. cit.*, ii, 392.

and ascertained for ever, and shall be at no time hereafter questioned or questionable.'[1]

The Irish Revolution had run its course—' I trust,' said Burke, ' the last Revolution in Ireland.'[2]

From first to last, as we have seen, in their origin and purpose as in their progress, the Irish and American Revolutions had been linked together. But in their results they had broken apart. At a great price, by the schism of the Empire, by the sacrifice of all that its continued unity might have meant in happier circumstances for the peace and welfare of the world, the thirteen colonies had obtained a freedom as general, as entire, as any state in a world of states could enjoy. The Irish, on the other hand, had obtained free trade and a free parliament and nothing more. They still professed allegiance to George III ; and, though they might call him King of Ireland rather than of Britain, his royal prerogatives in his Irish kingdom as in his British were still exercised on the advice of British, not of Irish, ministers. The Irish Government, moreover, was still appointed and controlled by the British Government. Nor were even those liberties of trade or legislation quite complete. There were still certain areas and markets in the Empire un- equally barred to Irish trade. Members of the Irish legislature—as the unclean story of 1800 was soon to prove—were still amenable to British bribes.

[1] 23 George III, c. 28.   [2] *Irish Letters, etc.*, 370.

And, lastly, the Catholic majority of the Irish people were still deprived of any political liberty at all. Far less, then, was the Irish freedom of 1783 than the American : far less, too, than the Irish freedom of to-day. Ireland, it is true, is not even yet a united nation : the descendants of the Protestant Irish who voted for ' Grattan's Parliament ' and created the Volunteers are still sundered for the most part from their Celtic fellow-countrymen. But the majority of Irishmen are citizens of a Free State, ' equal in status ' with Great Britain and its sister Dominions in the British Commonwealth of Nations, and ' in no way subordinate ' to it or to them ' in any aspect of [its] domestic or external affairs.'[1]   And in 1930 these are not words only, like so much that was said and written in 1782 and 1783 : they are facts. It is only for convenience and by common agreement that the British Parliament still retains its legal right to legislate for a Dominion ; and it can only exercise it ' at the request and with the consent of that Dominion.'[2]   If

[1] Report of Inter-Imperial Relations Committee of Imperial Conference of 1926 (Chairman, Lord Balfour), unanimously adopted by the members of the Conference, including the Prime Ministers of Great Britain and all the Dominions except the Irish Free State, whose senior representative was the Vice-President of the Executive Council. (Cmd. 2768, 14.)

[2] Report of the Conference on the Operation of Dominion Legislation, etc. Cmd. 3479, 20. The British representatives, including the Secretary of State for Dominion Affairs, signed this unanimous report. It has yet to be considered by the Imperial Conference which meets in September, 1930, and to be given

appeals from Dominion courts can still be made to
the Judicial Committee of the Privy Council in
Britain, it is again only for convenience and pending
further consultation and discussion.[1] More important—indeed the decisive factor—is the equal
status of the Free State Government with that of
Britain. The Governor-General is no longer the
agent of the British Government : he is ' the representative of the Crown, holding in all essential
respects the same position in relation to the administration of public affairs in the Dominion as
is held by His Majesty the King in Great Britain.'[2]
The Ministers of the Free State are in no way responsible to British Ministers or their agents ; they
are responsible to the Free State Parliament alone.[3]
And it is not only their right to advise the Crown
in all matters relating to the Free State's own affairs,
but it would be unconstitutional for British Ministers to tender contrary advice.[4] Comparison need
go no further—or, rather, contrast : for, in truth,
Irish liberties in 1783 and 1930 are scarcely com-
parable.

Nor had the Irish Revolution failed only to secure
an adequate measure of national freedom and equality. It had failed yet more completely to fulfil the

such statutory enforcement as it requires. But the use of the
British Parliament's right is already, in practice or *de facto*,
confined in the manner stated in the text above.

[1] Cmd. 2768, 19-20.   [2] Cmd. 2768, 16.
[3] Constitution of the Irish Free State, Articles 51 and 53.
[4] Imperial Conference, 1926. Cmd. 2768, 16. Reaffirmed
by Dominion Legislation Conference of 1929, Cmd. 3479, 14.

second and no less essential condition of any lasting settlement—imperial unity. It had left the British and Irish Parliaments, theoretically equal and independent, standing on no common ground, floating in the void with no appropriate or durable connexion to keep them on a common course of policy.[1] At the moment, it is true, there were safeguards of a sort. Negatively, the British Government could advise the King or instruct the Viceroy to veto measures of the Irish Parliament. Positively, the British Government through its agent, the Irish Government, could, as a rule and within limits, ' influence ' the Irish Parliament to pass the measures it desired. But the suppression of political corruption had already begun in Britain : it could not be long delayed in Ireland : there was already talk of Irish parliamentary reform on both sides of the Channel. And what then ? How long would the other link endure ? How long would an honest

[1] In case it be supposed that there is no better inter-imperial connexion to-day, it may be worth while to point out that the joint declaration of 1926 laid stress on consultation and co-operation for common purposes as well as on national autonomy and equality as between the nations of the British Commonwealth. ' Free institutions are its life-blood. Free co-operation is its instrument.' The Prime Ministers who agreed on that Report, and the public opinion which accepted it are pledged to observe both principles. Consultation and co-operation are effected (1) by the Imperial Conference of Prime Ministers which meets every four years, and more often 'if necessary, (2) by the presence of agents of the Dominion Governments in London and of agents of the British Government in most of the Dominion capitals, and (3) by constant correspondence between the Governments. No doubt this machinery could be improved.

and really representative Irish House of Commons submit to the authority of an Executive it could not control ? And, when the last link was gone, what was to prevent Ireland from pursuing a divergent course in the common affairs of the Empire, economic or political, from that of Britain—from establishing a tariff against Britain, from forming commercial ties with France, from adopting a distinct foreign policy, from refusing to engage in wars arising from that of Britain ? Those questions— and they could, of course, be multiplied—were not unreasonable in 1782 ; and it is to the credit of British statesmen that at least they asked them. When the Irish crisis came to a head after York Town, when Portland advised complete surrender, ' Are we to look,' Shelburne asked him, ' for any agreement which may answer the purposes of keeping up the appendancy and connexion of Ireland to the crown of Great Britain and of preventing that confusion which must arise in all cases of common concern from two Parliaments acting with distinct and equal powers and without any operating centre ? ' [1] And when he announced the surrender to the Lords, he gave such force as words could give to the disclaimer of ' the idea of treating England and Ireland as distinct dominions united under one sovereign ' and by nothing else.[2] Fox, on the same occasion, foreshadowed the negotiation

[1] 29 April, 1782. Fitzmaurice, *op. cit.*, ii, 97.
[2] *Parl. Hist.*, xxiii, 43.

of a ' treaty ' to establish ' a firm and solid basis '
for ' the future connexion of the two kingdoms ';[1]
and, three years afterwards, he confessed that
Britain's ' precipitate ' surrender of the power of
' external ' or ' imperial ' legislation had made it
necessary to establish some ' general and superin-
tending authority ' in its place—of what nature he
did not say.[2] Nor did Burke, of course, though he
congratulated Ireland on the settlement and extolled
the ' justice and moderation ' of Britain, ever really
acquiesce in abandoning the basic element of his
ideal imperialism. Shortly before his death in 1797
he dictated his unchanged opinion on the Irish
question—' that the whole of the superior and what
I should call *imperial* politics ought to have its
residence here [in Britain]; and that Ireland,
locally, civilly, and commercially independent, ought
politically to look up to Great Britain in all matters
of peace or of war ; in all these points to be guided
by her ; and, in a word, with her to live and to die.'[3]
There was logic, though not enough, as well as
sentiment in Burke's idealism. There was a practical need for Shelburne's ' operating centre ' and
for Fox's ' treaty.' But Grattan ignored it. He
refused, almost violently, even to consider a ' treaty.'

[1] *Parl. Hist.*, xxiii, 26.   [2] *Ibid.*, xxv, 966.
[3] *Irish Letters*, 270, 380. Burke had only accepted *commercial*
independence with reluctance : see his condemnation in 1780
of the virtual surrender of the legislative power as to trade in
1779. *Ibid.*, 319.

' There must be no negotiation,' he told Fox.[1]
And so—because of York Town—there was none.

So imperfect, so ill-balanced and unscientific, was
the actual settlement that emerged from all the ro-
mance and rhetoric of the Irish Revolution.   Yet
the worst settlement can last, the clumsiest political
machinery can work, for a time, if there is enough
good-will among those concerned with it.   And
unquestionably there was some good-will between
Britain and Ireland in 1782 and after.   The expression of it, indeed, was sometimes quite exuberant.
' It was not the King,' said Fox at Westminster,
' that was the chief bond of union : it was a
communion of affection, of regard, of brotherly love,
of consanguinity, and of constitution.'[2]   ' Let experience teach you wisdom,' said Hely Hutchison
at Dublin to Britain ; ' take Ireland to your bosom,
protect her infant commerce, respect her liberty :
she will prop the tottering fabric, heal the wounds
of your dismembered Empire, her youth will in-
vigorate your old age.'[3]   No doubt such purple
passages invite distrust ; yet no one can read through
the debates in the British and Irish Parliaments
without receiving a definite impression that behind
the sobriety of the one and the brilliance of the
other lay a substantial measure of genuine good-

[1] 6 May, 1782.   Froude, *op. cit.*, ii, 362.
[2] 17 May, 1782.   *Parl. Hist.*, xxiii, 32.
[3] 22 Feb., 1782.   *Irish Commons Debates*, i, 273-4.   Flood, in
the same strain in 1785 : ' If there be a string by which Britain
can recover the affections of America, it is a string which Ireland
holds out to her.' *Ibid.*, v, 403.

will. But it was not enough. Not enough even on the British side, where it was naturally less difficult to feel it—not enough to overcome the deep-rooted prejudices of mercantile imperialism, the unquestioning assertion of 'supremacy,' the almost instinctive denial of equality; not enough, it has been seen and will be seen again, to resist the clamour of the British commercial class. Nor could there be enough on the Irish side unless Britain's concessions had been as free as they were wide, so free, such a cogent proof of a real 'change of heart,' as to cancel out Irish memories of the past. And, of course, those concessions had not been free at all. Once more the dominant part played by the American Revolution in all this story looms out of the background. It was all very well for Fox to say of the concessions in 1782 that 'he would have been as ready to grant them if Ireland made them now in the same unarmed and modest manner in which she preferred her complaints four years ago.'[1] He might speak for himself, but nobody in Ireland supposed he spoke for Britain. Grattan, indeed, while he certainly believed and wisely tried to make his people believe in Britain's good intentions, was under no illusion as to what had prompted them, and at times the truth would out. 'The American war was the Irish harvest,' he confessed in 1785:[2] and

[1] *Parl. Hist.*, xxiii, 23.

[2] *Speeches*, i, 237. See also the speech in 1780 in which he represented Ireland as dreading the approach of peace: p. 126 above.

in the great speech of 1782, unconscious perhaps of all he was admitting, he had traced Ireland's progress from injuries to liberty through *arms*. Some of his fellow-countrymen were blunter. ' Gratitude to Britain ? ' asked one of them : ' It is not to the liberality of Britain but to circumstances, to necessity, to your own virtue, to America that you owe your advantages. To America your temple and statues are due.'[1]   And as early as the autumn of 1783, when Britain's final surrender was fresh in mind, it could be argued that on a matter of imperial concern—it was the old question of the size of the Irish army—Ireland could only get her way if she acted quickly, before the peace had had its full effect. ' You will never have such another opportunity. . . . You will never have another American war.'[2]

The American Revolution had made the Irish Revolution possible, but, in so doing, it had also made it sterile and short-lived. All Grattan's eloquence could not smother the hard facts or maintain in face of them the good-will which alone could save the Revolution from its own inherent vices. And so, within a year or two, Ireland, free and independent, began to drift towards an open rupture with Britain, and that—in peace-time—could have but one result.

[1] Arthur Browne, one of the two members for T.C.D. *Irish Commons Debates*, ii, 100.
[2] *Ibid.*, 102.

Such was the situation which confronted Pitt when he came to power in 1784 and examined the post-war Empire. His hands were free. He had taken no active part in the settlement of 1782-83. An attempt to rescue Anglo-Irish relations from the dangerous consequences of that settlement was the obvious beginning of his task of imperial reconstruction. ' After the severe calamities under which this country has so long laboured,' he said in the House of Commons in 1785, ' after the heavy loss she has sustained from the recent division of her dominions, there ought to be no object more impressive on the feelings of this house than to endeavour to preserve from further dismemberment and diminution, to unite and to connect *what yet remains of our reduced and shattered Empire, of which Great Britain and Ireland are now the only considerable members*, in the bonds of mutual affection and reciprocity of interests.'[1] Towards this end Pitt made three distinct moves during his tenure of office. The first was an effort to secure through the Irish Government and Parliament a similar measure of Reform for Ireland as that which he was then advocating in Britain. ' Parliamentary Reform,' Pitt told the Viceroy, at the end of 1784, ' *must* sooner or later be carried *in both countries* ' ; and he asked for ' unanswerable proofs that the case of Ireland and England is different.'[2] He had not yet outgrown

[1] Pitt's *Speeches* (1806 ed.), i, 258-9.
[2] Pitt-Rutland Correspondence, cited by Fisher, *op. cit.*, 177, 179. Pitt's italics.

his sanguine youth. It was quickly evident that the
case of Ireland and England was too much the same.
In both countries Reform was blocked by the vested
interests of the parliamentary class. Within a year
Pitt's moderate British Reform Bill had been rejected and the hope of Reform in either country
indefinitely postponed. So much for Pitt's first
move. His third and last move—a legislative
Union linked, as he intended, with Catholic emancipation—is a familiar story and lies beyond the scope
of this lecture. We are here concerned with the
second move—the move immediately required to
forestall the crisis that was fast approaching in
1784.

The root of the trouble, as often before in Ireland
and often after, was poverty. Free trade had not
restored prosperity to Irish commerce and industry.
Unemployment was still rife. Food itself was scarce
and very dear. And, not unnaturally, Irishmen
began to ask what was the use of economic liberty
if it did not do for Ireland what it did for other
independent countries. Let the free Irish Parliament give to Irish industries the tariff-protection
which all other nations gave to theirs. Was it not
absurd, for instance, that Irish woollens should be
not only excluded from the British market but also
beaten by cheaper British woollens in the Irish
market ? The questioners forgot that the British
Parliament was also free and would almost certainly
counter an Irish tariff by erecting further barriers

against Irish imports into Britain. The agitation
grew.[1]

To a pupil of Adam Smith the prospect of a
tariff war between the major British Isles was intolerable. Unlike most Englishmen and many
Irishmen, Pitt had accepted his master's view that
a free trade, unlimited in scope or time, between
Britain and Ireland would promote the welfare of
both countries. The threatened conflict, moreover,
underlined the obvious fact that the settlement of
1782-83 had been left dangerously incomplete.
Surely Grattan himself must now confess that only
some further engagement, only a ' treaty,' could
preserve the Anglo-Irish harmony he had always
preached. And the basic principles of any such
treaty were as clear to Pitt as they ever were to
Grattan. Better than most Englishmen, Pitt had
learned the lesson of the American Revolution.
He had recognised that the cardinal sin of the old
imperialism was inequality—the dominance of the
mother-country, the subjection of the colonies—
and that no part of the ' colonial ' field had suffered
as much therefrom as Ireland. The aim of a new
imperialism, therefore, in Ireland as elsewhere,
should be to promote, as far as practicable, a new
relationship, a new sense of an imperial communion
whose members would share equally in its rights
and privileges and, because of that equality and only
so, would solve the problem that had destroyed the

[1] Lecky, op. cit., ii, 382-6

old Empire by willingly accepting equal duties. And so, when Pitt introduced his proposals for an Irish ' treaty ' in the House of Commons in February, 1785, he declared at the outset that in settling the relations between the two islands there were only two possible policies. One was that of keeping ' the smaller completely subservient and subordinate to the greater.' ' This system we have tried.' The other was ' a system of equality and fairness,' involving ' a community of benefits ' and also ' a community of burdens.' On these principles he proposed, on the one hand, that all the remaining barriers to a free and equal trade between Britain and Ireland should be removed in perpetuity : that Irish imports should be admitted once and for all to the great British market and that their admission to the colonial markets, which the British Parliament had conceded but might at any time withdraw, should be declared to be ' permanent and irrevocable '. On the other hand, he proposed that Ireland should ' contribute a share towards the protection and security of the general commerce of the Empire ' : that, when the Irish ' hereditary revenue,' mainly derived from Customs and Excise, rose above a fixed sum as the result of the expected increase in Irish trade, the surplus should always be appropriated ' towards the support of the naval force of the Empire.'[1]

[1] Pitt's *Speeches*, i, 194-209. The ' naval ' Resolution was the tenth of the Ten Resolutions as proposed in the Irish Com-

There, in that last item of Pitt's programme, lay the crux. Ireland, it has been seen, had never refused the burden of imperial defence : in peace and in war, indeed, she had accepted more than her fair share of it. But would she bind herself to a permanent contribution as part of a compact with Britain ? Would she realise that she got by the compact, as a purely business proposition, far more than she gave, and that duties as well as rights were implicit in that recognition of her equality with Britain which far more than any material profit she desired ? Was there enough good-will still flickering in Ireland to illuminate the sincerity of Pitt's offer as well as its justice ? Or had the bitter memories, the jealousy and suspicion, recovered all their old hold since 1783 ? The issue trembled in the balance. And unhappily, yet once again, the precedents of the American Revolution weighed down the anti-British scale. To identify the Irish cause with the American had become a habit in Ireland, not to be outgrown in two or three years ; and it was easy, too easy, to detect in the proposal for a naval subsidy a resurrection of the Stamp Act and the Augmentation Scheme. No sooner had the Resolution which embodied that part of Pitt's plan been read in the House of Commons at Dublin

mons on 7 Feb., 1785 (*Irish Commons Debates*, iv, 120-5), and the eleventh of the Eleven as proposed in the British Commons on 22 Feb. (*Parl. Hist.*, xxv, 312-4). The 'hereditary revenue' in Ireland was still controlled by the Government and not Parliament. See Lecky, *op. cit.*, ii, 433.

when one impulsive member leapt to his feet to denounce, in broken and indignant sentences, so bare-faced an attempt to make Ireland ' a tributary nation.' ' Is this,' he cried, ' the boasted extension of our commerce ? Is this the reciprocal advantage we were to enjoy ? Sir, I reject the gift ! ' And then the old sinister comparison—' Such propositions were formerly made to America, and we have seen their effect. . . . I will not say *Timeo Danaos*.' [1] But he had said it : and in the hearts of most Irishmen who heard him, whatever their politics, there must have stirred at least a faint response. Only one man, perhaps, could have checked the tide of Irish feeling from rising with a rush, in Parliament and outside it, to overwhelm the scheme ; and that Grattan did check it is a better proof of his statesmanship than anything else in his life. He had not only recovered his ascendancy in the Irish Parliament but also his balance of mind. Three years ago he had denied the need for a ' treaty ': he admitted it now. He trusted Pitt. He believed in his principles : they were his own. The proposals seemed to him ' such as the British minister can justify to both nations.' And he was not afraid to say so. ' The plan,' he declared, ' is open, fair, and just.' [2] Those brave monosyllables were worth an hour of rolling oratory. The great majority of the House

[1] W. Brownlow, one of the two members for Armagh County. *Irish Commons Debates*, iv, 125.

[2] *Speeches*, i, 214.

voted with him. There was no hitch in the Lords. Flood and the malcontents could do nothing in the country at large. Ireland had accepted the ' treaty.'

And thereupon it was promptly rejected by the business men of Britain. They had learned little enough from the *Wealth of Nations*, as we shall see in our next lecture, about the virtues of free trade, and nothing at all from the American Revolution about the virtues of equality. So the sordid spectacle of 1778 was seen again. Again the British cities grasped their threatened money-bags and screamed. No less than 120,000 signatures were set to the so-called ' Manchester Petition ' to the House of Lords against Pitt's scheme.[1] Representatives of industry from all parts of the country met in London, and with Wedgwood, the great potter, at their head, established for their defence ' The Great Chamber of the Manufacturers of Great Britain.'[2] And this time there was another yet more piquant novelty. No louder voices were to be heard inciting that spirit of commercial jealousy in Britain which had so long kept Ireland in economic servitude and inciting in the same breath that spirit of unforgetting, unforgiving enmity in Ireland which was so long to make atonement difficult and reconciliation impossible, than the voices of Fox and his fellow-champions of freedom and ' brotherly love.' Burke's opposition to the scheme was not unqualified, but even he did not scruple to rehearse the old American analogy. ' I hope to God

[1] *Annual Register*, 1784-85, 362.   [2] Lecky, *op. cit.*, ii, 444.

the conclusion of this business will not be like that of the contest with America.'[1]   Fox was more thorough.   Many sentences of his, spoken on other days, were long to be remembered, some of them to feed the hopes of the world; but it would be better for his memory if we could forget that one famous sentence, spoken in the early hours of 13 May, 1785, in which he so deliberately misconstrued Pitt's principles and so adroitly appealed to the conflicting interests of his opponents.   ' I will not barter English commerce for Irish slavery.'[2]

Not for the only time in his career, Pitt's policy on a great issue was absolutely right, and yet—was it because he was too far ahead of his party or because he had not quite Chatham's strength or merely because he was so young?—he failed to carry it.   He was a bigger man than Grattan, but he could not do at Westminster what Grattan had done in Dublin.   He was a bigger man than North, but not big enough to break the storm, and so, like North, he bowed to it.   Part I of the story of 1778 had been repeated.   Part II now followed.   The proposals were transformed so as still to bar Irish trade from rivalry with British in certain fields and goods, and a new condition was inserted requiring the Irish Parliament automatically to enact all past and future laws enacted by the British Parliament regarding navigation and inter-imperial trade.   Even

[1] *Parl. Hist.*, xxv, 647.   See also Lecky, *op. cit.*, ii, 447, note 1.
[2] *Parl. Hist.*, xxv, 778.

in this new guise, Pitt only succeeded after long debate in forcing the proposals through the Commons.[1]   In any case, as he ought to have known, he was wasting his time.   His policy had lost the balance on which both its justice and its acceptability depended.   The community of burdens remained : the community of benefits was gone.   There was to be no real, no full equality for Ireland. Even the legislative freedom she had won in 1782-83 was to be surrendered—in that very field of trade wherein she had suffered her worst oppressions—to the old ' supremacy ' of the British Parliament : and the old subordination was to be stiffened now by a permanent obligation to contribute to imperial defence.   When the second edition of the Resolutions was submitted to the Irish Commons and when the cry was raised again that Britain was trying ' to treat Ireland as America was treated,'[2] this time Grattan echoed it.   ' Whence the American war ? ' he asked :   ' Whence the Irish restrictions ? . . .   Whence but from the evil of suffering one country to regulate the trade and navigation of another, and of instituting, under the idea of general protection, a proud domination, which sacrifices the interest of a whole to the ambition of a part and arms the little passions of the monopolist with the sovereign   potency   of   an   Imperial   Parliament ! '

[1] *Parl. Hist.*, xxv, 713-78.   The revised Resolutions, now twenty : 707-13.

[2] C. O'Hara, member for Sligo County.   *Irish Commons Debates*, v, 452.

And in words as direct and true as those in which, six months back, he had blessed Pitt's policy, he cursed its perversion. ' Here is an end of your free trade and your free constitution.'[1]   And this time, though the ' influence ' of Government was still strong enough to secure a slight majority on the first division in the Commons, Irish opinion was more decidedly with Grattan than before. The Resolutions were withdrawn, and Dublin blazed with illuminations.[2]

So one more item had been added to the list of lost chances that runs through Anglo-Irish history. If public opinion in Britain and in Ireland had fully understood and sincerely accepted the principles of Pitt and Grattan, it is not impossible that the foundations of a real union between the sister islands might have been built in 1785.   And even if the ' treaty ' had been made without a real appreciation of its meaning on either side, at least it would have stopped the drift that had set in since 1783, a drift that was leading, as Pitt had warned the Commons, from latent jealousy and suspicion to an ' open war of interests and passions.'[3]   As it was, it would have been better, perhaps, if Pitt had never made his effort.   For the circumstances of its failure threw back the more impulsive Irish patriots to the mood of an earlier day.   The force of the American example was not yet exhausted.   Too

[1] *Speeches*, i, 239, 241.   [2] Lecky, *op. cit.*, ii, 450.
[3] *Speeches*, i, 258.

little and too much had been taught by the American Revolution. That British business men had learned too little had been made crudely clear by their new exhibition of commercial selfishness, by their instant and fierce rejection of Pitt's gospel of equality. And so Irish patriots set themselves to show that they had learned too much. Why, they began to ask, had they not followed the American lead to the bitter end ? The American colonies were now independent States: they were now constituting themselves an united republic. Could Ireland ever be free unless she did the same ? And how had the Americans done it ? Not by a show of force, but by the use of it. . . . A few years later the French Revolution came to reinspire and reinforce such thoughts, and, hard on its heels, the Revolutionary War, giving Ireland, beyond her expectations, ' another opportunity.' And this time the ' patriots ' were not content to use their arms for drilling and saluting only. Listening still to the voice from over the Atlantic, heartening themselves with the watchwords of defiant Massachusetts, parading the American flag, toasting the names of Washington and Franklin, they broke into open rebellion. And this time the French did land and were welcome. And this time the hopes of Irish unity were blasted by the revival in all its bitterness of the old strife of race and faith. So, not for the first time nor the last, unhappy Ireland became a devil's playground.

V.

THE ATTACK ON MERCANTILISM.

IN 1798 Ireland was in far worse plight than in
1775. In that field, it might well be thought, the
effects of the American Revolution on the character of the British Empire were more injurious
than otherwise. If there were any change in its
character, it might well seem, it was a change for the
worse : the Irish spirit of antagonism to Britain,
the spirit of British domination over Ireland, those
primary barriers to peace and harmony were raised
and stiffened. But let us look deep and look ahead
before we jump to that conclusion. Remember,
first, that too much was not to be expected. No
imperial problem, not even the American, was half
so difficult to solve as the Irish problem. The tissues
of Anglo-Irish relations had been poisoned by
history—by what Englishmen had done to Irishmen
and by what Irishmen had done to one another—and
generations were still to pass, the American Revolution was to fade from men's minds, before that
poison could be diluted and disinfected and filtered
away. And remember, secondly, that this process,
long and dreary as it proved to be, did actually
begin at the period of the American Revolution.
It was observed in the last lecture that the debates

in the Houses of Parliament during the war revealed a new attitude towards Ireland, a new understanding of what her economic subjection had meant. There were other Englishmen besides Townshend who could see the contrast that was so plain to Irishmen, who began now to think about Ireland's case as they had never thought before. Though Pitt found himself in a minority, he was not, of course, alone. Other representatives of young post-war England thought as he did. And Pitt, in 1785, was still a prophet of the future, not a defender of the past. The true, the only antidote for the Anglo-Irish poison was the recognition of equality between the English and Irish nations; and that was the essential principle of Pitt's prescription in 1785. His own conception of the union of 1800, however perverted in the event, was based on that principle : every liberal effort in the nineteenth century pursued it : the settlement of 1921 conformed to it. Remember, lastly, that Pitt's Irish policy on its economic side was one of the first moves in an attack aimed at the very heart of the old imperialism—at Mercantilism itself—and that, though British industrialists could easily repel it in 1785, it was one day to prevail. For it had behind it a stronger instrument than the Great Chamber of the Manufacturers of Great Britain : it had the brains of Adam Smith.

Great changes in the organisation of human society can seldom be so largely ascribed to the work of one man as the downfall of the Mercantile System can be ascribed to the work of Adam Smith ; and seldom are the dates attached to the world's great books of such historical significance as the date attached to the first edition of the *Wealth of Nations*. The two quarto volumes which appeared on 9 March, 1776, were not, of course, the instant outcome of a year of civil war. Their creation from first to last had taken nearly thirty years, and most of the ideas they contained were already formulated in the lectures their author gave in Glasgow between 1759 and 1763. But the most famous chapter in the book, the long chapter ' Of Colonies,' had no prenatal existence in those lectures. It was the production of the twelve years between the conclusion of the Peace of Paris and the Battle of Lexington. The sudden presentation and rapid exacerbation of the colonial question during those crucial years attracted to it a mind which had hitherto neglected it, but which, once engaged on it, soon proved itself the clearest mind in Britain. Moreover, in the third edition of the book, which was published at the end of 1784, Smith inserted a wholly new chapter with the premature but at least prophetic title, ' The Conclusion of the Mercantile System.' It is obvious, then, that the American Revolution was not the least important item in the complex of facts and ideas which inspired and shaped the *Wealth of Nations ;* and it would be difficult, surely, to ex- aggerate the ultimate effects of that great book on the thoughts and policies of the Western World in general and of Britain in particular.[1]

Circumstance, meantime, was reinforcing doctrine. The upshot of the Revolution, the transformation of the thirteen British colonies into thirteen foreign states, had made the old Empire economically as well as politically lop-sided. The territorial field, wherein the system Adam Smith attacked was operating, had greatly shrunk between the issues of the first and third editions of his book ; and to him and his disciples, at any rate, it seemed that not only economic theory but immediate practical needs required a change in the old system to meet the changed conditions. It was argued (as will appear) that Britain herself would not greatly suffer if the Americans were prevented—as the Navigation Acts automatically prevented them—from enjoying as foreigners the same access for their shipping and goods to British ports and markets which they had enjoyed as colonists. But the British West Indies were bound to suffer if no change were made. Their trade had been moulded by the old system. The greater part of it was with the North American mainland and mostly carried in American ships. 'What had been created under monopoly,' to quote a recent author, ' was now in danger of

[1] On the composition of the *Wealth of Nations*, see E. Cannan's introduction to his edition of it (London, 1904). Its colonial doctrine is fully examined in J. S. Nicholson, *A Project of Empire* (London, 1909).

being destroyed under exclusion.'[1] 'The lumber and provisions of the United States,' wrote Adam Smith to William Eden, ' are more necessary to our West India Islands than the rum and sugar of the latter are to the former. Any interruption or restraint of commerce would hurt our loyal much more than our revolted subjects.'[2]

To Pitt, who was proud to describe himself as a pupil of the great professor, this lesson seemed one of the most obvious to be learned from examining ' what was left ' of the Empire at the close of the War ; and he attempted to apply it without delay. On 3 March, 1783, some six weeks after the conclusion of the preliminaries of peace, when his chief, Shelburne, had just resigned and his own political future seemed quite uncertain, he boldly introduced a Bill to enable the American States to continue to enjoy their previous privileges in British ports and markets.[3] Like Shelburne, who had also been convinced by the *Wealth of Nations*, Pitt believed that British commerce would gain more than it lost by such a concession and was prepared to face the risk of American competition in the

[1] A. Brady, *William Huskisson and Liberal Reform* (London, 1928), p. 77.

[2] *Journal and Correspondence of Lord Auckland* (London, 1861-62), i, 64 ; cited by Brady, *op. cit.*

[3] The best account of the Bill and the discussion of it is by E. C. Burnett in *American Historical Review*, xviii, 769-73. An abstract of the Bill appears in the *London Chronicle*, 6-8 March, 1783. The more important parts of the debates on it in Parliament are given in *Parl. Hist.*, xxiii, 602-15, 724-9, 894-5.

carrying-trade. A great part of the ' City ' agreed
with him. ' We beg leave to declare it to be our
firm persuasion,' said the Lord Mayor, Aldermen,
and Commons in an address to the King, ' that the
great commercial interests of this country and of
North America are inseparably united.'[1] And a
similar address was presented by the firms trading
with America, asking that commerce between Britain
and America be regulated ' with that liberality which
we conceive to be the true policy of commercial
states.'[2] ' The Press teemed with pamphlets,' it is
recorded in the *Annals of Commerce*, ' written in
support of these new maxims of commercial policy.'[3]
And, of course, the West Indian interest was wholly
for the Bill. On the spot, indeed, it seemed such
an obvious concession to economic necessity as to
be almost a mere formality ; and ' some of the governors of the islands,' to quote the *Annals* again,
' acted as if they thought the peace had placed the
Americans precisely in the same condition they were
in before the revolution, and freely admitted them
into their ports.'[4] But, strong as it was on its commercial side, Pitt's motive was more than commercial.

[1] Burnett, *op. cit.*, 772, note 13, citing *London Gazette*, 25 Feb.,
—1 March, 1783.

[2] *Ibid.*, p. 772. See also the *Observations* of the London
merchants engaged in American trade, printed in full, pp. 773-80.
This document is dated 22 July, 1783 ; but it is probably (as
Burnett argues) the same or much the same as the report they
gave to Pitt in March.

[3] Macpherson, *op. cit.*, iv, 18 (cited by Brady, as above).

[4] *Ibid.*

It was an attempt to ' reconciliate our ancient friends.'
Might not the old ties of kinship and tongue and
tradition be reknitted and grow stronger than they
had ever been, once the imperial control which had
frayed and finally severed them had been abandoned ?
Many other Englishmen thought so. In his ode to
the next new year the Poet Laureate depicted, not
very felicitously, Britain and America, linked in
amity and commerce, as ' The Tyre and Carthage
of a wider sphere.'[1] And Burke went farther still.
In one of the debates on Pitt's Bill, he declared that
the principle that he wished to lay down with
respect to America was not to treat her people as
aliens. ' I. would still treat them as fellow-subjects
as far as I could.'[2] Nor was the American attitude,
on the whole, less friendly. The Peace Commissioners, who were still in Paris, were shown the
outlines of the Bill ; and they were highly pleased,'
Pitt told the House of Commons, ' at the generosity
of Britain, and made no doubt but America would
do everything in her power to promote the interests
of this country.' ' Mr. Pitt's Bill,' wrote Jay to the
British Minister at Washington, ' was a good one,
a wise one, and one that will forever do honour to
the extent and policy of his views.'[3]

For a moment British opinion seemed about to

[1] Macpherson, *op. cit.*, iv, 18.
[2] Debate of 7 March, 1783. *Parl. Hist.*, xxiii, 614.
[3] Burnett, *op. cit.*, p. 770, note 4. As against Jay, Henry
Laurens was ' rather antagonistic.'

follow Pitt's lead ; but then the current turned. Toryism protested against so revolutionary a departure from the old commercial tradition.[1] The shipowners, of course, were up in arms. And with the fear of American rivalry went, humanly enough, a dislike of restoring to those ' ungrateful ' recusants the very privileges which they had so deliberately thrcwn away. Arguments were added to instincts. In an able and widely-read pamphlet Lord Sheffield showed—and it was true—that the new American States would still be obliged to import most of the goods they wanted from British lands ; declared—less truly—that Britain and the West Indies would soon obtain from Canada and Nova Scotia all the raw materials previously supplied by the thirteen colonies ; affirmed, accordingly, that British trade, whether inter-imperial or Anglo-American, would gain nothing by abandoning the wisdom of the past ; and in his closing sentence threatened ministers with impeachment if they dared to ' desert the Navigation Act and sacrifice the marine of England.' As for reconciliation with the Americans, ' If in some instances, as in the loss of the carrying-trade, they feel the inconvenience of their choice, they can no longer complain ; but, if they are placed on the footing of the most-favoured nation, they must surely applaud our liberality and friendship, without expecting that, for their emolument, we should sacrifice the navigation and the naval power of

[1] See the debates, cited in Note (3), p. 164 above.

Great Britain.'[1]   A similar pamphlet followed from
Mr. Chalmers' pen.[2]   Between them they did their
easy work. The Bill was amended almost out of
recognition before Pitt resigned the Chancellorship
of the Exchequer on 31 March. And the Coalition,
which assumed office on 2 April, took little interest
in the mangled remains of some one else's child.
Fox, who, though he welcomed the idea of reconciliation, had been unusually cautious about the
Bill from the first, was still more cautious now he
was in office. He suggested that it might be wiser
to proceed by treaty than by statute. That was
enough. Pitt's Bill faded into limbo.[3]

Historians must be cautious about ' might-have-

[1] *Observations on the Commerce of the American States with
Europe and the West Indies*, London, 1783. The popularity of
this pamphlet is shown by the fact that it quickly reached its
sixth edition. Gibbon, an intimate friend of the author, wrote
in his *Autobiography* (World's Classics edition, 1907 ; p. 206) :
' The sale of his *Observations on the American States* was diffusive,
their effect beneficial ; the Navigation Act, the palladium of
Britain, was defended, and perhaps saved, by his pen ; and he
proves, by the weight of fact and argument, that the mother-
country may survive and flourish after the loss of America.'

[2] *Opinions on Interesting Subjects of Public Law and Commercial Policy arising from American Independence*, London, 1783.

[3] See Fox's speeches in the debates of 7 March and 9 April,
1783 ; *Parl. Hist.*, xxiii, 615, 724. Fox's highly conservative
attitude on the commercial question is illustrated by his opposition to Pitt's treaty with France. He attacked the ' new principles of commercial reciprocity ' which constituted ' altogether
a new system, in which not only were the established doctrines
of our forefathers departed from, but by which the great and most
essential principles in our commerce, principles which, whether
wise or erroneous, had made us opulent, were to be completely
changed.' *Speeches* (London, 1815), iii, 264.

beens.' Greater privileges, as it was, were conceded to the Americans than to any other ' foreign '
people ; but the Orders-in-Council admitting certain of their raw materials into Britain in American
as well as British ships were inspired by the interests
of British traders.[1] They were indeed the main
factor in that great increase of British trade with
America which seemed to prove that Sheffield had
been right.[2] But a really generous and whole-
hearted move, a move which could only have been
construed as selfish in that Britain confessed thereby
her wish and her need for American friendship, a
move which sought to close the breach by treating
the seceders, at whatever risk to British sea-power,
as if, after all, they were still brothers, might possibly
have stemmed the tide of anti-British sentiment in
the United States, created an atmosphere on both
sides of the Atlantic in which the points of friction
left over from the Peace might have been amicably
adjusted, and prevented the illogical and futile war
of 1812. If, indeed, there was a chance of that
in 1783, then the missing of it must rank very high
among the tragic blunders of history.[3]

[1] *Acts of Privy Council, Colonial* (1766-83), v, 527-30. Macpherson, *op. cit.*, iv, 28. American ships were excluded from
the West Indies and Canada.

[2] S. E. Morison, *Oxford History of the United States* (London,
1927), i, 48-9. ' By 1789 the Lords of Trade could boast that
British exports to the United States had recovered pre-war
dimensions ; and that their excess over imports from America
was even greater than in 1772.'

[3] On the lost opportunity, see S. E. Morison, *op. cit.*, i, 47 ;
Holland Rose, *op. cit.*, vol. i, p. 121, note 2.

Young Pitt had lost his Bill, but he was not to be diverted from his attack on Mercantilism by one defeat. On 11 November, in the same year, in one of the endless and useless debates on the peace treaties, he suddenly demanded something like an economic revolution. ' The nation has a right,' he said, ' to expect that, without delay, a complete commercial system, suited to the novelty of our situation, will be laid before Parliament. I am acquainted with the difficulty of the business and will not attribute the delay hitherto to any neglect on the part of Ministers. . . . But I expect that the business will soon be brought forward, not by piecemeal, but that one grand system of commerce, built upon the circumstances of the times, will be submitted to the House for their consideration.' [1] As vague, no doubt, as it was ambitious, this talk of a grand new system came much more easily from the Opposition than from the Government benches. None the less, though Pitt must have known that the Coalition Ministry entertained no such ideas, he was sincere enough himself ; and if, when he came to power, he had believed that his position was so strong and safe that he could take the risk of forcing new ideas down Tory throats, he might have attempted some large-scale application of Smith's doctrine. But, in fact, the cause of Free Trade fared only a little better in his hands

[1] In the debate on the Address at the opening of the session. *Parl. Hist.*, xxiii, 1143.

than the cause of Parliamentary Reform. He applied the ' piecemeal ' process he had scorned, and applied it only to two specific fields—Ireland and France. In the former he failed, as we have seen, because the business firms concerned joined with Fox against him. In the latter he succeeded because business was on his side and Fox alone. The Anglo-French Commercial Treaty, which was signed in 1786 and came into operation in 1787, was doomed soon to disappear in the general convulsion of Europe : but the fact of its unquestioned benefit to British trade and industry, while it lasted, was evidence at least that a breach could be made in the old system, even in the Navigation Acts themselves, without immediate disaster. Whether the needs of inter-imperial and international trade would have prompted Pitt to renew the assault on Mercantilism if the interval of peace had been longer is a matter of speculation. Englishmen were not to be easily or quickly convinced that they and their fathers were quite mistaken in their main economic ideas and that the whole imposing edifice of British commerce rested on false foundations. As it was, the long French war distorted the normal course of trade and postponed the controversy ; and it was not till after Waterloo that the second generation of Pittites—the party of Canning and Huskisson who spoke of Pitt as ' our great master '—reopened the attack.[1]

[1] Canning's best-known eulogy of Pitt occurs in his speech at Liverpool in 1812 (cited by Brady, *op. cit.*, p. 6). A more

The new advance towards Free Trade, begun by
Wallace and Robinson in 1822 and carried to bolder
lengths by their greater successor, Huskisson, in
the next four years, was two-sided. It aimed partly
at the relaxation of restrictions on international trade
in general and partly at a reconstruction of the
economic system of the Empire. And in both fields
the ideas behind the movement were Pitt's ideas,
confirmed by the lessons of the intervening years.
Thus, while Huskisson's reciprocity treaties with
European States were, like Pitt's treaty with France,
an attempt to create a wider market for British
exports than the old colonial field, the most urgent
and most vexed question for Huskisson as for Pitt
was not trade with Europe but trade with the United
States. The maintenance of the Navigation Acts
had by no means prevented the growth of the American mercantile marine. Something like a third,
moreover, of the British export trade was directed
to the United States and therefore subject to its
interference. And, denied free intercourse, Congress
had quickly shown that restriction was a weapon it
could use no less easily and even more effectively
than Parliament. The American Navigation Act of
1818 was almost literally a leaf out of the British
statute-book. And, though this Act, as it happened,

interesting, because discriminating, tribute may be found in a
speech of 1826 (Canning's *Speeches*, London, 1828, v, 529-30).
For a reference by Huskisson to Pitt's principles of ' commercial
good-will,' see his *Speeches* (London, 1831), iii, 120.

precipitated a stubborn battle of retaliation which lasted till 1830, the initial force behind Huskisson's reforms was a desire to conciliate the United States.[1]

It was, similarly, the existence of this new independent factor in the world's politics and trade, the United States, that did most to break down the barriers which still enclosed colonial commerce. The plight of the West Indies was the same in the 'eighteen-twenties' as in 1783.[2] They could not obtain their timber and the other imports they required from Nova Scotia and New Brunswick as Sheffield had predicted; and they were precluded from selling their rum and molasses in the United States. Again they pleaded that their 'distress and difficulties' might be relieved by the admission of American shipping to their ports.[3] And in Newfoundland and Canada there were similar complaints against the restrictions of a system that had outlived its logic.[4] But more significant was the demand that came from Nova Scotia. In 1819 the Council and Assembly of that province appointed a committee to examine the condition of trade; and, on the basis

[1] Brady (cited note (1), p. 164 above), chap. iv. This book meets a long-felt need and will help to bring Huskisson out of the background where a too exclusively political tradition has hitherto left him. See also S. E. Morison, op. cit., i, 344; B. Holland, The Fall of Protection (London, 1913), 31-2.

[2] Jay's Treaty (1794) permitted small American ships to enter British West Indian ports; but this concession was not renewed after the War of 1812. Brady, op. cit., 81-2.

[3] See the complaint from Granada, ibid., 84-5.

[4] Ibid., 86.

of its report, they drafted a joint address inviting
' all the inhabitants of British America . . . to unite
with us ' in an appeal to the ' confidence and assistance of the Mother Country.' ' It is immediately
necessary that the Colonies, in addition to the
privileges they now enjoy, should be allowed the
same freedom of trade with all the world which
the people of the United States have acquired.'[1]
No common action, apparently, was taken as the
result of this appeal; its importance lies in the
argument implicit in it—a new argument and one
which (as will be explained more fully in our last
lecture) went far to determine the political as well
as the economic development of the Second British
Empire. What was this latent argument ? In plain
terms it was that British North America ought to
enjoy as much liberty as the United States. Were
the colonists who had remained British to be less
free, to stand on a lower footing, than the ex-
colonists, next door to them, who had seceded from
the Empire ? To say ' yes ' to that question, it
might be said, was to justify the Revolution and
provoke its repetition.

It may be doubted whether the legislators of
Nova Scotia, who were strongly impregnated with
the ' loyalist ' tradition and who expressly disavowed
any ' factious or seditious murmurings,' had thought
out their case to this conclusion. Nor is it known

[1] Chester Martin, *Empire and Commonwealth* (Oxford, 1929),
160. Brady, *op. cit.*, 86.

what effect this or similar appeals from oversea had on Huskisson's mind. But unquestionably it was the memory of the American Revolution and the position of the United States alongside what remained of British North America that combined to bring about the opening of the colonies to foreign trade and the transformation of the old system of monopoly into a new system of imperial reciprocity. Let Huskisson confess it himself.

' It is generally believed [he said in the speech which preluded the great reforms of 1826] that the attempt to tax our American colonies without their consent was the sole cause of the separation of those colonies from the mother-country. But, if the whole history of the period between the year 1763 and the year 1775 be attentively examined, it will, I think, be abundantly evident that, however the attempt at taxation may have contributed somewhat to hasten the explosion, the train had been long laid in the severe and exasperating efforts of this country to enforce, with inopportune and increasing vigour, the strictest and most annoying regulations of our Colonial and Navigation Code.' ' The peace with America [he went on] gave the first great blow to the Navigation System of this country. There had now arisen an independent state in the New World. Our colonies had fought for, and had taken, a station in the rank of nations. They had now interests in navigation to attend to and a commerce of their own to protect. It therefore became imperative on this country, unless we were prepared to relinquish all trade with America, to conform to circumstances. It was impossible for us in this new state of things to enforce the system of our Navigation Laws.'[1]

[1] Huskisson's *Speeches*, iii, 8-11.

And when he develops his ideas of a new ' colonial system,' he starts from the same point.

' I would ask any man whether the disseverance of the United States from the British Empire, viewed as a mere question of commerce, has been an injury to this country— whether their emancipation from the commercial thraldom of the colonial system has really been prejudicial to the trade and industry of Great Britain. If the answer must be that it has not been prejudicial, is there no useful ad- monition to be derived from this example ? Contemplate the possibility of another set of Provinces, emancipated from commercial thraldom, but firmly maintaining their political connexion—their commercial marine a part of our com- mercial marine—their seamen a part of our seamen—their population a part of our strength. Consider whether it be not worth while to attempt a course which promises, both to these Provinces and the Mother Country, all the com- mercial benefits of a free trade, together with all the political advantages of our continuing parts of one great Empire and enjoying alike, under the sway and protection of the same Sovereign, all the rights and privileges of British subjects.' [1]

It would be interesting, if time permitted, to show how the political ideas of Huskisson's colonial policy ran side by side with its economic ideas ; how he trusted that the British North American colonies, ' connecting their prosperity with the liberal treat- ment of the Mother Country,' would ' neither look with envy at the growth of other States on the same continent, nor wish for the dissolution of old and the formation of new political connexions ' ; how he hoped that, if one day Canada desired and secured

[1] Huskisson's *Speeches*, ii, 312-13.

independence, it should come about ' by the course of natural events,' ' by the growth of national honour, opulence, and population,' and that the separation it involved would be a kind of separation that ' instead of alienating, would strengthen the foundation of those feelings of mutual good-will which arise from the considerations of family and blood.'[1]

Nor is it possible here to pursue the economic development of the Second Empire through its further stages—to show how Huskisson's system, far better though it was than that which it replaced, was necessarily not final but transitional, because the control of it still rested solely with the Government and Parliament of the mother-country : how even Durham and his school maintained the principle that in the economic interests of the Empire as a whole the regulation of inter-imperial trade must remain in Britain's hands : how even Grey, when the final triumph of Free Trade had swept away the last vestiges of the Mercantile System, assumed that the colonies would accept Free Trade, as they had once accepted monopoly and then preference, at the bidding of Westminster : how this new kind of Mercantilism—a Mercantilism turned inside-out— was blown up and blown away for good when Alexander Galt told the Duke of Newcastle that, if he wanted to prevent the Canadian people from adopting such fiscal arrangements as they desired, he must govern Canada himself : and how, lastly,

[1] Huskisson's *Speeches*, ii, 321-2 ; iii, 368.

the opinions and policies, which developed in Canada and led to the acceptance of complete fiscal auto-nomy throughout British North America and after-wards in all the self-governing colonies, were deeply influenced by the old dominating fact that the American Revolution had produced an independent ex-colonial nation on the other side of the Canadian frontier. Indeed, at the end of the study, we should be tempted to adapt the famous sentence in which Burke linked the old Trade Laws with the old thirteen colonies and to say that the movement of the Empire away from monopoly and ' supremacy ' in trade and towards freedom and equality attended American Independence from its infancy, grew with its growth, and strengthened with its strength.

But that would take us too far afield. This lecture is only concerned to point out that the process which reached its logical conclusion in 1859 began in 1783 ; that the opening of the long battle against Mercantilism—Adam Smith's attack in theory all along the line, Pitt's local attacks in practice—was the immediate sequel and result of the American Revolution. And, however slight the first advance, nothing else that happened in that post-war decade reveals more clearly the advent of a new era in British history. If men could begin to dig up and sift the very ground, the almost sacred ground, on which commercial England stood, then, in truth, the future was challenging the past. Nor was this irreverent examination purely economic, concerned only with rival methods of getting rich. It went deeper than that, and, going deeper, was more dangerous. The economic structure of Mercantilism could stand the new strain for many years; it might be more than half a century before the last girder fell; but its spirit was not so tough nor so enduring. It is of the first importance, therefore, to observe that Pitt's new economic policy, as much as Huskisson's, differed from the old not only in technique but also in purpose. And the difference lay in this—that the purpose now was not economic only. ' To reconciliate our ancient friends ' was a stronger motive than commercial profit in Pitt's Bill of 1783. To establish a ' friendly connexion,' an *entente cordiale*, with ' inveterate enemies,' was at least a secondary motive in his Treaty of 1786.[1] Still more obvious is the wider aim of Pitt's commercial approach to the Irish problem. And, as our examination proceeds into other sections of the British Empire, we shall find that the spirit of Mercantilism is everywhere in retreat; that the battles it fought and won on the American issue in 1783 and on the Irish in 1785 were rear-guard actions; that, in fine, it is being slowly but surely driven from the field by a new imperialism which still seeks, of course, its due commercial profit but now confesses also other obligations and works for other ends.

[1] See R. Coupland, *The War Speeches of William Pitt the Younger* (Oxford, 1915), pp. 8-14.

VI.

THE NEW IMPERIALISM.

PITT, of course, was not the only British statesman who was impelled by the disaster of the American Revolution to reconsider the whole structure of the surviving Empire. ' I think I can trace all the calamities of this country,' said Burke in 1785, ' to the single source of our not having had steadily before our eyes a general, comprehensive, well-connected, and well-proportioned view of the whole of our dominions, and a just sense of their true bearings and relations. . . . If we make ourselves too little for the sphere of our duty, if on the contrary we do not stretch and expand our minds to the compass of their object, be well assured that everything about us will dwindle by degrees, until at length our concerns are shrunk to the dimensions of our minds.'[1] That indictment, that warning, were directed at the Empire as a whole, but they were uttered in the course of one of Burke's finest speeches on India. Nowhere else, as we have seen, was the Old Imperialism so much too little for its

[1] Speech on the Nabob of Arcot's Debts. *Works* (1826 ed.), iv, 201.

duties, nowhere did the narrow mind of Mercantilism need so much stretching and expanding, as
in the field of contact with coloured and backward
peoples—in the Indies, East and West, and, linked
with the latter, West Africa. And nowhere else was
the change from the old ideas and methods to the
new so profound. It is the object of this lecture to
discuss first the nature of that change and then the
extent to v:hich it was influenced by the American
Revolution.

It is interesting to observe at the outset that the
vices of the old imperialism in British India and
in the American colonies, subjected as they were
in both areas to a sort of forcing process by the
aftermath of the Seven Years War, came to a head
at precisely the same period. In 1765 the Stamp
Act so aggravated and advertised the old-standing
fact of the subordination of the American colonies
to the mother-country as to thrust its full meaning
for the first time into colonial minds. In 1765 the
evils of the old imperialism in Bengal—happily more
recent but infinitely more grievous—reached the
worst point they had yet attained. Then, for a
space, in both countries, the tide turned. The repeal of the Stamp Act restored harmony in America.
Clive's return for his second governorship brought
relief to Bengal. But in 1767 the Townshend duties
re-opened the American quarrel, and in 1767 Clive's
final departure from India let loose the flood of

tyranny and corruption for five more terrible years. In both countries there followed a period of unrest and controversy, culminating in a revolution : for so complete was the transformation of British rule in India, both in its purpose and in its method, as to deserve no lesser name. And again the process synchronised. The American Revolution began in 1775 and ended in 1783 or, in a fuller sense, in 1788. The Indian Revolution was accomplished between 1772 and 1784.

To describe the onset of the Indian Revolution, as of the American, we must return to the morrow of the Seven Years War. The Battle of Plassey was an incident in that war, and the peace of 1763 was still young when the terrible results of Plassey on the people of Bengal began to reach the eyes and ears of Englishmen at home. It was through their eyes, as is usual with Englishmen, that they noticed first that something must be wrong. That a reasonable fortune could be acquired in India, if one cared to face the tedium of exile and the appalling risks (as then indeed they were) of sub-tropical diseases, had long been known. Ambitious young men like Clive would never have entered the Company's service without such expectations.[1] But never before had fortunes been ' hatched ' (to use Clive's phrase) so fast and on such a scale. The home-coming of the ' nabobs '—still so relatively young and so very rich

[1] See Sir G. W. Forrest, *Life of Clive* (London, 1918), i, 15, 16, 224, 267, 353, for evidence of Clive's pecuniary objective.

and flaunting their wealth with such vulgar osten-
tation—was a social event which no Englishman
could ignore and few approve. Could honest
wealth, they asked, be won so quickly? As yet,
however, Mercantilist England was not so much
concerned about the means by which the money
had been got—to infer the sufferings of Bengal
demanded an unusual effort of imagination—as
about the use to which it was put. These *nouveaux
riches*, it appeared, were not content to buy old
estates and set up as country-gentlemen : they
were usurping also the political privileges of country-
gentlemen and buying seats in the House of Commons. It was this that presently provoked an open
storm and brought down the thunder of no less a
censor than Chatham. ' The riches of Asia have
been poured upon us,' he declaimed in the House
of Lords, ' and have brought with them not only
Asiatic luxury but, I fear, Asiatic principles of
government. Without connexions, without any
natural interest in the soil, the importers of foreign
gold have forced their way into Parliament by such
a torrent of corruption as no private hereditary
fortune could resist.'[1] But that is all. There is
nothing in the rest of the speech to show that
Chatham had detected the root of the evil. His
anxieties were all for the good government of
England, not for the good government of Bengal.

[1] Speech of 22 Jan., 1770 ; B. Williams, *op. cit.*, ii, 269.

Observe, once more, the limitations of Chatham's mind, the limitations of his age. And contrast, presently, the attitude of the younger Pitt and the atmosphere of 1784.

Parliament, meantime, had been stirred to action, but its outlook was similarly narrow. The average member may not have hated corruption on principle as much as Chatham—he was used to it—but he resented that new torrent flowing through this odious new channel. That the wealth, again, was presumably ill-gotten did not yet so much distress him as that it had found its way into the private pockets of those upstarts and not into the more public coffers of the Company or the State. Such was the mood in which Parliament began to meddle with the affairs of British India ; and in such a mood it did more harm than good. In 1767, the year in which it imposed the Townshend duties on the American colonies (one of which, it will be remembered, was a threepenny duty on Indian tea), it enacted five small Indian Bills, the most important of which required the Company to pay the State £400,000 a year as a sort of rent for the territories it claimed to possess in India. Parliament, in fact, was not troubling itself about tyranny and extortion in Bengal : it was simply appropriating to the State a share of the loot. And, naturally, it was disappointed by the result, since it had overlooked the fact that the looters were not so much the Company as its officials. It was, no doubt, a wholesome shock

to learn in 1772 that the Company was virtually
bankrupt. So far from being able to pay the State
its annual rent, it demanded from the State a loan
of a million pounds as the condition on which alone
it could carry on at all. Meanwhile, the facts in
Bengal which lay behind the unpleasing spectacle
of the ' nabobs ' in England were at last beginning
to reach Englishmen's ears. And once rumours
started, they spread fast. A shadow fell even on
Clive's name. It was said that the hero of Plassey
had acquired a huge fortune from his victory—how
huge was not yet known. Public sentiment, moreover, could not but be stirred by the news of the
terrible drought and famine in Bengal in 1770. No
less than one-third, it was reported, of the entire
population had perished. It was soon no longer
possible for Parliament to ignore what had happened
or was happening in India. In 1772 a Select and
a Secret Committee of the House of Commons were
appointed to find out the truth. And the revela-
tions of the former's first reports were staggering.
They dealt with the sequel to Plassey and they
declared, *inter alia*, that Clive had received more
than a quarter of a million sterling. The critics of
the Company were quick to use this ammunition.
Already, in the previous year, Colonel Burgoyne,
their leader in Parliament, had argued—with more
insight than most of his contemporaries—that ' if
sovereignty and law are not separated from trade,
India and Great Britain will be sunk and over-

whelmed.'[1]   And now, in the spring of 1773, having
carried a set of resolutions declaring in general that
all acquisitions, territorial or other, obtained by
arms or treaty with foreign princes belonged to the
State, the destined victim of Saratoga crossed swords
with the victor of Plassey and moved that Robert
Clive had ' abused the powers with which he was
entrusted.'[2]   The upshot is an old story—Clive's
passionate defence and the vindication of his honour
by the unanimous vote of the House.   Burgoyne,
none the less, was right in principle.   The two greatest Englishmen of the Mercantilist Age (let it be
repeated) could not free themselves from its obses-
sions—and Clive still less than Chatham.   He had
gone to India solely to make his fortune ; and even
in the days of Plassey, on the morrow of the victory,
his letters betray him thinking of his fortune at least
as much as anything else.   When he went out for
his second Governorship, it is true, he protested—
and his conduct proved him sincere—that he sought
no further wealth.   But how significant that protest
is ! ' I am determined to return to England without
having acquired one farthing addition to my fortune.
Surely then I cannot possibly design anything but
public good.'[3]   Bitter irony, betraying Clive's resentment at the criticisms that had already reached
his ears—or can it be sheer simplicity ?   In any case
it is not for us to disparage, without understanding,

[1] *Parl. Hist.*, xvii, 458.   [2] *Ibid.*, 881-2.
[3] Sir G. W. Forrest, *Life of Clive* (London, 1918), ii, 258.

this very great, yet characteristic, creature of his Age. And certainly he paid his account in full. Disordered already by disease and pain, the assault on his honour strained his melancholic temper to the breaking-point. On 2 November, 1774, when Clive killed himself, the Fates of Asia were linking fingers with the Fates of America. The greatest soldier England had possessed since Marlborough died was lost to her, when he was only forty-nine, six months before the outbreak of the American War.[1]

Meantime the financial collapse of the Company and the reports of the Committees had forced Parliament to interfere again—more vigorously this time and yet not vigorously enough. Good Governors might achieve a transient reform, but there could be no lasting assurance of good government until responsibility for it was definitely assumed and the chain of that responsibility clearly defined from top to bottom of the administration, or, in more concrete terms, until the sovereignty of the Crown over British India was indisputably asserted and its government subjected to the supervision and control of the British Government and Parliament. But that, of course, implied a drastic, a revolutionary change. It meant the abandonment of the old Mercantilist view of Britain's connexion with India. It meant the acceptance of the idea that another and more

[1] Lecky makes this point. *History of England in the Eighteenth Century*, iv, 286.

urgent task than that of trade had now, by the course of circumstances, been imposed on the British in India—the task of government. It meant that, for the efficient performance of that task, the time-honoured privileges, even perhaps the legal rights, of an ancient Chartered Company must be curtailed. To be persuaded to open their eyes and look so straight and far as that, to swallow so much new-fangled doctrine, Parliament needed some more potent argument than anything that had happened yet. So, though the step it took in 1773 was a long bold step by the standards of that day, it was only half-way to the goal. The famous Regulating Act did much. It remodelled the governing body of the Company in London : it concentrated, but not sufficiently, the control of British India in the Government of Bengal : it forbade officials to engage in private trade or to accept presents and substantially increased their salaries in lieu thereof. But it did not declare the sovereignty of the Crown or even of the Company. It provided no means by which the British Government or Parliament could continuously or effectively control the Company's administration. And it weakened and confused the responsibility of the Governor-General by attaching him to a Council which could outvote him. The Regulating Act, in fact, was not by any means enough to redeem the situation : and it was despite the Act, not because of it, and through his own unaided force of character, that Warren Hastings, who had already picked up the broken threads of Clive's reforms, was able to do as much as he did to weave into the fabric of the British Raj the new principles of honesty and justice.

Hastings had been barely three years in office when the American Revolution began ; and a month before the battle of Lexington the Bombay Government signed the foolish treaty which led at once to war with the Mahrattas and then to war with the Sultan of Mysore. So again the destinies of East and West were in conjunction. For the next eight years the fate of the British Empire in India as in America depended on the issue of a long drawn-out and fluctuating conflict ; and the result would probably have been the same in India as in America if Lord George Germain had been Governor-General. The British in India were practically isolated. The Government at home was hard put to it to find troops and money for the war in America : there were none to spare for the war in India. After 1778, communication itself was (as we have seen) in constant danger ; once at least it was cut.[1] And France was as quick to renew the old conflict in the East as in the West. French fleets appeared in Indian waters and French troops were landed on Indian soil. Never before, and never after—not even in 1857—was the British position in India so precarious : and nothing less than the capacity and the courage of a Hastings could have

[1] See p. 7 above.

saved it. Difficulties and dissension within the camp could no more bend that stubborn will than disastrous tidings from without. When Hastings heard the news of Saratoga, ' If it be really true,' he said, ' that the British arms and influence have suffered so severe a check in the western world, it is the more incumbent upon those who are charged with the interest of Great Britain in the East to exert themselves for the retrieval of the national loss.' [1] In such high spirit Hastings and the fine soldiers who worked with him threw their weight into the wavering scales of the world-wide war, and in some degree—as far indeed as could be expected under the circumstances—they forced the balance down. The exploits of Goddard and Popham in 1780 were at least something to contrast with the indecisive fighting in America and the black outlook in Europe ; Eyre Coote's victories at Porto Novo and Solingar in 1781 were at least something to set off against York Town ; and, if the Indian peace-treaties of 1782 and 1784 were not much more glorious than the Treaty of Versailles, at least they made no sacrifice of British territory in the eastern world.

Meantime, despite the pre-occupation of the war,

---

[1] P. E. Roberts, *Historical Geography of India* (Oxford, 1916), i, 193. With his usual malignant unfairness, Francis quoted this passage from the Bengal records in a debate in the House of Commons in 1784, to show that the Mahratta war was solely due to Hastings' unjustifiable aggression. *Parl. Hist.*, xxiv, 1106.

the question of Indian government had been kept alive at Westminster. In 1781 Select and Secret Committees were again appointed ; and it was on the former of these that Burke first appeared as the champion of the Indian people. Then, in 1783, the Coalition Government produced its—or rather Burke's and Fox's—India Bill. That Bill, as every-one knows, was the lever which George III used for the overthrow of the Coalition ; but the change of ministry did not mean the shelving of the Indian question. Fox's India Bill was instantly followed by Pitt's. And when, in 1784, Pitt's Bill became law, the Indian Revolution was accomplished.

It was a revolution of the British type. The Act of 1784 did not wipe the slate clean and write some-thing entirely new on it. On the contrary, it retained most of the old script. The Company's adminis-trative machine, though strengthened and improved, was left intact. The Directors still sent their orders to India, still appointed the officials. But it was none the less a revolution because now for the first time the whole system was definitely subjected to the continuous and effective control of the British Government in London. The six new ' Commis-sioners for the Affairs of India ' could review and, at need, amend all orders sent by the Directors ; in urgent cases they could send their own orders direct to India ; and they could recall any of the Com-pany's officials. There was no doubt now where the supreme authority lay. The Board of Control, in fact, as the Commissioners came to be called, was practically the Indian Department of the Government ; the President of the Board, as its chairman was termed after 1793, was practically a Secretary of State for India ; and, long before its formal dissolution in 1858, the Company, in politics at any rate, was little else than a name. In other words, the Parliament of 1784 had taken at last the decisive step. Whigs and Tories alike—for, though the battle over Pitt's Bill was as hot as it had been over Fox's, both parties were agreed on the basic principle—had recognised that the connexion with India had laid other and greater duties on the British people than the pursuit of trade, and that these duties were such as no trading company could properly perform. The main fortress of eighteenth-century conservatism—the rights of property—had been surrendered. The Act of 1767, requiring a rent from the Company for its ' territorial ' possessions, had been bitterly denounced—a group of peers had entered a formal protest against it—because it violated the sanctity of contract. The City of London had petitioned against the relatively timid interference of the Regulating Act because the ' privileges ' of the Company stood on the same ground as its own.[1] But in 1784 there were few who dared openly assert that the Company was

---

[1] *Parl. Hist.*, xvi, 353 ; xvii, 889 : cited by Roberts in *Cambridge History of India* (Cambridge, 1929), v, 184, 188.

capable of governing British India uncontrolled or that reverence for its vested interests should be permitted to bar the road to reform. The failure of the Company, the sufferings of the Indian people, the dishonour cast on the name of Englishman— these topics were the theme of speech after speech in both Houses during the frequent debates on India between 1780 and 1784. There were some, indeed, who went so far as to suggest that it would be better for both countries if the only status of Englishmen in India was that of merchants who came and went as in China. But it was reserved for Burke to lift the true arguments out of the mass of parliamentary verbiage and in a speech as noble as his more famous speeches on America to expound the philosophy on which the new order in British India was to rest. He stated—at times, indeed, he greatly overstated—the case against the Company's administration ; but, in solemn terms, he refused to accept its failure as an argument for leaving India in anarchy. ' There we are ; there we are placed by the Sovereign Disposer ; and we must do the best we can in our situation. The situation of man is the preceptor of his duty.' And what was the nature, what was the sanction, of our duty in India ? ' All political power which is set over men . . . ought to be some way or other exercised ultimately for their benefit,' and such rights and privileges as those involved in the government of India are ' all in the strictest sense a trust ; and it is of the very essence of every trust to be rendered accountable, and even totally to cease, when it substantially varies from the purposes for which alone it could have a lawful existence.'[1] Those are historic words. They announced the end of the old imperialism and the beginning of the new Trade with India was to continue; and since, as we have seen, the structure of Mercantilism was not easily or quickly to be overthrown, the Company was to retain its old monopoly. But the spirit of Mercantilism had been dispelled. The powers of government in British India might remain for many years in the hands of the Company's officials ; but henceforth they were to be the instruments of a policy controlled by the British Government and Parliament, and, as the regulations of the College founded for their instruction at Calcutta in 1800 reminded them, they were to regard themselves no longer as ' the agents of a commercial concern ' but as ' the ministers and officers of a powerful Sovereign,' charged with ' sacred trusts ' for ' the good government ' of British India and ' the prosperity and happiness ' of its people.[2] Set that idea of the duties of an Indian civil servant beside the ideas generally held in Clive's day, and so measure the magnitude of

[1] *Speeches* (1826 ed.), iv, 11, 44.

[2] Minute in Council at Fort William by the Governor-General (Wellesley), 18 Aug., 1800, pp. i-v, xv-xvi, printed in T. Roebuck's *Annals of the College of Fort William* (Calcutta, 1819).

the change in public opinion which was registered
by the Act of 1784.

And then, like a rider to the verdict, came the
trial of Warren Hastings. Outwardly what an unpleasant, an improper stage-performance ! Society
crowding to the show. The reigning beauties flirt-
ing or fainting in their boxes. The indecent tableau
at the outset—Hastings on his knees, Hastings who,
whatever his faults, had endured what none of his
accusers could ever have endured, not for profit,
still less for applause, but only to serve the British
Empire by saving British India. And then the
wearisome, interminable scenes of rancour and
rant—Sheridan over-acting in his own melodrama—
Burke pathetically throwing sense and decency
away in the frenzies of his genuine passion—and,
all the while, Francis lurking in the wings, with an
old scar on his arm, dripping venom. But, however
unpleasant the spectacle, there was something of value
in it to Britain and to India. That the method of
impeachment was utterly unsuitable, that the prosecution was a parody, that the ultimate verdict was
acquittal—all those things are unimportant. The
important thing is that Hastings was tried at all.
Ten years earlier it would have been impossible.
But, when in 1785 Pitt declared that the practice
of extortion, though for public and not private ends,
though from the rich and not from the poor, and
though by no means an infringement of oriental
custom, was not permissible to Englishmen in India,

and by that declaration decided the question as to whether Hastings should be tried or not, he was once again the spokesman of the new post-war age.[1] The last impeachment but one in English history had thus as wide a significance as any of the others. With a noise that echoed round the world, it proclaimed the fact that the transformation of the British Raj was not only a reconstruction of political machinery but that far rarer thing in the records of mankind, a ' change of heart.' [2]

No less a ' change of heart,' and even more striking because more drastic and more widespread, occurred in this same period as regards the second field of the ' subject ' Empire. The moral blight of Mercantilism lay nowhere, as we saw, so thick and black as on the West Indies and their connexion with West Africa. In 1783 Slavery and the Slave Trade seemed rooted for ever in that imperial field. Yet, in less than twenty-five years, one was dead and the other dying. Never has so great a triumph of

---

[1] For Pitt's conduct in the Hasting's case, which has been misrepresented by Macaulay and other historians, see J. H. Rose, *Life of Pitt*, i, chap. x ; P. E. Roberts, *Cambridge History of India*, v, 307 ; and R. Coupland, *Wilberforce*, 64-7.

[2] An account of the practical application of the new principles in India after 1784 lies beyond the scope of these lectures. Students should examine the administrations of Cornwallis (Governor-General, 1786-93) and his immediate successors, and the work of such officials of the early nineteenth century as Munro, Metcalfe, and Elphinstone. A good conspectus of the period can be obtained by reading the selection of documents in Ramsay Muir's *Making of British India* (Manchester, 1917).

humanity been so swiftly won. And the huge impulse needed to achieve it, the great irresistible wave of public opinion, began to move in that remarkable post-war decade.

It was no new thing, of course, in 1783 for the slave-system to be criticised. Individual attacks on it, and especially on the barbarities of the Slave Trade, were almost as old as the thing itself. But no organised body of opinion, no community or society, had joined together to condemn it with the one noble exception of the Quakers ; and Quaker idealism was too impossibly Christian to make much impression on hard-headed Englishmen in the eighteenth century. For more than a generation past, however, new ideas about the backward races of the world had been slowly permeating British minds. Doctrinaire conceptions of human equality and the ' noble savage ' had drifted over Channel from France. The voyages of Captain Cook and others had excited a fresh interest in the aborigines of distant lands. Coloured people had been sympathetically treated in fiction and poetry and even, recalling Othello, on the stage. ' Man Friday ' had become a children's hero. And this new atmosphere had enabled an individual— for it was Granville Sharp's doing and practically his alone—to destroy Slavery in England. As the result of his efforts and with the general assent of public opinion, without which indeed his efforts would probably have been fruitless, the famous Somerset Judgment had freed at a stroke the 14,000 negro slaves that were then in England, and the subsequent Knight Judgment in Scotland had completed the eradication of Slavery from the British Isles.[1]   But there were still hundreds of thousands of slaves in British ownership on British soil overseas ; and still, as far as the dislocation of trade caused by the war permitted, their numbers were being maintained by the theft of men from Africa. And still, it seemed, the crime was to continue. When the Quakers presented to the House of Commons a petition against the Slave Trade in 1783, Lord North, on behalf of the Coalition Government, urbanely complimented them on their humanity but regretted that there was no hope of abolishing the Trade, since most of Europe regarded it as a necessity.[2]   No one in Parliament dissented.   The question seemed permanently shelved.

But Quakers have never despaired.   A committee of six continued to ventilate the question, and in the course of the next few years two or three other gifted individuals were drawn into the work.   Ramsay published his pamphlet on the *Treatment and Conversion of the African Slaves in the Sugar Colonies* in 1784.   Clarkson wrote his famous prize-essay in 1785.   Wilberforce underwent his evangelical ' conversion ' in the same year.   And in 1787 the

[1] See E. C. P. Lascelles' attractive study of *Granville Sharp* (London, 1928), chaps. iii and iv ; and F. J. Klingberg, *The Anti-Slavery Movement in England* (New Haven, U.S.A., and London, 1926), chap. ii.

[2] See p. 84 above.

Committee for the Abolition of the Slave Trade was created. Granville Sharp was its first chairman, and Wilberforce became its parliamentary spokesman. From that moment the issue of Abolition, which had been smoothly bowed out of politics only four years before, began to make its way to the very front of the public stage. In 1789 Wilberforce opened the campaign in Parliament, while Clarkson was scouring the country-side. By 1792 public opinion had been so thoroughly awakened, instructed, and organised that over 500 petitions poured into the House of Commons; and its members, though all the finest eloquence, including the greatest speech Pitt ever made, could not quite persuade them to vote for immediate Abolition, did actually decide that the Slave Trade should be gradually abolished in the course of the next few years. Such a convulsion of public opinion, such a conversion of the House of Commons, would have seemed literally incredible in 1783. The decision of 1792, it is true, was not carried into effect owing to the reaction and diversion caused by the French Revolution and the War: but the conscience of the British people had been so deeply stirred that in 1807—eight years before the War ended and while the material arguments against the sacrifice had lost nothing of their force—the bestial Trade was 'utterly abolished, prohibited, and declared to be unlawful' by Act of Parliament. Nor was the British conscience satiated by this act of atonement. It was bent on compelling the other maritime nations to follow Britain's example. In the re-settlement of Europe in 1814 and 1815, nothing interested British public opinion so much as the attempt to get all Europe to agree to Abolition : it was indeed the only mandate which his people gave to Castlereagh. And in the years that followed, the most persistent activities of British diplomacy and the British navy were directed to the same end. Meantime, the humanitarian crusaders had pressed on from the abolition of the Slave Trade to the abolition of Slavery. In 1834 the slaves in the British colonies, not far short of a million, became free men.[1]

Various changes in the principles on which the first British Empire rested have been described in the course of these lectures, and there are more to come ; but none of them is quite so startling in its magnitude as this. Within a few years, as history goes, the whole moral basis of the relations between Englishmen and Africans was transformed. If we look at history as world-history, if we consider, as we should, the inter-connexion not merely of nations

[1] A detailed contemporary account of the abolition of the British Slave Trade is given in T. Clarkson, *History of the Abolition of the African Slave Trade* (London, 1808) : the fullest modern account is in Coupland's *Wilberforce*. For the suppression of the non-British Slave Trade, see W. P. Mathieson, *Great Britain and the Slave Trade* (London, 1929) ; and for the abolition of British Slavery, the same author's *British Slavery and its Abolition* (London, 1926). See also Klingberg, *op. cit.*

but of continents and races, we must recognise that the destruction of the slave-system was one of the greatest achievements of the modern world. And just as Englishmen should feel ashamed at the English share in that system, so they should feel proud of the English share in its destruction. Nor is that all. Beside the destructive, the negative policy, the leaders of that great crusade insisted from the outset on a positive policy too. It was Britain's duty not only to stop barbarising Africa but to help to civilise her. From that same impulse in that same decade, from the speeches of Wilberforce and Pitt and their comrades, sprang the idea of a positive duty, an active ' trusteeship,' which was to dominate David Livingstone and the great company of his disciples, to lead to the penetration and occupation of vast areas of the ' Dark Continent,' and to inspire all that is best in the administration of British Tropical Africa and in the public opinion in this country on which its destiny depends.[1]

Such, in outline, was the great transformation, the birth of the New Imperialism. What, we can now ask, had the American Revolution to do with it? If we were to accept the *argumentum a silentio* of the text-books, the answer would be ' nothing.'

[1] The development of the ' positive policy ' and the part played by Livingstone are described in Coupland, *Kirk on the Zambesi* (Oxford, 1928). See also *Memoirs of Sir W. F. Buxton* (reprint in Everyman's Library); Mathieson, *Great Britain and the Slave Trade* ; R. J. Campbell, *Livingstone* (London, 1929).

But that silence is misleading—for two reasons. First, our historians have only recently begun to free themselves from the bad habit of studying and writing the history of the British Empire in geographical compartments : the true synthetic narrative, which describes the development of our great inter-oceanic society as one whole and traces the interaction of each part upon its fellows, still awaits its author. And, secondly, as was suggested in our first lecture, the force of the impact of the American Revolution on British politics in general seems to have been somewhat under-estimated. But do not let us rush to the other extreme. He is a frail historian who is so mesmerised by mere synchronism or sequence that he falls blindly into the fallacy of *post hoc, ergo propter hoc*. Because the Indian Revolution reached its climax in 1784 and the organised crusade against the Slave Trade began in 1787, it does not follow that the American Revolution was the cause of either. It would be strange, however, if the juxtaposition of such great events, occurring within the bounds of a single political system, had no significance at all. It would be strange if the only connexion between events in America and events in India was the fact that the tea consumed at the ' Boston tea-party ' was Indian tea. The truth would seem to lie, as usual, between the two extremes. Let us try to find it.

On 11 April, 1775—eight days before the battle of Lexington—a debate took place in the House of

Commons on a proposal to continue in force part
of an Act of 1773 which was now due to expire.[1]
This Act was a companion of the Regulating Act,
and the clause in question had continued the obligation laid upon the East India Company in 1768 to
export every year to India a specified quantity of
British goods. The financial position of the Company (as we have observed) had very seriously
declined in the course of the last seven years ; its
payment of rent to the State for its ' territorial '
possessions had necessarily lapsed ; and it could not
unfairly claim to be relieved also of an obligation
which limited its commercial freedom for the sake
of other business interests. But the representatives
of those interests had never been so keen on the
arrangement as they were in 1775. And the reason
is plain. The quarrel with the American Colonies
had been very damaging to British business. The
non-importation and non-exportation agreements on
the one side and the prohibition of all commercial
dealings with New England on the other had blocked
one of the main channels of the export trade ; and
British exporters would have been no business men
if they had not clung to any advantage, however
small, which they enjoyed in other parts of the world.
Burke, who had not yet become the Company's
most passionate assailant, put the case neatly, if not
quite justly, in attacking the North Government
for supporting the measure. ' What circumstance,'

[1] 13 Geo. III, c. 64.

he asked, 'is the father of the motion? I will tell you, Sir. The late American measures have threatened the manufactures of this country with ruin or at least with stagnation. . . . While Administration annihilates the American markets, she cooks up others in the East Indies.' [1]

The outbreak of the War and its disastrous course drove the obvious economic lesson home. Englishmen had never belittled the importance of the Indian trade; but, when the hopes of a quick settlement with New England were frustrated, when Saratoga came and the French alliance, when it seemed that the Colonies might actually be lost, the value of India to the Empire seemed progressively to rise. Public discussion of the Indian Question acquired a place second only to that of the American Question. 'The affairs of India,' reports the *Annual Register* early in 1781, and the pages of *Hansard* confirm it, ' now began to require and to attract the most serious attention of the House of Commons.' In that year a parliamentary inquiry was held into the operation of the judicial system established by the Regulating Act in Bengal, two Acts were passed dealing with this question and with finance, and the Select and Secret Committees were appointed whose deliberations led to the great measures of 1783 and 1784. There can be no question that this burst of active public interest in India was mainly due to the spread of

[1] *Parl. Hist.*, xviii, 617.

that new humanitarian spirit which was soon to affect the African Question even more strikingly than the Indian. The wordy warfare of those debates consisted chiefly of the advancement or the rebuttal of charges concerning the misgovernment of India and the sufferings of her people. But human motives are seldom unmixed ; and with all that genuine moral idealism was mingled a good measure of political and economic realism. No business man in Britain could fail to observe that the American Revolution was threatening to swing the whole balance of British trade over from West to East ; and Mercantilists of the harder type, who upheld the rights of chartered companies on principle and had little sympathy to spare for Indian peasants, became more and more ready, as the American War proceeded, to acquiesce in interference and reform in India for the simple reason that bad Indian government meant bad Indian trade. And public opinion at large was influenced in the same direction by a livelier recognition of what the Indian connexion meant to the wealth and strength of Britain. Already before York Town, Wraxall was contrasting ' our losses and disgraces in America ' with ' the splendour of our arms ' in India, and even declaring that on India ' the future glory, grandeur, and permanent greatness of England must ultimately depend.' [1]   And if the House of Commons

[1] *Parl. Hist.*, xxi, 1206-7. Writing in 1815, Wraxall could assert that his prophecy had been fulfilled. ' The third source

as a whole was not yet quite prepared to go so far as that, it was becoming accustomed to think of America and India as the twin pillars on which the Empire rested. Thus, for the purposes of party conflict, the Government was represented as undermining both pillars by the same mischievous methods. ' Was Lord North not content,' asked Fox in an Indian debate of 1780, ' with having lost America ? Or was he determined not to quit the situation in which he stood till he had reduced the dominions of the Crown to the confines of Great Britain ? ' [1] ' It was the rapacity of the Minister to gain a great revenue in America,' said Burke in the same Indian debate, ' that had lost us the thirteen colonies. Let that be a warning to the House not to let the revenue mislead them again.' [2] From another angle, one of the defenders of the Company's chartered rights reminded the House ' of the consequence of violating the charter of Massachusetts.' [3]

And then came York Town, finally confirming this eastward drift of thought. One pillar had gone for ever. The great swing-over of the Empire was

of our [recovered] prosperity came from the East where . . . the sun of Britain rose as it set in the West. . . . All our losses on the Delaware and on the Chesapeake have been more than compensated by our conquests on the Ganges or on the coasts of Coromandel and Malabar,' and so on. Wealth derived from India enabled Britain to defeat Napoleon. *Memoirs*, 519-20.

[1] *Parl. Hist.*, xxi, 310.
[2] *Ibid.*, 314. Cf. Burke in 1781, *ibid.*, xxii, 555.
[3] Dempster, *ibid.*, xxii, 311. Cf. Wilkes in 1783, *ibid.*, xxiv, 22.

now a completed fact ; and a century and a half
were to pass before its equilibrium was restored by
the growth of other oversea dominions, before, for
instance, the eastward twist given to British foreign
policy, not always with good results, could be
straightened out. Naturally, therefore, that combination of motives for bettering and strengthening the
British connexion with India now reached its climax.
Whatever Lord Sheffield and Mr. Chalmers might
say, British merchants were convinced that their
market in the independent States of America could
never be as big or safe as it had been in the colonies :
let the Indian market, then, be made bigger and safer.
And those who took wider views than those of profit
and loss were now obliged to accept the definition of
British India—coined by Dundas and reproduced by
Fox—as 'the brightest jewel *that now remained* in
His Majesty's crown.'[1] The same idea, the upset
of the imperial balance, the enhancement given by
the result of the American Revolution to the relative value of India to the Empire, must have been
among Pitt's first thoughts when he ' examined
what was left ' ; and it was first on that unassailable
ground that he commended the great Bill of 1784
to Parliament. The third sentence of the imperfect
report of the speech with which he introduced it
runs as follows : ' India had at all times been of
great consequence to this country from the resources of opulence and strength it afforded ; and

[1] *Parl. Hist.*, xxii, 1285.

that consequence had, of course, increased in proportion to the losses sustained by the dismemberment
of other great possessions; by which losses the
limits of the Empire being more contracted, the
remaining territories became more valuable.'[1] Pitt,
in fact, in proposing to do virtually what Clive had
asked his father to do nearly twenty years before,
was giving as his first reason for doing it the same
reason that Clive gave—a reason which the father
had rejected but the son could not reject because
something had happened in the interval to make it
irresistible. The elder Pitt may well have doubted
in 1765 whether India in the long run would prove
more valuable than the American colonies with a
whole continent at their back. But the younger
Pitt could scarcely doubt in 1784 that India was
more valuable than nothing, or, more strictly, than
the foothold in North America, seemingly so bleak
and unproductive, which Britain had retained at
the mouth and on the banks of the St. Lawrence.
No one, indeed, can question that the transformation
of British policy in India was largely due to the
determination of British statesmen and business
men to make good in the East the resources of
imperial power and wealth which had been lost in
the West.

That motive, however, as we have seen in the
earlier part of this lecture, was not the only motive.
Pitt had another and a better reason than Clive's,

[1] Pitt's *Speeches* (1806 ed.), i, 179.

a higher object than ' opulence and strength,' for desiring to bring the government of India under effective State control. In the next sentence to that just quoted from his introductory speech, he explained that his Bill was intended not only ' to confirm and enlarge the advantages derived by this country from its connexion with India,' but also ' to render that connexion a blessing to the native Indians.' The new system was meant to do what one of its most high-minded administrators in India believed, only twenty years later, it had already done, when he said it had ' founded British Greatness upon Indian Happiness.' [1] What, then, of that higher motive, that ' change of heart,' that initiation of the doctrine of ' trustee-ship ' ? Did the American Revolution react only on the material side of the Indian Question ? Or had it something to do with the moral issue also ?

Before considering the answers to these questions, we must look again at the other field of race-contact, the African field. It was the same awakening of conscience, the same ' humanitarian movement,' that created at about the same time the new sense of obligation towards the victims of misrule in India and the victims of the slave-system. But with regard to the Africans there was no secondary motive. The moral issue stood alone ; and, for that reason,

[1] Lord William Bentinck as Governor of Madras in 1804, Muir, *Making of British India*, 283.

the material results of the American Revolution
could not affect the African Question as they affected
the Indian. Clearly the abolition of the Slave
Trade could not be regarded as a means of economic
reparation for the damage of 1783. The Abolitionists argued, indeed, quite truly, that a great, varied,
and profitable ' legitimate ' trade might be developed
in Central Africa, once the curse which prohibited
its penetration and civilisation had been lifted : but
to business men of the day these vague potentiali-
ties of future gain were of little account beside the
hard fact of immediate loss. And in the West
Indies the end of the Slave Trade and still more of
Slavery was bound to be regarded, whatever the
Abolitionists might say, as the beginning of ruin.
None the less, there was one direct link between
the achievements of Washington and Wilberforce.
When the thirteen colonies secured their independence, one of the chief obstacles to the success
of the Abolitionist cause—an obstacle which must
otherwise have proved, for many long years at least,
almost insurmountable—was instantly and automatically reduced by more than half its size.

That the crusade against the Slave Trade which
began in 1787 did not achieve its end in 1792 was
largely due to the stubborn opposition of the colonial planters. They, after all, were the men who
bought the slaves and owned them. They were the
' men on the spot.' They, not the philanthropists,
were to pay the price of idealism. It was their case,

far more than that of the Traders, that made fair-
minded Englishmen inclined to hesitate and compromise. And when the crusaders, victorious at
last, pressed on to attack Slavery itself, the planters
and their friends and agents in England fought
again to the last ditch. In both battles, not unnaturally, the political issue was repeatedly raised,
the joint between colonies and mother-country continually strained. Not content with denouncing the
unconstitutional interference of the British Parliament in a question which in their eyes was essentially
domestic, the planters of Jamaica threatened, more
than once, to break the imperial tie.[1] Now, if the
American Revolution had not occurred, if the
thirteen colonies had remained British colonies
after 1783, this obstruction in the path of Abolition
would have been far more formidable. The first
community, it is true, to raise its voice against the
Trade had been the Quakers of Pennsylvania ; and
before the period of the Revolution some of the
' middle ' and southern colonies had attempted to
diminish the Trade by restrictive legislation, not
so much, however, on account of its iniquity as
because of the alarming growth in the numbers of
the slaves and the danger of their rising in revolt
against their masters. Naturally the colonies had
resented the veto laid on some of these measures
by the British Government; but Jefferson was not

[1] See Mathieson, *British Slavery and its Abolition*, chaps. ii
and iii ; Coupland, *Wilberforce*, chap. xii.

altogether fair when, in that outspoken passage in
his first draft of the Declaration of Independence,
he denounced King George III for waging the slave-
war against Africa and forcing its victims on the
reluctant and protesting colonies. In any case,
Jefferson's hatred of the Trade was not shared by
all his fellow-countrymen. The southern colonies
were steeped in Slavery and therefore in the Trade
as deeply as any West Indian island ; and ' in
complaisance,' as Jefferson frankly confessed, to
their feelings—and also, in some degree, to those
of ' our northern brethren ' who were engaged in
supplying them with slaves—the dangerous sentences were struck out.[1]   But the schism of opinion
lasted and grew deeper. When, under northern
influence, Congress passed and Jefferson signed the
Bill prohibiting the importation of slaves into the
United States, just three weeks before the Bill
abolishing the Slave Trade became law throughout
the British Empire, the American Act, unlike the
British, was not effectively enforced. Like the
Acts passed later to supplement and strengthen it,
it became a dead letter in the South, where the
illicit Slave Trade lasted virtually as long as Slavery
itself. Suppose, then, these Southern States had
still been British colonies when Wilberforce opened
his campaign. Suppose the planters of Virginia

[1] Details of the restrictive policy in each colony are given by
W. E. B. Du Bois in *The Suppression of the African Slave Trade
to the United States of America*, 1638-1870 (Cambridge, Mass.,
1896), chaps. ii-iv. Jefferson and the Declaration, pp. 48-9.

and the Carolinas and Georgia and their agents and
friends in England had been added to, or rather had
dominated and led, the anti-Abolitionist forces.
What then could the crusaders have achieved?
Wilberforce and other idealists might still have
acted as they did; for they relied on more than
human agencies to gain their end. But what of
the realists? What of Pitt? What of Parliament?
Threats of rebellion would have been less contemptuously brushed aside if uttered not only by Jamaica
and her feeble consorts but by half the American
colonies. . . . But if idealism had none the less prevailed in Britain and if the South had risen, which
kind of civil war would have resulted? Would
Britain and the northern colonies have fought
together for the negroes' cause? Or would this
' interference ' by the mother-country—so far more
drastic than anything that actually happened in the
eighteenth century—have healed the schism between
North and South, united them to sacrifice the black
man's to the white man's liberty, and precipitated
a pan-American Revolution? . . . Or suppose the
abolition of the Slave Trade somehow achieved
without a rupture, what would have happened
when Slavery itself became the issue? . . . But
enough of vain speculation. It has been indulged
in so far in order to emphasise the historical fact
that, if the American Revolution had not happened
when it did, the abolition of the Slave Trade and
Slavery within the British Empire would not have

happened when and as they did. It is, perhaps, a consoling thought for latter-day Englishmen that the unity of the old Empire could only have been preserved at the price of impeding and postponing the destruction of the British Slave Trade and the liberation of nearly a million British slaves.

The American Revolution, then, provided a material reason for reforming British rule in India and it removed a serious obstacle to the destruction of the British slave-system. But was that all ? Let us now attempt to answer those postponed questions as to the influence of the Revolution on the moral issue.

We may start from the two facts—familiar facts by now—on which the thesis of these lectures mainly rests. The first is the fact of synchronism, of which too much must not be made nor yet too little : the fact that the humanitarian movement received a new impetus at the time of the Revolution ; that it grew quickly to a head during the later years of the Revolution ; that it achieved its first great triumphs immediately or soon after the close of the Revolution. Can that be mere coincidence ? Is there no connexion ? And the second fact is that the loss of the thirteen colonies forced Englishmen to think as they had never thought before about the principles on which their maimed and shaken Empire rested. In the discussions and decisions that resulted, is it possible to separate the ideas of political reconstruction and economic reparation from those of moral obligation ? Is it possible to assert that the effects of the American Revolution, which so largely prompted and shaped the one, had no influence at all upon the other ? The new humanitarianism, it is true, was already on the move before the American Revolution, and England was ripe for a ' change of heart ' quite apart from anything that happened on the other side of the Atlantic. The reaction from the moral atmosphere of the first half of the eighteenth century was manifestly due, and the swiftness and the heat with which the fire of the new Evangelicalism was spreading over England before 1775 showed that it had already begun. None the less, it seems only reasonable to suppose that the ' change of heart ' in the relations of Englishmen with Asiatics and Africans, though not of course initiated, was hastened and intensified by the process of examining ' what was left ' of their Empire.

The American Revolution, moreover, had brought something into the atmosphere of British politics that was congenial to the growth of idealism. The effect of the American Revolution on liberal-minded men in every country was akin to that of the French Revolution. The causes and the characters of those two immense events were very different. The revolt of the French people against Louis XVI was impelled by practical grievances, by real suffering, as much as by the doctrines of Rousseau and the

intellectuals. The revolt of the American colonists
against George III, a revolt of prosperous, not on
the whole ill-governed, largely indeed self-governing
people, was almost entirely a matter of theories and
principles—a point to be commended, by the way,
to those who never tire of repeating the hackneyed
contrast between the French and the British mentality in politics. But both Revolutions had this
much in common : they were both battles for
freedom ; and it was not merely the bitter prompt-
ings of party spirit, it was a natural instinct, that
made a lover of liberty like Fox feel about Saratoga
something akin to what he felt about the fall of the
Bastille. Other Englishmen may have been less
enthusiastic, have regretted more deeply the sever-
ance of the colonies from their mother-country,
and yet have confessed in their hearts that, if indeed
there was no other choice, the victory of Washington
and his colleagues was better for the world and better
for Britain than the victory of George III and North.
And when, as we saw in our first lecture, the end
of the unhappy conflict coincided with the end of
the Georgian ' system,' there was a feeling in the
air as if an incubus had been removed, as if a new
era had begun. In such an atmosphere men find
the faith to pursue ideals and sometimes the courage
to attain them.

Remember, too, that for Englishmen the issue of
the American Revolution, accept it though they
might as the lesser of two evils, was a national

defeat—the most disastrous and humiliating defeat in all their records. Is it of no significance that, so soon afterwards, Englishmen set themselves, in their crusade against the Slave Trade and Slavery, to write, as Lecky put it, what ' may probably be regarded as among the three or four perfectly virtuous pages comprised in the history of nations '[1] and what is certainly the most virtuous page in the history of England ? Defeat may be better for a nation than victory. It may not only teach it political wisdom, it may brace it also to political virtue, especially perhaps if in its conscience it questions the justice of the cause for which it fought. Again, then, is there no significance in the attitude of the humanitarian crusaders, of the founders of the new imperialism, to the American War ? Of the older generation, Fox and Burke had regarded George III's American policy as not only foolish but immoral ; and Granville Sharp had resigned his post in the Ordnance Office, though it was, he confessed, his ' only profession and livelihood,' because of his conscientious objection to taking a part, however small, in providing munitions for use against the colonists. ' I cannot return to my ordnance duty,' he said, ' whilst a bloody war is carried on, unjustly as I conceive, against my fellow-subjects ' ; and he had then devoted himself to repeated attempts to persuade the Government to seek for peace by

[1] *History of European Morals* (1911 ed.), 153.

negotiation.[1] Of the younger generation, Pitt and
Wilberforce had served their political apprentice-
ship sitting side by side in the gallery of the House
of Commons and listening to Whig denunciations
of the War : and as soon as they descended to the
floor of the House, they had lost no time in joining
in the chorus. The War, said Pitt with youthful
vigour, was ' a most accursed, wicked, barbarous,
cruel, unnatural, unjust, and diabolical war.'[2] It
had been conducted, echoed Wilberforce, ' in a cruel,
bloody, and impracticable manner.'[3] And both of
them looked back on it in after years, and Wilberforce with deeper feeling after his ' conversion,' as
not only a blunder but a crime.

Those were the spokesmen of young post-war
England. That is what young post-war England
thought. Is it, then, too much to assume that the
moral atmosphere out of which the attitude of this
new England towards the two great race problems
of the Empire grew must have been coloured and
deepened in some degree by an admission of fault
and a feeling of contrition for the part which the
older generation had taken in the American tragedy.
' It takes a great many blows to knock down a great
nation,' wrote the poet Cowper, soon after hearing
the news of York Town ; ' and in the case of poor
England, a great many heavy ones have not been
wanting. They make us reel and stagger indeed ;

[1] Lascelles, *Granville Sharp*, chaps. v-vi.
[2] Rose, *Pitt*, i, 88.   [3] Coupland, *Wilberforce*, 11.

but the blow is not yet struck that is to make us fall upon our knees. That fall would save us.'[1] Perhaps Cowper was wrong. Perhaps York Town had forced England, as nothing else could have done, to examine her conscience and, in the light of what she found there, to resolve not merely to heal the body of her stricken Empire but to save its soul.

[1] R. Southey, *Life and Works of Cowper* (London, 1836), iv, 162.

VII.

THE FOUNDATION OF CANADA.

WE have now 'examined what was left' of the British Empire in 1783 in every field but one, and found that its subsequent development in each of them was influenced, with variations of manner and degree, by the American Revolution. It remains to consider the true colonial field, the field of European settlement overseas. It was in this field that the Revolution occurred, a tragic attestation of the failure of the First British Empire to retain communities of European stock on both sides of the Atlantic within the frame of one political society. But it is this same field that has witnessed the no less conspicuous success of the Second British Empire in which, to-day, British subjects of European stock at least ten times as numerous as those who broke away in 1783 are living beyond the oceans as members of a single commonwealth. That there are some links of historical causation between that great failure and that great success is indisputable. It is the purpose of this lecture and the next to lay them bare and test their strength.

If the American insurgents had had their way, there would have been no colonies of European settlement left to the British Empire in 1783. At the outset of the Revolution, its leaders naturally desired that the whole of British North America should present a solid front to the 'tyranny' of the Home Government, that the so-called 'fourteenth colony' should be ranked beside the other thirteen. The fact that it was regarded as standing apart and that there should be some difficulty in bringing it into the common cause was due to its different character. The 'fourteenth colony' was actually composed of the colonies which dominated the entrance from the Atlantic to the St. Lawrence —Nova Scotia, Cape Breton, and Prince Edward Island—and, separated from that group by a long stretch of more or less unoccupied country on the river banks, the colony or province of Quebec, a huge area stretching from the mouth of the St. Lawrence to the Great Lakes and vaguely beyond them into the unexplored West. Now these colonies were not, for the most part, colonies settled by Britons like the thirteen to the south.[1] They had been settled by Frenchmen and had passed to the British Empire by conquest and annexation. Considerable British settlements had been subsequently made in Nova Scotia, where Halifax

---

[1] New York and New Jersey were Dutch settlements, annexed while still small and undeveloped. North of Quebec lay the territories of the Hudson's Bay Company.

was a naval station and garrison-town ; but in Quebec in 1775 there were only a few hundred recent British immigrants, largely from the thirteen colonies, who had followed on the heels of the conquering British army at the close of the Seven Years War. The rest of the population of all this area, apart from the Indians, was French ; and it might almost be said that New France, as it had been called till 1763, had nothing in common with New England except its location on the same continent. The people of New England were vigorous, progressive, engaged in commerce and industry as well as agriculture, Protestant and rather bigotedly Protestant, and passionately attached to their old inherited rights of self-government. The people of New France were mainly simple and old-fashioned peasants and farmers, ill-educated and very conservative, with little aptitude or care for business, Roman Catholics practically to a man and devoted to their church, and though they had occasionally chafed a little at the bonds of Bourbon absolutism and the relics of feudalism, neither acquainted with self-government nor keenly interested in it. These differences were enough in themselves to make a breach between the neighbours, and the breach had been widened by the border-warfare which had inevitably accompanied the intermittent conflict of Britain and France in North America. But the revolutionaries were none the less determined to cross and close it.

It was a natural, an obvious policy, both with a view to the struggle with Britain and with a view to its sequel. For the purpose of the war, Canada might be made the main enemy base, and, despite the freezing-up of the St. Lawrence in winter, a base of great strategic value, since it would enable the British enemy to do what the French enemy had done—to threaten an attack on the sea-board colonies from the rear which, if pressed home as Burgoyne failed to press it, might cut their whole military and political system in two with disastrous and probably decisive results. No competent soldier could overlook this cardinal point in the strategic geography of North America; and Carleton, who was more than competent and had served on the St. Lawrence with Wolfe, had repeatedly dwelt on it in the dispatches he had sent home during his governorship of Quebec. Rightly assuming the refusal of France to accept the Seven Years War as the last round of her old conflict with Britain and resentfully observing the ' democratic ' temper of the southward colonies, he had pleaded for the strengthening of Quebec against just such an emergency as, except for the order of events, was actually to occur. ' Should France begin a war,' he wrote in 1768, ' in hopes the British colonies will push matters to extremities and she adopts the project of supporting them in their independent notions, Canada will probably then become the principal

scene where the fate of America may be determined.' [1]
Had Carleton, indeed, been in supreme command
and allowed to conduct the war from Montreal
without interference from Lord George Germain,
he might conceivably have won it. Nor was it only
for its strategic importance in the war that the
Americans dreaded the retention of this Canadian
base by Britain. They looked ahead. Suppose the
issue of the war were victory and independence.
Would their victory be more than half won if its
scope were less than continental ? Would their independence be more than half assured as long as
the British Government had any foothold left in
North America ? That foothold, as we know now,
has aided rather than obstructed the maintenance
of peace and harmony between the United States
and the British Empire. But such a happy future
can scarcely have been expected in 1775 or 1783.
To the Americans of that day the retention of Canada
in British hands must have seemed a permanent
menace to the security of a new Republic—a source
of constant friction, a breeding-ground of inevitable
disputes arising from a common frontier, and, if
the worst came to the worst, a sally-port for British
aggression.

By all the means at their disposal, therefore, by

[1] Carleton to Hillsborough, 20, xi, 1768 (Coupland, *The
Quebec Act*, Oxford, 1925, p. 60). This dispatch is more valid
evidence of Carleton's real expectations in 1768 than the *post
eventum* dispatch of 1776, cited by Chester Martin, *Empire and
Commonwealth* (Oxford, 1929), 114.

propaganda, by force, by diplomacy, the Americans tried to annex Canada. In the little group of British immigrants there was a party which favoured and kept in touch with the revolutionary cause to the southward ; and among the local Correspondence Committees which did so much to organise the Revolution were Committees at Quebec and Montreal. In October, 1774, a few weeks after the similar address to the people of Great Britain, the Congress at Philadelphia issued a formal appeal to ' the inhabitants of the Province of Quebec ' for co-operation in obtaining the redress of their ' afflicting grievances ' in which the shade of Montesquieu was invoked to point out the path to ' the natural sagacity of Frenchmen.'

Seize the opportunity presented to you by Providence itself. You have been conquered into liberty if you act as you ought. This work is not of man. You are a small people compared to those who with open arms invite you into fellowship. A moment's reflection should convince you which will be most for your interest and happiness, to have all the rest of North America your unalterable friends or your inveterate enemies. The injuries of Boston have roused and associated every colony from Nova Scotia to Georgia. Your province is the only link which is wanting to complete the bright and strong chain of union. Nature has joined your country to theirs. Do you join your political interests.

This document was sent to the Montreal Committee ; copies of it, translated into French, were distributed throughout the province ; and agents were busily employed in trying to undermine the

allegiance—so recently accepted and still uncertain
—of the French-Canadians to the British Crown.
At the end of six months the Montreal Committee
took a sanguine view of the results of this propaganda.
In April, 1775, a few days before Lexington, they
reported to the Committee of Safety of Massachusetts that the bulk of the population of Canada,
French as well as British, wished well to their
cause.[1]

With the outbreak of the war, the situation changed.
However effective persuasion might be, force was
now needed to back it. To leave Carleton and his
little garrison of British regulars in command of the
St. Lawrence might (as has been seen) be strategi-
cally fatal ; nor, while he was there, could the
French-Canadians be expected to join actively in
the Revolution. Already, before Lexington was a
month past, the adventurous 'Green Mountain Boys,'
founders of Vermont, had invaded Canada north
of Lake Champlain on their own account and inflicted
some damage before they were forced to withdraw.
After Bunker Hill the capture of Canada became at
once a vital part of the official plan of campaign.
For Washington agreed with Carleton on the
strategic essentials of North America. 'Upon your
conduct and courage,' he told Benedict Arnold who
led one of the two columns which invaded Canada
in September, 1775, 'and that of the officers and
soldiers detached on this expedition . . . the safety

[1] Coupland, *Quebec Act*, 144-51.

and welfare of the whole continent may depend.'
And during the American siege of Quebec a few
months later, ' To whomsoever it belongs,' he wrote,
' in their favour probably will the balance turn. If
it is in ours, success, I think, will most certainly
crown our virtuous struggles. If it is in theirs,
the contest at least will be doubtful, hazardous,
and bloody.'[1]

The invasion failed—partly through Carleton's
spirited defence, partly through the effects of the
Canadian winter on the health and morale of the
American troops and the failure to reinforce them
in time, but mainly through the stubborn neutrality
of the great majority of the French-Canadians.
Their social leaders, the *seigneurs* and the priests,
were actively pro-British ; but the mass of the
habitants or peasantry took neither side.[2] Even
when France joined in the war and when the French
admiral appealed ' in the King's name to all the old
French of North America,' though for a time the
situation was tense enough, they did not rise. They
might have risen if a French fleet had sailed up the
St. Lawrence and if Lafayette had led a French army
on to Canadian soil ; but Washington, for obvious

[1] Coupland, *Quebec Act*, 173-5.
[2] Of the minority which did take an active part in the campaign,
it seems that more joined the Americans than the British, especially in the early stages when Carleton, for lack of troops
and because Arnold's column threatened Quebec, was forced to
abandon Montreal. This question has long needed the fuller
research which (the present author is informed) is now being
conducted in Canada.

reasons, opposed and defeated the proposal for an invasion of Canada by land under French auspices ; and, when the chance came for a naval attack, de Grasse preferred the fatal waters of the West Indies to those of the St. Lawrence.   So, when hostilities ceased, Canada was still British.[1]

Still British, also, were its maritime neighbours. On the eve of the Revolution the political atmosphere in 'New Scotland' was different, though not, of course, so different as in New France, from that of New England.   Long neglected and very sparsely settled, Nova Scotia had recently come to the front of imperial politics.   Its position on the Gulf of the St. Lawrence and its fine harbours gave it a strategic value at least as great as that of Canada. If Canada commanded the entry to the interior of the Continent, Nova Scotia commanded the entry to Canada.   It was ' the Key,' said Governor Shirley of Massachusetts, ' to British interests and dominion in America ' ; and it was to secure that key against the French that the first organised British settlement of Nova Scotia was made in 1749.   From that year the colony had begun a new life.   It was virtually a new colony, the youngest of Britain's offspring, and in some degree her Benjamin.   Some of the new settlers came from New England and

[1] D'Estaing's manifesto of 28 Oct., 1778, is given in Kingsford, *History of Canada* (Toronto and London, 1893), vi, 342.   In the treaty of alliance the French King had renounced any purpose of recovering the lost French colonies ; but difficulties might have arisen if French troops had re-occupied Quebec.

some were Germans, but most of them were fresh
from the mother-country and unaffected by those
long and varied processes of estrangement which distance and divergent conditions and ways of life had
inevitably brought to bear on the older colonies to
the south. The politics of Nova Scotia similarly
were too new, too young, to be poisoned and distorted
by a long tradition of friction with imperial authority.
The new colonists had claimed and soon obtained
the rights of representative government inherent
in a ' settled ' colony. The obstacle of a Roman
Catholic French population, the Acadians, out-
numbering the other Europeans—the insurmountable obstacle to the grant of representative government before the Revolution in Quebec—had been
removed by the tragic expulsion of three-quarters
of them. The opposition of Governor Lawrence,
who like most eighteenth-century Governors regarded popular legislative chambers as needless and
tiresome checks on the executive power and
dangerous nurseries of ' heats, animosities and disunion,' had been overruled. The only Assembly
in North America which was to survive the Revolution and remain British had met in 1758, nearly a
century and a half after the meeting of its prototype
in Virginia. And it had succeeded in asserting its
due privileges with scarcely any heat, animosity or
disunion at all. Nor was this due only to its youth,
nor only to the moderation and good temper which
seems from the outset to have distinguished Nova

Scotian politicians. It was mainly due to a closer identity between the interests of mother-country and colony than existed south of the Bay of Fundy. The British Government favoured and fostered Halifax as a trans-Atlantic Gibraltar. It spent money freely in the colony for military and naval needs. It ungrudgingly made good the deficits in the colonial budget from British revenue. And the colonists on their part, owing their increased prosperity mainly to the commercial side of this military connexion, looked forward to the day when their ' infant colony ' should become ' the headquarters of the British land and sea forces in America ' and accustomed themselves without complaint to the measure of imperial control which such a destiny implied. So it was that in 1770 Governor Campbell could report no sign in the Nova Scotia Assembly of ' any of that licentious principle with which the neighbouring colonies are so highly infected.' And so it was that, despite their many links with contiguous New England, the Nova Scotians as a whole felt no sympathy with her side of the quarrel. They did not question the supremacy of Parliament. They did not dislike the idea of taxation for the purpose of imperial defence in North America, centred perhaps at Halifax. They only proposed that they should levy the requisite taxes themselves. The imperial cause, in fact, even as handled by George III and North, was safe in Nova Scotia, provided the impossible were not asked of her ; and the only serious crisis during the war was provoked by the attempt of that headstrong patriot, Governor Legge, to conscribe the men and money of the colony for active operations against their relatives and friends in Massachusetts. Thus, in 1783, Nova Scotia and with it the island colonies in the Gulf remained, like Canada, detached from the revolutionary ' chain of union.' [1]

At the close of the war, therefore, it must have seemed as if No. XI in the Articles of Confederation adopted by the American States in 1781—the article which provided for the admission of Canada into the Union—was likely to remain a dead letter. There was still, however, one chance left. Where propaganda and invasion had failed, diplomacy might still succeed ; and at an early stage of the peace-negotiations Benjamin Franklin began to press gently for the cession of the surviving British colonies in North America to the United States. Their surrender, he suggested to Oswald, the British emissary in Paris, would be regarded by the Americans as a reparation for the injustice of the war and would thereby promote that true reconciliation which both parties desired. It is one more illustration of the narrow vision of Mercantilism in

[1] The materials of this paragraph are mainly derived from Chester Martin, whose essay in *Empire and Commonwealth* (56-89), provides a long-needed study of Nova Scotian politics before and during the Revolution. For the period before 1758, see also J. B. Brebner's scholarly work, *New England's Outpost* (New York, 1927).

England that this proposal should have found English supporters. Just as in the negotiations for the Treaty of Paris a strong body of opinion had urged the retention of the sugar-island of Guadeloupe instead of the whole of French Canada, so now there were some Englishmen who agreed with Franklin's subtle suggestion that Britain's ' chief advantage from the possession of Canada consists in the trade for peltry.' Oswald himself was in favour of the cession. He even urged it on Rockingham, Shelburne, and Fox; and he got the impression that the two former, though they did not commit themselves, were ' not very averse to it.' ' Fox, however, seemed startled at the proposition.' But Shelburne, though he was certainly as anxious as any one for a true reconciliation, had already rejected the idea. The memorandum he had given Oswald contained the following reply to the American claim for Canada. ' 1st. *By way of reparation.*—Answer. No reparation can be heard of. 2nd. *To prevent future wars.*—Answer. It is to be hoped that some more friendly method will be found.' Happily for the future of the British Empire—and not, it is now agreed, unhappily for the future of the United States—this first attitude was maintained until the end. As the long diplomatic wrangle went on, it became more and more evident that the old and more congenial division of 1756 to 1763 was re-establishing itself across the new and unnatural division of 1778 to 1783 ; that

the interests and ideals of Britain and her some-
time colonies were more akin to each other than to
those of France and Spain. On the issue of the
freedom of the Mississippi—the vital issue for the
future expansion of the United States—it was
almost as if the Americans had changed allies;
and the terms of the final settlement as a whole
are a proof that the British and Americans were
making a sincere attempt at lasting peace and
understanding. In such an atmosphere maximum
claims were dropped. Britain conceded a new
frontier which transferred to the Americans a vast
area of the Old Quebec province in the basin of
the Ohio, but north of the Great Lakes she held
her ground. The cession of all Canada and Nova
Scotia faded out of the discussion.[1]

So from the Peace as well as from the War a
fragment of British North America emerged. But,
because it was now a fragment, this little group of
colonies was different from what it had been before
the Revolution. Their political outlook had necessarily been affected by the change in their political
situation. Instead of being the northern fringe of
a compact block of British territory stretching to the
Gulf of Mexico, they were now isolated British outposts on the borders of a foreign state. The population of this state was about twenty times as
numerous as theirs: they had just been fighting it,

[1] Fitzmaurice, *Life of Shelburne*, ii, chaps. iv and vi.

and might soon have to fight it again : and the long frontier between them was not easily defensible. This instant and obvious result of the American Revolution will require our attention in the next lecture. It became at once, it remained, it still is, one of the paramount factors in the life of Canada. But it is enough to say now that this sense of isolation, of possible danger, of relative helplessness, was bound to affect the attitude of these colonies to Britain and the Empire. In 1783 their political allegiance, for the time being at least, had been decided—partly by deliberate choice and action on their part, partly by a passive acceptance of destiny —and, that being so, they were obliged to give more thought to this allegiance, to be more interested in the strength and continuance of the imperial connexion, to be more ' loyal ' (to use the old-fashioned word) than they would otherwise have been. This attitude, moreover, had been strengthened by the experiences of war-time. If the personality and policy of Governor Legge had seemed for a moment to justify the New England view of imperial ' tyranny,' his unceremonious recall had confirmed the colonists of Nova Scotia in their belief that the constitutional liberty they possessed was all they needed and was not in danger from King or Parliament. ' The issues of the Revolution,' says the latest historian of Nova Scotia, ' left the province . . . in many respects more stolidly British than they found it.' [1]

---

[1] Chester Martin, *op. cit.*, 87.

And the same may be said of the small British minority in Canada. Carleton had refrained from attempting to repress the disaffected element within it. The Quebec and Montreal Committees had been left to their own devices; some of the extremists joined the Americans at the outset of the invasion; and most, if not all, of them accompanied the invaders on their withdrawal. Thus the British in Canada after the war were a more ' loyal ' community than before it, purged of the more vigorous and vocal malcontents, and stirred by memories of a victorious campaign.[1]

But the effect on the attitude of the great majority of the Canadian population—on the 80,000 or so of French-Canadians—was yet deeper. Though they had, in the mass, been neutral in the war, the breach between them and their southward neighbours, which the Americans had tried in vain to close, had been definitely widened. The *habitants* had not been very favourably impressed when they observed the old enemies of their race—the ' Bastonnais ' as they used to call them—at close quarters. The invading armies, it is true, were welcomed at some of the villages they passed in the course of their advance. But they were then, to all appearance, the victors of the morrow. Carleton and the remnants of his tiny force were falling back on Quebec. And when, in the following spring, the siege of

---

[1] Coupland, *op. cit.*, 151, 178, 182. The loyalist immigration will be dealt with later.

Quebec was relieved by reinforcements from England, when the invaders were now seen in disorderly retreat towards the frontier, the *habitants*, simple, but shrewd folk, welcomed their departure as much as they had welcomed their arrival.   In their better days, too, the conduct of some of the Americans had not been calculated to disarm old suspicions and antagonisms.   Happy the nation that can stand the test of an invasion in the judgment of the invaded ! And Washington, at any rate, well aware of the danger, had carefully impressed on the officers in command the need of treating the Canadians with the utmost respect, especially in the matter of their religion, and of punishing any breach of these instructions, if necessary with the death penalty. But, though the record of this invasion compares very favourably with that of many others in history —with that, for example, of the invasions of certain American colonies by British and Hessian troops in the course of this same war—it proved impossible to prevent a number of insults and minor outrages, including the kind which Puritans were likely to commit among Papists.   'Their clergy,' reported one of the officers, ' have been neglected and sometimes ill-used.'   And the *habitants'* resentment was deepened when they found their food and fuel taken by force at less than the current price, and, still worse, when such payment as they did receive was often in paper notes of little value.   Again there was a contrast.   For there were many *habitants* who remembered how well those other invaders had behaved, under the strict discipline of which Amherst had been rightly proud, in the course of the British conquest only fifteen years before.[1]

Circumstances could palliate and time efface these impressions; and it is sometimes suggested that the Revolution had a far more important and lasting effect on French-Canada than any such by-product of the actual fighting. Was not the notorious Quebec Act, it is asked, an outcome of the Revolution in the sense that it was an organic part of the British Government's attempt to repress recalcitrant New England? And did not the Quebec Act solidify and perpetuate French-Canadian nationalism and so doom the future Canada, for good or ill, to a bi-national destiny? To answer these controversial questions requires a brief digression.[2]

The French-Canadians in 1775 were a conquered and a recently conquered people. No student of history or human nature need be told, therefore, that they were intensely conscious of their nationality and deeply concerned to maintain its primary elements—the Roman Catholic faith, the French language, and a peculiar system of civil law—in the inevitable conflict with the nationality of their

[1] Coupland, *op. cit.*, 165-6.
[2] For a more detailed account, with authorities, of the events summarised in the next few paragraphs, see Coupland, *op. cit.* A further note on the Quebec Act will be found in the Appendix, p. 317 below.

Protestant, English-speaking conquerors. For the
first few years after the Peace the prospect had seemed
dark enough. Regarding its new possession from
the same angle as Nova Scotia, the British Government had decided to apply the same policy and to
transform Quebec into a British colony. It realised
that the great majority of the population would be
French-Canadian ' for a very long period of time ' ;
but it hoped that the balance might be steadily
reduced and eventually reversed by British immigration from the home-country and the neighbouring
colonies. Obviously British settlers would not be
attracted to a colony still governed more or less on
the principles of the old French *régime*. Canada,
therefore, though it could not yet be made British
in fact, was to be made British in form without
delay. Instructions were given for the introduction
of English law, and a representative assembly, as
recently established in Nova Scotia, was promised
as soon as conditions permitted. The effect of this
declaration of policy was not quite what was intended. It did not set flowing a stream of new
British settlers into Canada, but it did, not unnaturally, confirm the racial pretensions of those
few who were already there. Quebec was to be a
British colony ? Well, then, all Roman Catholics
should be excluded from civic rights as in Britain,
and the promised Assembly—an Assembly, of course,
of Protestants—should be convoked at once. There
could be no clearer example of that inordinate

nationalism which has become so unhappily familiar to the modern world. New England and New France, it may be said, were at open issue. Was the one, backed by British statesmen, bent on trying to repress, ' anglicize,' absorb the other ? Was the tragedy of Ireland to be repeated without its historical excuse ?

Fortunately the two soldiers who governed Quebec between the Conquest and the Revolution, though they betrayed the weak as well as the strong points of their class and time, were men of vigorous common sense. To Murray it was preposterous that three hundred British newcomers should dominate a colony of seventy thousand French-Canadians, and he said as much, with more vehemence than good manners. Under his auspices the more important provisions of the French-Canadian civil law were temporarily kept in force, and a judgment was obtained from the Law Officers that Roman Catholics in Canada were not subject to the same civic disabilities as in Britain. A striking proof, moreover, was given of the Government's determination, whatever its ultimate political aims might be, to honour and more than honour the pledge given in the Treaty of Paris that the ' free exercise ' of the Roman Catholic religion would be guaranteed. Despite the tacit recognition it involved of the Pope's authority, a bishop was allowed to be surreptitiously consecrated in France and duly installed at Quebec. Carleton saw deeper than Murray and went further.

He was convinced that the hardy and prolific French-
Canadians would never be outnumbered on the soil
in which they had rooted themselves for more than
a century. ' Barring a catastrophe shocking to think
of,' he said, ' this country, must till the end of time,
be peopled by the Canadian race.' He realised,
secondly, as we have already observed, that a renewal
of war with France was probable and a colonial
rebellion possible in the near future, and therefore
that the primary purpose of statesmanship in Canada
should be to reconcile the French-Canadians to
British rule as fully and as quickly as might be.
Clearly this meant a complete reversal of the ' Nova
Scotia ' system ; but, none the less, Carleton pressed
it to its logical extreme ; and, since his opinions
were received in London with more than the usual
respect accorded to ' the man on the spot,' his
programme, intact in almost every item, was finally,
after some years of discussion and delay, embodied
in an Act of Parliament.

The essence of the Quebec Act of 1774 was
that it frankly recognised and legally confirmed the
French character of the province. It wiped out
the instruments embodying the ' Nova Scotia '
policy. It restored the whole body of French-
Canadian civil law. It virtually recognised the
Roman Catholic Church as ' established ' by giving
it the legal sanction for the collection of tithes
which it had enjoyed under French rule.[1] It main-

[1] Burke, of course, supported this part of the Quebec Act.
Writing in 1792, in favour of Catholic emancipation in Ireland,

tained the ' arbitrary ' government of a Governor and
nominated Council, since, as was explained in the
debates, the only justifiable kind of Assembly would
be dominantly Roman Catholic, and few Englishmen were yet prepared—it was six years before
the Gordon Riots—to go so far as that.[1] Finally,
in order to regulate relations with the Indian tribes
and promote the fur-trade, it brought the *hinterland*
south and west of the Great Lakes within the frontiers
of the province.[2] A maximum measure, in fact, of
toleration and conciliation. But the circumstances
of its enactment made it only too easy for its critics
to construe it as something else. It was framed
under the shadow of the impending Revolution. It
was actually passed side by side with the penal Acts
against Massachusetts. The crisis Carleton had
foreseen was at hand. To him and to ministers
and bureaucrats who thought as he did, it mattered

he makes an interesting comment on the predictions of ' an
eminent divine ' in 1774, that the concessions to Catholicism
in Canada would ' lose our dominions in America . . . that
the Canadians would fall in with France, would declare independence, and draw or force our colonies into the same design.
The independence happened according to his prediction, but
in directly the reverse order. All our English Protestant colonies
revolted. They joined themselves to France : and it so happened
that Popish Canada was the only place which preserved its
fidelity—the only place in which France got no footing—the
only peopled colony which now remains to Great Britain.' *Irish
Letters*, 275.

[1] See Appendix, p. 319 below.
[2] On this aspect of the Act, see Alvord's authoritative *Mississippi Valley in British Politics* (Cleveland, 1917).

little whether a colonial rebellion or a war with France came first; and, as the passions of that tragic summer reached their climax, they made no secret of their hopes that, as the first-fruits of the policy of conciliation, the French-Canadians would be willing to fight for George III. Inevitably, therefore, the Americans and some of their sympathisers in England conceived the Quebec Act, coming in such bad company and in such a sultry atmosphere, as nothing more than another ' Penal Act ' and the most provocative of them all, and the whole policy it summarised as inspired from first to last solely by the idea of renewing the old French menace in the north, of bribing the French-Canadians to intimidate and, at need, to dragoon the British colonies. The wholesale concession of the French-Canadian claims, the wooing of the Roman Catholic Church, the appropriation of the *hinterland*, the denial to British settlers of British rights, the maintenance of a strong unchecked Executive—everything fell into its place. It was Strafford and his Irish army over again.

If this were true, it might indeed be said that the Quebec Act was a child of the Revolution. But it is not true. Despite the circumstances of its enactment, despite the military use to which its sponsors hoped in the end to turn it, its original purpose was merely security and not aggression. Its policy was the policy of Murray from 1763 to 1766 and the policy of his successor Carleton from 1766 onwards; and Murray and Carleton were appointed and their policy of conciliation eventually accepted by the Whig Governments that held office from 1763 to 1769.[1] If its spirit changed in those last clouded days, its content remained essentially the same. And, supposing there had been no question at all of trouble with the colonies to the south, what else should it or could it have been ? No, the American Revolution did not give birth to the Quebec Act ; but, from the moment it was born, the Revolution did immediately and intensely affect its character and history. It sharpened its outline and heightened its colour and hardened its tone. It thrust it to the front of politics. It gave it its place in North American tradition. It intensified the conflicting sentiments which still attach to it. For the Americans, on the one side, viewing it as they did, were bound to make the worst of it, to denounce it as ' the ministerial plan for enslaving us,' as a deliberate reinforcement and extension of French absolutism and Popery on the free soil of America. And, on the other side, Carleton and Haldimand, the practical Swiss soldier who succeeded him as Governor of Quebec, were bound to make the best of it.

---

[1] For the policy of the Board of Trade from 1763 to 1769, see Chester Martin, *op. cit.*, 119-22. It differed from Carleton's in so far as it maintained the purposes of the Proclamation of 1763 and specifically in recommending an Assembly : see Appendix, p. 319 below. For the acceptance of Murray's and Carleton's principles by the Government as a whole, see Coupland, *op. cit.*, 49-57, and Hillsborough's dispatch of 6 March, 1768 (*Canadian Constitutional Documents*, 1759-91, 297).

Against the arguments and threats of the Revolution, still more against the appeal of France, it was the only card they had to play. Its effect on the uneducated peasantry, already restive under the relics of French feudalism, was disappointing, as Carleton angrily confessed ; but, because the Act conceded all they asked, because it proved the sincerity of the policy of conciliation, because it attested the British Government's willingness to accept and protect the survival of an alien nationality under the British Crown, it determined the allegiance of the *seigneurs* and the Church, and their attitude and influence, and predominantly that of the Church, determined the destiny of Canada.[1] Naturally, therefore, Carleton set his face against any tampering with the whole-hearted ' French-Canadianism ' of the Act, against any compromise with the claims of the British minority, even against opening the door which Parliament had inserted in the Act itself for letting in some concession to British commercial interests. And Haldimand followed suit. ' The Quebec Act,' he said, ' is a sacred charter, granted by the King in Parliament to the Canadians as a security for their religion, laws, and property.' And, indeed, that was exactly how the French-Canadian leaders regarded it. Attack consolidates defence. Not a stone may be shifted from the walls

[1] Not only in 1775, but more decisively in 1779-82, and again in 1812 and in 1837 : see W. P. M. Kennedy, *Constitution of Canada* (Oxford, 1922), 69.

while the fort is in danger. The future of French-Canadian nationality depended, it seemed, on the Act, the whole Act, and nothing but the Act. On its social and religious side, if not on the political, it was the Ark of the Covenant. Enshrined in the deep-rooted patriotism of old Quebec, it won for itself a jealous devotion rarely accorded to the law-making efforts of imperfect men.

With the tradition that the American Revolution created the Quebec Act goes the tradition that the Quebec Act created the national dualism of modern Canada. The second is as unhistorical as the first. The national dualism of Canada was created, of course, by the British conquest and annexation of an old-established French colony. No one who has studied the chequered history of nationality and nationalism in other quarters of the world can suppose that by anything done or left undone in the last quarter of the eighteenth century, French-Canadian nationality, planted so firmly in its home by the St. Lawrence, stiffened in its peculiar mould by its isolation from the life of other peoples, strengthened and sustained by its fidelity to so powerful a Church, could somehow have been eliminated or absorbed. The Treaty of Paris, not the Quebec Act, was the document which made it inevitable that the Canadian nation of the future should be composed of two primary nationalities, drawing its blood from two historic races and its culture from the two greatest living languages and literatures of the Old World. But there is this much truth in the tradition. The Quebec Act set the seal of Parliament on the policy which Murray and Carleton had pursued. It was a public, a statutory recognition of race-dualism in Canada. It solemnly attested the deliberate incorporation of an alien nationality within the British Empire. It gave the French-Canadians a guarantee of national rights such as the Act of Union of 1707 gave the Scots and such as the Act of Union of 1800 unhappily did not give the Irish. And this also is true. The American Revolution, breaking out concurrently with the enforcement of the Act and darkening the Canadian scene with the twofold danger of American invasion and French propaganda, compelled the local authorities to administer the Act in even stricter accordance with its primary purpose than its ministerial authors had intended. Compromise is at a discount in war-time. And so, perhaps, if the French-Canadians of a later day were tempted or provoked to give their ' charter ' too hard and one-sided an interpretation, to regard Britons in their St. Lawrence valley as *étrangers et intrus*, to forget that minorities have their rights, they may have been influenced by the precedent set between 1775 and 1783.

The survival of French-Canadian nationality, then, was accepted and safeguarded in the stormy years of the Revolution. But the Revolution did not make

French Canada. It would be truer to say that it made British Canada—for reasons that we will now examine.

The area of British territory in North America which emerged from the wreck of 1783 was larger than that of all the lost colonies together; but its pre-war population was relatively very small—some eighty to one hundred thousand French and five to ten thousand British, concentrated in Nova Scotia and in the St. Lawrence valley from below Quebec to above Montreal. Between them lay the coast-lands of the Gulf, occupied by a handful of settlers from New England. Beyond them to the west lay the forests and waters of the Great Lake country, traversed only by the Indians and a few French-Canadian *coureurs de bois*, and beyond that again stretched the leagues of virgin prairie towards the Rockies and the Pacific. Clearly those surviving British outposts in the East were not big enough, nor was the character of its dominant population, the French peasantry, adventurous or ambitious enough, to explore, to penetrate, to occupy, to develop that vast *hinterland*. New settlers were needed, and settlers of a progressive, pioneer type. Without them, indeed, the Canada of 1783 could not conceivably have grown to the Canada of 1929. If British immigrants had not been available at this early stage to occupy the Lake country and to estab-lish a base for the later occupation of the prairies, it can hardly be doubted that the ' Middle-West ' of Canada would have been absorbed in the waves of migration from the American Republic which, as it was, produced, before the middle of the nineteenth century, the dangerous disputes over the Oregon Boundary now best remembered, happily, through such slogans as ' The Roaring Forties ' or ' Fifty-four Forty or Fight.' There was need, then, for new British colonists on the morrow of the American Revolution if the British Canada of the future were ever to be made. How was that need met ?

Before that question is answered, let us go farther afield. Three other great trans-oceanic Dominions besides Canada are now partners in the British Commonwealth of Nations—Australia, New Zealand, South Africa. How came it that the second British Empire was able to retrieve in those far quarters the losses of the First ? Was there any connexion between the loss and the retrieval ? As to South Africa, very little. For in 1783 Cape Colony, then limited to Cape Town and its neighbourhood, was still a Dutch possession, beyond the scope of British enterprise. But it is perhaps worth suggesting that the idea which led to the first British annexation of the Cape in 1795 and its permanent retention after 1815— namely, the need for a port of call and naval station to safeguard the route to India—had been strengthened in British statesmen's minds by the lessons of the conflict with the French in India which arose

from the American War.[1]   With regard to Australia
the connexion was far more substantial.   The long
struggle between France and Britain was literally
world-wide.   The conflict in Europe had not only
spread across the Atlantic and across the Indian
Ocean ;   it had penetrated the Pacific.   In those
waters, however, there was no fighting.   On the
contrary, the French and British explorers and
scientists who discovered or rediscovered Australia
and New Zealand and the multitudinous South Sea
islands established a remarkable tradition of friendly
and courteous rivalry.   ' Des Europeans,' said La
Pérouse, ' sont tous compatriotes à cette distance
de leur pays ' [2]—a lesson Europe still needs to learn
in her dealings with the backward peoples.   But
French and British never forgot that they were
rivals.   Wherever they landed, they left a record
of discovery :   and some day, they hoped, those
discoveries would be followed by that ' occupation '
on which their respective nations could base a valid
claim to sovereign ownership.   That no occupation
was actually attempted was mainly due to distance.
Why embark on such a precarious and costly adventure as the colonisation of Australasia when America

[1] See Pitt's speech of 30 Dec., 1796, on retaining the Cape
and Ceylon in order to checkmate the ' long cherished ' plans
of France ' of undermining our Indian empire and destroying
our Indian commerce.' *War Speeches of William Pitt* (Oxford,
1916), 180.
[2] J. D. Rogers and R. N. Kershaw, *Australasia* in *Historical
Geography of the British Dominions* (Oxford, 1925), p. 25.

was less than half as far ?   When, however, in the
course of events, America was closed, in whole or
in part, to further French or British settlement, the
situation changed.   After 1763 French imperialists,
besides their designs of reconquest and expansion
in America and India, were seriously thinking of
new colonies in Australasia.   De Bougainville set
out for the Pacific in 1766 and Surville in 1769 :
the first had been in Canada, the second at Pondi-
cherry.[1]   And it would have been strange if similar
thoughts had not occurred to British minds after
1783.   Captain Cook and his companions had
already interested public opinion in the South
Seas before the Revolution ; and in 1776 he had
made his third voyage with secret instructions, it
was said, to take possession in the King's name of
any countries undiscovered by other nations.   No
wonder that a French observer declared in 1781
that Cook's mission was to retrieve in another hemi-
sphere the loss of England's Empire in America.[2]
Cook's alleged instructions, however, are apparently
the only evidence that British statesmen were definitely contemplating settlement in the Pacific as
early as 1776 when, after all, the thirteen colonies
had not yet been lost.   But in 1783 and after ?
Certainly the idea was in the air.   Sir Joseph Banks,
for instance, the most eminent of Cook's companions,

[1] Rogers and Kershaw, op. cit., p. 23.
[2] N***, Oeuvres Posthumes, i, 11 (cited by Rogers and Kershaw,
op. cit., p. 44).

had come back full of dreams and schemes.[1] But nothing, it seemed, was going to happen. The British Ministers made no move. Nor did the French. For three or four years the fate of Australasia hung poised between two hesitating governments. And the reasons for their hesitation were probably the same. An Australian colony could not be founded by a stroke of the pen. It needed an elaborate plan. It needed money. Above all, it needed colonists. If Britain was to act first, if Australia was to be British, those colonists had to be found.

They could not be found in Britain in 1783 as easily as in earlier days. The springs of emigration which had fed the thirteen colonies in America were no longer available for the expansion of the 'fourteenth,' still less for the far greater adventure of peopling remote and unknown Australia. Throughout the history of British imperialism the behaviour of the mother-country has been marked by alternate periods of expansion and contraction. And this period immediately succeeding the American Revolution was emphatically a period of contraction. In most Englishmen's minds the result of the Revolution had produced a complex of ideas antagonistic

[1] Though Banks favoured the idea of an Australian colony, he described the coast of New South Wales, on Cook's first voyage in 1770, as 'in every respect the most barren country I have seen.' *Journal of Sir J. Banks* (ed. Sir J. Hooker, London, 1896), 307.

to further colonial enterprise. Adam Smith and Lord Sheffield, from their different platforms, proclaimed that colonies did not pay. What then, asked the business man, could be the use of them ? Others required no economic disputation to convince them of the manifest absurdity of troubling to found colonies which were bound, sooner or later, to bite the hand that fed them and break away. Others, again, assuaged their wounded pride by a studied lack of interest in a field of activity in which their country had so conspicuously failed. Perhaps Britain had lost her colonies *because* they weren't worth keeping ? The British sun, it seemed, might rise again, but not over a colonial Empire. Scarcely anybody dreamed that new British colonies would ever replace the old. There was no Raleigh, no Penn, no Gibbon Wakefield to inspire Englishmen to follow the old quest overseas. Most members of the governing class, indeed, believed at this period that emigration weakened the man-power of the mother-country and was therefore not to be encouraged. Nor was there any impulse of expansion from below. The economic results of the war had been disastrous ; but the tides of emigration from England have not always coincided with the tides of adversity ; and there was no impulse among the classes that suffered most in 1783 to seek a new life in a new world. The British people, in fact, defeated, disheartened, disillusioned, had retired into its island home to nurse its wounds. And if this had been the only effect of the American Revolution on the course of British colonial policy, then indeed the destinies of Canada and Australasia must have been diverted into other paths. But by a singular play of circumstances there were two other effects of the Revolution—quite minor, incidental effects in themselves—which provided, in two very different groups and for two very different reasons, the human material required for the essential first steps in a further process of British colonial expansion.

The first group were the convicts. Transportation was regarded in the eighteenth century as a cheap and simple method of ridding England of her ' undesirables,' and before the Revolution a variety of convicts, most of them guilty only of what would now be considered quite minor offences, were dumped, at the rate of about five hundred a year, in the American colonies, especially those in the south where they could be set to work on the plantations. But already, before 1775, the colonists, obtaining from the negro slave-market all the labour they required, had begun to resent this imposition ; and after 1783, of course, independent America could no longer be used as a British dustbin. Where, then, were the convicts to go ? Gambia, in West Africa, had been tried in the early years of the war ; but since of the seven hundred unfortunates sent there nearly half had quickly died and the rest had disappeared into the bush, this experiment had been abandoned. So the notorious ' hulks,' which were used as a temporary substitute for exile, had become more and more horribly crowded ; and it had long been recognised as a public scandal when, in 1785, Burke in the Commons and Beauchamp in the Lords forced the matter on the Government's attention. But the problem of locality seemed insoluble. West Africa, again suggested, was now finally ruled out on humanitarian grounds. The healthier coast farther south was surveyed and found to be too dry and barren for a settlement. Kaffraria was mentioned—a better thought, but nothing came of it. And all the time Banks' great idea, fully set forth in a letter written in 1783 by one of his fellow-voyagers, James M. Matra, was lying in some departmental pigeon-hole. In 1785 a similar scheme was submitted by Admiral Young. And, at last, in the latter half of 1786, Lord Sydney, the Home Secretary, came to the conclusion, and Pitt agreed, that Australia was the place they sought. They knew next to nothing about it, and the difficulties awaiting a penal colony on a continent in which no Europeans had yet tried to make a home were obviously considerable. No matter : the tiresome question had to be settled ; there was nowhere else for the convicts to go ; and the climate at any rate was said to be tolerable. Thus boldly—almost recklessly it seems now—Captain Philip set sail in the spring of 1787 with over 750 convicts and some 200 marines, and on 20 January, 1788, he landed at Botany Bay, where Banks had botanised. Six days later La Pérouse with a French squadron cast anchor in the same waters ; but, finding himself forestalled, he exchanged civilities with Philip and sailed away. It is, perhaps, too much to say that thus, and by so narrow a margin, the American Revolution had secured Australia for the British Empire. But at least the Revolution by creating the convict problem had brought into being a British settlement that would not otherwise have been attempted at that time. And though, it is true, La Pérouse had no instructions to annex, it is possible that the Australian coast might have been proclaimed French territory. If that, again, had happened, it might well have remained French territory in Britain's generous settlement of colonial issues in 1814-15. And in that case—to carry speculation one step further—New Zealand which was nearly annexed by France, as it was, in 1840 would probably have shared Australia's fate.[1]

Seeley's famous but misleading dictum that ' we seem, as it were, to have conquered and peopled half the world in a fit of absence of mind ' applies more legitimately to the first occupation of Australia than to any other major incident in the so-called (and mis-called) *Expansion of England*. The first occupation of Australian soil by Englishmen was

[1] The documents are in *Historical Records of New South Wales*, vol. i, part 2 (Sydney, 1892). See also Holland Rose, *Life of Pitt*, vol. i, chap. xix ; and Rogers and Kershaw, *op. cit.*, 44-8. Philip moved on to a finer harbour, eight miles north of Botany Bay and there founded his settlement at ' Sydney Cove.'

not, it is clear, the product of any far-sighted imperial design.   In one sense it was an accident in
that it seemed to be the only way of dealing with
an unforeseen domestic emergency.   But was that
all it meant to Pitt ?   He had little, doubtless, of
his father's imperial imagination ; but was he content to examine and reconstruct ' what was left ' of
the Empire without a thought of also making good
by new colonial enterprise what was lost ?   The
records provide no certain answer ; but it is clear
that Pitt did not regard the Australian colony as
limited for all time to a penal settlement.   How
could he ?   Most of the convicts were merely petty
thieves or poachers and condemned to serve the
minimum sentence of seven years.   Provision was
made for their emancipation, and it was certainly
hoped that on recovering their freedom they would
not all attempt the long voyage back to England.
Some of the marines, moreover, had taken their
wives with them.   Might not their children settle
in Australia ?   With this and more than this in
view the Lord Chief Justice had suggested to Pitt
that the establishment of the English judicial system, including trial by jury, would presently be
desirable ' if the colony thrives and the number of
inhabitants increase ' ; and the Act for the creation
and regulation of the settlement provided for a
criminal court on the ground that ' it may be found
necessary that a colony and civil government should
be established.'   Still   more   significant,   Captain

Philip had been appointed Governor not merely of a site for the convicts but of half of all Australia ! ' Our territory called New South Wales ' was defined in his Commission and Instructions as including the whole continent eastwards of longitude 135°, and all islands likewise, off the coast ; and Philip was to take command ' of all towns, garrisons, castles, forts, and all other fortifications or other military works which may be hereafter erected upon the said territory or any of the said islands.' The coast, moreover, was to be explored, and a post was to be established on Norfolk Island to preclude its occupation by a foreign Power. Finally, Philip was to report, ' with all convenient speed,' on the agricultural prospects of the country, since others, besides the garrison, ' may resort thither upon their private occupations . . . desirous of proceeding to the cultivation and improvement of the land ' and should be afforded ' any reasonable encouragement in such an undertaking.' He was empowered, further, to make grants of land and to ' appoint fairs, marts, and markets as also such and so many ports, harbours, bays, havens, and other places for conveniency and security of shipping and for the better loading and unloading of goods and merchandises ' as may be needed. From these instructions, from the very size of the territory annexed, from the evident desire to forestall the French whose expedition was known of in London, it is manifest, surely, that the Government was at least contemplating the possibility of an ultimate colonial expansion far beyond the bounds of Botany Bay. And that this idea was firmly fixed in Philip's mind at any rate is indisputable. He felt himself to be —indeed he was—an Empire builder despite the narrow design and imperfect materials of his immediate task. He had not been more than a few months at Sydney before he was asking for fifty farmers to be sent out with their families ; and, though he made no secret of his initial difficulties, he told the Secretary of State that he had no doubt ' but that this country will prove the most valuable acquisition Great Britain ever made.' [1]

But, if indeed Pitt shared this vision of the future, he was not the man to pursue it with Chatham's fire and energy. He would let it work itself out. He would take no risks. And there, probably, lies the key to what his critics have regarded as the missing of a golden opportunity. For it was not as the site of a penal settlement in the first instance that Matra and Young had recommended Botany Bay. ' I am going to offer an object to the consideration of our Government,' so Matra began his memorial of 1783, ' that may in time atone for the loss of *our American colonies*.' And for this, for the foundation of a second New England, as he had

[1] Philip's Commission and Instructions, *Hist. Rec. of N.S.W.*, vol. i, part 2, pp. 61 and 85. Act, 27 Geo. III, c. 56, *ibid.*, 67. Philip to Sydney (9, vii, 88), *ibid.*, 151. Chief Justice Camden,' Holland Rose, *op. cit.*, i, 439,

pointed out, the requisite human material was also available. Besides the convicts there was another and very different group of British subjects for whom also, and again as a result of the American Revolution, a new home was needed.[1]

The American Revolution, like all Revolutions, was not the unanimous uprising of a whole people. From first to last there was a party in each of the thirteen colonies, larger in some than in others, which supported the British Government. Their enemies called them ' Tories ' or worse names. Their friends called them ' Loyalists.' At the outset they constituted, it is reckoned, about a third of the population ; but, as the war dragged on and Independence came slowly nearer to attainment, the number dwindled. At least 20,000 joined the British armies and fought against their fellow-colonists—a fact which students of the period should remember before they blame too hardly the persecuting spirit of the victors. At the close of the war, their position was unenviable. They were regarded as traitors and outlaws ; their estates were confiscated ; they could not recover their debts. Nor could the British Government, in whose support they had lost all, protect them. All that could be obtained in the Treaty of Versailles was a promise that Congress would earnestly recommend the States to restore the Loyalists' rights and

[1] *Hist. Rec. of N.S.W.*, vol. i, part 2, p. 1.

260 THE FOUNDATION OF CANADA

properties. The inadequacy of this provision was angrily denounced in Parliament; it was on that issue, indeed, that Shelburne's Government fell : but, in view of the situation described in the first of these lectures, it is difficult to justify the abuse with which, amongst others, Lord North and Lord George Germain, with more than the usual effrontery of ex-ministers in opposition, assailed the peacemakers. ' I had but the alternative,' replied Shelburne, ' either to accept the terms proposed or continue the war. . . . A part must be wounded that the whole of the Empire may not perish.' [1] To many Englishmen, none the less, this sacrifice of friends gave the bitterest taste to the cup they drank in 1783. And it was a sacrifice. All the States except South Carolina ignored the recommendation. ' After all,' it was argued, in effect, ' these men had done their best to defeat the American cause. They had helped the enemy to destroy patriots' property in the war. Was it unjust, then, to confiscate theirs ? ' And so the Loyalists—all of them at least that remained stalwart to the end —were ruined. Some of them abandoned their homes and fled the country before the war was over. The rest followed in a stream when the peace brought neither restitution nor protection. From first to last, it is reckoned, over 60,000 left the country. The great majority of them made for the

[1] *Parl. Hist.*, xxiii, 412. For a different view see Lucas, *History of Canada*, 1763-1812 (Oxford, 1909), 217.

nearest patch of soil that was still British—just across the northern border. Some hundreds came to England. Others took refuge in the West Indies.[1]

The British Government did all it could, once the Treaty had been perforce accepted, to pay its debt of honour. Those Loyalists who had crossed into Canada were freely granted lands and food and clothing ; and, after a lengthy examination of claims, the whole body received over three million pounds in monetary compensation—in those days a considerable sum.[2] Public opinion, indeed, could scarcely fail to recognise how valuable, how timely, was this spill-over from the old Empire into the new. These 60,000 were not men who, finding the tide running against them, had modified their opinions or submitted in silence to a change of allegiance. They had clung to their old faith to the bitter end, and suffered all things for their convictions. And, though many of them had been well-to-do professional or business men, they were all ' colonials,'

[1] On the Loyalist question, see C. H. Van Tyne, *The Loyalists in the American Revolution* (New York, 1902), and *The War of Independence* (London, 1929) ; L. Sabine, *Loyalists of the American Revolution* (Boston, 1864) ; A. C. Flick, *Loyalism in New York* (New York, 1901) ; W. H. Siebert, *Loyalists of Pennsylvania* (Columbus, 1905), and other writings ; F. R. Diffenderffer, *Loyalists in the Revolution* (Lancaster Co. Hist. Socy., 1919).

[2] See J. E. Wilmot, *Historical View of the Commission, etc.* (London, 1815), and the Coke MSS. in *The Royal Commission on the Losses and Services of American Loyalists* (Roxburghe Club, Oxford, 1915), with H. E. Egerton's Introduction. Subsistence allowances were paid during the enquiry.

acclimatised, so to speak, to the demands of overseas life, able to endure, as soon they showed, the difficulties and discomforts of pioneering. Here, then, was something that was ' left ' of the old Empire, a human fragment to set beside the territorial ; and, as we have seen, precisely what was needed to strengthen the surviving colonies. And to people new ones ? In Australia ? Was not that Pitt's golden opportunity ? Matra certainly thought so. New South Wales, he wrote, may afford an ' asylum ' where ' those unfortunate American Loyalists . . . may repair their broken fortunes.' ' That the Ministry may be convinced,' he added, ' that this is not a vain idle scheme, taken up without due attention and consideration, they may be assured that the matter has been seriously considered by some of the most intelligent and candid Americans, who all agree that, under the patronage and protection of Government, it offers the most favourable prospects that have yet occurred to better the fortunes and to promote the happiness of their fellow-sufferers and countrymen.' Banks ' highly approved ' the plan and Young reproduced it. A certain Mr. de Lancey was ' active in procuring the consent of many people to go.' Lord Mansfield was interested. And yet nothing came of it all— except the convict settlement. Why ? The probable reason, good or bad, was just distance. A settlement, so isolated and far off, was bound (it may be repeated) to be both hazardous and costly.

Sydney submitted Matra's scheme to Lord Howe at the Admiralty and received a chilling opinion. ' The length of the navigation, subject to all the retardments of an India voyage [does] not, I must confess, encourage one to hope for a return of the many advantages in commerce or war which Mr. M. Matra has in contemplation.' And so, probably, thought Pitt. It might seem legitimate to try the experiment with convicts. If a penal settlement failed, it could be easily abandoned. But to found a colony of Loyalists, already victims of British policy, on the good faith of the British Government, with the promise of its ' patronage and protection '—that was a very different matter. And in view of the desperate difficulties through which Philip and his companions had to struggle, can one blame Pitt's caution ? In any case, only a small minority of the Loyalists would ever have gone to Australia. The direction of the main stream of their migration did not rest with Pitt or any man. Geography decided it. The mass of the Loyalists —probably as much as five-sixths of them—poured of their own motion into Canada because it lay next door—roughly 28,000 into Nova Scotia and chiefly into its sparsely settled mainland area, 3000 into Cape Breton Island, 10,000 into Quebec and mainly into its unoccupied western district up among the Lakes.[1]

[1] Matra's Memorial ; *Hist. Rec. of N.S.W.*, vol. i, part 2, pp. 1-6. Young Plan, p. 11. De Lancey, pp. 8-9. Howe, p. 10.

'The flourishing state of the new settlements,' wrote Sydney as Secretary of State with reference to the Loyalists in Canada, 'affords his Majesty great satisfaction . . . on account of the advantages which the Province in general will derive from so valuable a body of people.'[1] 'That body of English loyalty planted in the West '—so Chief-Justice Smith of Quebec, himself a Loyalist, described them.[2] And Carleton, back again as Governor, declared his wish 'to put a mark of honour upon the families who had adhered to the unity of the Empire ' and carried an Order-in-Council at Quebec providing for an official registry of their names.[3] But no words or titles could do justice to the historic importance of the Loyalist immigration. It was not only an immense accession of strength to those remaining outposts of the Empire, increasing their population at a stroke by at least a third. It began the essential, immediate task of filling up the two great gaps in the chain of settlement between Niagara and the Atlantic. And it provided just the kind of material needed for the further task of expansion to the West. The foundation of modern Canada—of a Dominion bridging North America from ocean to ocean—was laid by the Loyalist

---

[1] *Canadian Constitutional Documents*, 1759-91, ed. A. Shortt and A. D. Doughty (2nd ed., Ottawa, 1918), ii, 808.

[2] *Ibid.*, 1019.

[3] 9 Nov., 1789. The title, ' United Empire ' Loyalists, derives from this.

immigration, and the Loyalist immigration was the direct result of the American Revolution.

Finally, it was the coming of the Loyalists into Canada that forced British statesmen to consider at last the real crux of the whole colonial problem— the political status of the colonists. The newcomers, it was clear, could not be refused in Canada at least as much self-government as they had possessed in their old homes in the thirteen colonies. Ruined through their steadfast devotion to the British Empire, they could scarcely be denied the primary right of British subjects—representative government. And there were questions of expediency as well as of principle. Many of those Loyalists who had entered Nova Scotia and settled mostly in its northern mainland area might have ' had enough of Assemblies '; but all of them felt the inconvenience of being governed from a capital so remote and in those days so inaccessible as Halifax. Nor can the old inhabitants have welcomed the prospect of their votes being swamped by those of the newcomers. But the solution of the difficulty was obvious and quickly adopted. In 1784 the mainland area was made into a separate province with the name of New Brunswick, with its capital at St. John ' the city of the Loyalists,' and with its own system of representative government.[1]

Westwards the problem was more complex. The

[1] Chester Martin, *op. cit.*, 91-2.

case of the little British minority in the province of Quebec which had demanded representative government and English law had been negligible before the Revolution ; but it had now been immensely strengthened both in point of numbers and in moral force. The British population had risen at a stroke from a hundredth to a tenth part of the whole ; and even the irascible Murray, had he still been Governor, could scarcely have described the new ten thousand settlers as ' licentious fanatics ' when they asked for relief from the *régime* of the Quebec Act with its bureaucratic rule and alien laws. Yet how could their just claims be met without violating the equally just claims of the French-Canadians who still out-numbered the British by ten to one ? After prolonged consideration and consultation— the representatives of local opinion ' said all they had to say '—Pitt's Government took the only way out of the *impasse*. They cut the knot by cutting the province in two ; and this, though a rough and ready solution, was at least a practical solution because, as in the maritime area, the majority of the immigrant Loyalists had settled in the unoccupied western part of the province, many of them, indeed, at a greater distance from the centres of government and justice at Quebec and Montreal than that of St. John from Halifax. So the Constitutional Act of 1791 provided for the division of Quebec into Upper Canada (now Ontario) and Lower Canada (now Quebec). In the former English law

was established, in t[...]
was retained. In b[...]
that what was conceded to [...]
not be denied to French—representativ[...] g
ment was instituted.[1]

Very great indeed, then, were the effects of the
American Revolution on the piece that ' was left '
of the British Empire in North America. It con-
solidated that fragment : it stiffened its allegiance
to the imperial connexion : it provided the men
and women needed to give it the strength and
energy to develop and expand : it confirmed and
for a space at least ensured the smooth working
of the old system of representative government
in Nova Scotia ; and, through its offspring, the
Loyalist migration, it extended the system to New
Brunswick and started it in Upper and Lower
Canada. And that was not all. The next and
last lecture will try to show how Pitt and his
colleagues, as they examined the Canadian problem
and framed the measure of 1791, were obliged,
almost of necessity, to formulate a new principle of
colonial policy—a principle which was destined to
become the basis of the Second British Empire.

[1] 31 Geo. III, c. 31. This Act will be further discussed in the
next lecture.

VIII.

THE GREAT EXPERIMENT.

'ALL are on an equality.' So Lord Balfour defined the relationship of the six nations of the British
Commonwealth when he explained to the House of
Lords the meaning of the historic Declaration of
1926. 'All are on an equality. That is the very
essence, as I understand it, of the British Empire.'
And later in the speech he spoke of ' that fundamental equality of status which can be the only
permanent bond between these self-governing por-
tions of the Empire.'[1] To compare those words
with any definition of inter-imperial relations a
century and a half ago is to measure the effects of
the American Revolution on the colonial field of
the Second British Empire. The proceedings of
1926 are a proof that we have learned the lesson of
1783.

There was, of course, no startling novelty in
those proceedings, no sudden conversion. The
secret of the Commonwealth did not flash into
men's minds in 1926. It had long been obvious
to anyone who thought at all about the matter that
British citizens oversea could not remain members

---

[1] *Hansard*, H. of L., lxv, 1332, 1335.

of the same political society as British citizens in the mother-country unless their equality was recognised in practice as well as in principle. It was as palpable an absurdity in the late nineteenth century as in the early twentieth to imagine that Canadians or Australians would be permanently content with an inferior status to that of Englishmen. None the less, 1926 did mark a step forward—a last step. It meant that the last letter of the lesson had been learned. The Dominions, on their side, having been gripped by the Great War and forced to recognise its political logic, realised that the time had come when the principle of equality could and should be applied in practice no longer partially and progressively but wholly and finally. Britain, on her side, agreed. She had made the same response to an ascending series of similar claims; but to this ultimate and highest claim her response was more immediate, more intelligent, more whole-hearted than ever before. It is sometimes *le dernier pas qui côute* : and the significant feature of 1926 was the easy and cordial unanimity with which the assembled statesmen of six nations greeted, not the beginning of a revolution, but the end of an evolution. The Second British Empire, born under black skies in 1783, had come of age in sunshine.

Let us now examine more closely the nature of that saving lesson. It is clear, to start with, from what has just been said, that it was twofold. If the Second Empire was not to repeat the failure of the First, two things were needed. First, a full recognition of *equality in principle* between the colonists and their kinsmen at home. Second, a progressive policy which conceded so much *equality in practice*, stage by stage, as the colonists in their growing and ripening communities required and desired. This does not mean that British statesmen could be expected at the outset or at most of the subsequent stages—either in 1791, or in 1839, or in 1849, or in 1859, or in 1867—to foresee the development of inter-imperial relations to its end, to follow a calculated track, to devise (so to speak) a time-table of concession. That has never been, for good or ill, the British method. The essential requirement of a progressive policy was a recognition of the fact that the political organisation of the Empire was not static but dynamic, that any particular concession at any particular stage was not the last but inevitably led on to the next, and that the process of development could not be halted just because nobody knew where it would end or because somebody thought he knew and did not like it.

The statesmen of the First Empire did not recognise even the first of those two needs. Mercantilism, as we saw in the second lecture, had blinded them. Though the colonists, taking with them across the Atlantic their heritage of English freedom, had begun their new political life with the same system of self-government as England had begun it, and were steadily developing it along the same lines as England had developed it, yet it does not seem to have occurred to the men who made and lost the War of Independence that the ' rebels ' were in principle their equals. Still less, therefore, could they think of putting the principle into practice. All that was needed, they supposed, was to re-affirm and reinforce imperial control and colonial ' dependency.' And, as we also saw, even Chatham and Burke, though they did recognise and loudly proclaimed the principle, took more or less the static view of its application. There would have been no trouble, they declared, if Britain had not tried to tax the colonies. There never would be any, if she would restore just that measure of control and dependency which had been in force before the Stamp Act.[1] Deeper insight was only shown by Adam Smith, and his concrete proposals were impracticable. From nothing less, perhaps, than a Revolution could the lesson have been learned.

The great story of how it was learned awaits its full and proper telling, and the teller of it will not only concern himself with British politics. The achievement confirmed and registered in 1926 was due as much to the foresight, patience, and political sense of overseas statesmen as to any similar virtues in the mother-country. But in this lecture we must confine ourselves to Britain's part in the story ; and, though it will be possible to touch

[1] For the one advance proposed by Chatham, see p. 72 above.

briefly on its cardinal chapter—that stage in the long development, associated with the names of Durham and Elgin, which went far to determine all the rest of its course—our main concern must be the prelude to the story, a prelude in three parts, enacted on the eve and on the morrow of the Revolution and so far detached by subsequent events from all that followed that its significance, like that of some other things that happened in that period, has been overlooked—so much so indeed that it is often said that British statesmen, before the time of Durham at any rate, had learned nothing at all from the Revolution.

The first scene of this prelude is dated 1774 and staged in the House of Commons during the debates on the Quebec Bill. The constitutional clauses of the Bill were being attacked by the Whigs because, as we saw in the last lecture, they did not provide for the establishment of an Assembly. Britons, it was argued, were entitled to British liberty. Were those few hundred of them in Quebec to be deprived of their natural rights for ever because they had chosen to settle in a part of the British Empire mainly populated by Frenchmen? Was the Bill 'meant to be a permanent measure,' North was asked, 'or to be qualified and made temporary by some provision?' If it were granted that the French-Canadians were not yet ready for representative government, ought not the Bill to contain some promise of advancement in the future? At this stage of the argument, Fox said a remarkable thing. ' The principle laid down in the course of these discussions has been this—that *the government of the colony ought to be assimilated as much as possible with that of the mother-country.*' [1]   In that sentence, and especially in the word ' assimilated,' the secret of the true colonial policy broke for a moment through the fog.   For ' assimilation ' implied more than the acceptance of the principle of equality : it implied also its progressive application in practice. It is doubtful, indeed, whether Fox himself realised all it meant.   He may have thought, like Burke, that the progress of colonial freedom could stop short at the measure of self-government enjoyed before 1765 and that to assimilate so far was to assimilate ' as much as possible.'   In any case (to judge from our imperfect reports) he did not enlarge on the principle, nor does it appear to have been ' laid down ' by anyone else in the debate.   All the Government speakers but one ignored it.   North admitted that the Canadians ought to have an Assembly when they were fit for it, and Wedderburn declared that the Bill was ' essentially a temporary one ' ; [2] but neither of them said a word about ' assimilation.'   Only that cynical and crooked politician, Edward Thurlow, then Attorney-General, mentioned Fox's pregnant phrase because he had

[1] Egerton and Grant, *Canadian Constitutional Development* (London, 1907), 88.

[2] Coupland, *Quebec Act*, pp. 100, 108, and note 1.

detected in it an opportunity of amusing himself and the House. ' Do you mean,' he asked, ' to vest the sovereignty of the province . . . in any other place than in the House of Lords and Commons of Great Britain ? Yet, if you follow your assimilating idea, you must do that. . . . Is their money, are their forces, to be applied to support the British Empire ? Are they content that the King, Lords and Commons shall be judges of the drawing forth of those forces and the applying of that money to the protection of the British Empire ? . . . To be sure, it is a grossness—it is making two allied kingdoms, totally out of our power, to act as a federal union if they please and, if they do not please, to act as independent countries.' [1] Thurlow would have been amazed, no doubt, if a vision had been granted him of the British Empire operating in the twentieth century very much on the lines he was deriding. But his logic was sound enough ; and it was only too easy to laugh the imperial secret out of court on its first appearance by simply demonstrating the apparently gross conclusion to which it led.

So the fog closed in again, and in the fog the War of the Revolution was fought out. Of the combatants no new ideas were to be expected. They had begun to fight on the old issue of the ' supremacy' of the British Parliament. They went on fighting because the colonies could only make good their

---

[1] Coupland, *op. cit.*, p. 100.

claim to legislative equality by the disruption of the Empire. And, though it was only by the satisfaction of that claim, by one method or another, that the American Question or the Irish Question could then have been settled, the quarrel over it gave little light for laying the first foundations of a new colonial system. Legislative equality comes at the end, not at the beginning. The old-established population of the colonies, numbering over two millions altogether, the ancient kingdom of Ireland —for those communities the time was ripe or ripening ; but, observe, it is only to-day—when the Second British Empire has endured for a century and a half, when its self-governing peoples oversea number more than twenty millions—that the full legal recognition of legislative equality is being asked for and conceded. And, of course, in 1783, nobody dreamed of asking for it or conceding it in the case of the surviving colonies. How could the little representative assembly in Nova Scotia, or the hundred thousand French-Canadians in Quebec, who had not yet got a representative Assembly, legislate with the same authority and scope as the Parliament at Westminster ? That idea, in itself, was useless for making a new start, for the development of colonies still in political infancy. Nor, indeed—as we saw in the last lecture—did many Englishmen think about colonies at all when the war was over. In fact, the whole Colonial Question would presumably have relapsed into its old pre-war stagnation, if the migration of the Loyalists into Canada had not necessitated a reconsideration of the constitution of Quebec and so forced the political problem to the front again.[1]

The result provides the second scene of our prelude. Its date is 1791. The place is again the House of Commons. And once more a ' Quebec Bill ' is being debated.

The Canada or Constitutional Bill of 1791 might seem at first sight to have been framed in blind imitation of the pre-Revolution system. It established almost exactly the same system of representative government which had creaked along in most of the old colonies. Only two points were new. First, the essential clause of the Act of Renunciation of 1778, forbidding imperial taxation, was solemnly repeated. And this, though obviously wise, was purely negative —a reversion to pre-Stamp Act custom. Secondly, the Act provided for the bestowal of hereditary honours on members of the provincial Legislative Councils or ' Second Chambers.' And this was

[1] For the identity of the conception of inter-imperial relations held by such American leaders as Jefferson, Franklin, Madison, and Wilson before 1776 (e.g. ' All members of the British Empire are distinct states, independent of each other, but connected together under the same sovereign '), with the conception accepted to-day, see McIlwain, *The American Revolution ;* R. G. Adams, *Political Ideas of the American Revolution ;* and W. P. M. Kennedy, *Theories of Law and the Constitutional Law of the British Empire* (an address to the Canadian Bar Association, 1929).

soon recognised to be wholly unsuited to the social conditions of the young pioneer communities of Canada. If that were all, then indeed it could be said that British statesmen had learned nothing from the American Revolution. It would have meant that Pitt, who had shown himself so fresh-minded and so liberal in every other field of imperial politics, had nothing better to offer for this colonial field than Burke's stale prescription. But that was not all : and, if we would discover the true meaning of the Act of 1791, we must look beneath the letter of it to its spirit and intent.[1]

It is clear, in the first place, that in the deliberations which led up to the framing of the Bill the American Revolution was never for a moment forgotten. How could it be ? The Revolution had created an independent Republic next door to the colonies whose fate was now under discussion. The Revolution had produced the new settlers whose claims had precipitated that discussion. From the very outset, therefore, the dominant thought was how to prevent those surviving colonies, when the first reaction from rebellion had cooled down, from following the example of the lost thirteen, as the pessimists, with Turgot's hackneyed dictum on their lips, asserted they inevitably would. ' Good

[1] A clear account of the Act, based on the documents in the Public Record Office, is given in an unpublished thesis by F. H. Soward, a copy of which is in the Rhodes House Library at Oxford. See also the same author's article in *Canadian Historical Review*, v, 314.

policy,' wrote Dorchester, at an early stage of the deliberations, 'requires that we should leave as little for them to gain by a separation as possible. All the advantages offered to Congress for a reconciliation should be reconsidered, and such of them as may now be judged advisable to grant, and are wished for by the Provinces which remain in their allegiance, cannot be granted too soon. That those benefits may have their proper effect, they should be conferred unasked as soon as may be and as flowing spontaneously from the benevolence of Government. It would be unwise to withhold from dutiful obedience what might have been obtained by tumults and rebellion.'[1] And Grenville, who, as Home Secretary, was more concerned with the Bill than any other member of the Government, was exactly of the same opinion. The concessions, he agreed, must be quickly and freely given, not extorted.[2] But what form were they to take? The Loyalists were asking for 'the blessings of the British Constitution.'[3] 'They were born British subjects,' to quote one of their petitions, 'and have ever been accustomed to the government and laws of England. It was to restore that government and to be restored to those laws for which from husbandmen they became soldiers, animated with the hope, even in the most gloomy aspect of public affairs,

[1] *Canadian Constitutional Documents*, 1759-91, 811, note. For the offer to Congress, see p. 118 above.
[2] *Ibid.*, 969.   [3] Petition of 1787. *Ibid.*, 949.

that, should they fail in their attempts to recover their former habitations by a restoration of Your Majesty's government, they would still find a resource in some part of the British dominions where they might enjoy the blessings of British laws and of the British Government.'[1] Now British laws and British government were precisely what Grenville wanted to give them ; for he had come to the conclusion that the primary cause of the loss of the thirteen colonies was ' the want of more resemblance in their constitution with that of Great Britain.'[2] Accordingly, the Act of 1791 established in Canada the representative government which had been withheld in the Act of 1774 ; and it was in the language of the Whig Opposition in 1774 that Pitt summed up the purpose of the Bill when he introduced it in the House of Commons. The Bill, he declared, was ' to bring the government of the province as near as the nature and situation of it would admit to the British constitution.'[3] ' I hope you will agree,' he said in the course of the subsequent debates, ' to give Canada a free constitution in the British sense of the word. . . . As much as possible of a constitution deservedly the glory and happiness of those who live under it and the model and envy of the world should be extended

[1] Petition of 1785. *Canadian Constitutional Documents*, 1759-91, 773.
[2] *The Simcoe Papers* (Toronto, 1923), i, 4.
[3] *Parl. Hist.*, xxviii, 1377.

to all our dependencies.' [1]   And Grenville preached
from the same text to the Lords.[2]

Clearly, then, the policy of 1791, though what it
conceded to the two Canadian provinces and maintained in Nova Scotia and New Brunswick was in
form no more than any of the lost colonies had
enjoyed, was not a mere mechanical continuation of
the pre-Revolution system.   It was making a new
start in a new spirit ; and the essence of that new
spirit was the belief or the hope that British subjects in the colonies would remain loyal to the
imperial connexion if they were permitted to share
' as much as possible ' with British subjects in the
mother-country in the ' blessings ' of the British
constitution.   In other words, the root of the policy
of 1791 was the ' assimilating idea.'   So far, so good.
But did the authors of the Act of 1791 look ahead ?
Did they realise that the principle of assimilation
entailed a progressive policy ?   Or was the system
of 1791 to be no more in actual practice than the
system of 1765, the new spirit to be no more dynamic than Burke's, the new start to be nothing but
a start ?   There is just sufficient evidence to provide an answer to those questions.   We know, first,
that Thurlow, now Lord Chancellor, was as much

[1] *Parl. Hist.*, xxix, 404, 414 ; cf. xxviii, 1377, 1379.
[2] *Ibid.*, xxix, 657.   Cf. Grenville's dispatch to Dorchester,
20 Oct., 1789 : ' The general object of this plan is to *assimilate*
the constitution of that province to that of Great Britain as
nearly as the difference arising from the manners of the people
and from the present situation of the province will admit.'
Can. Con. Doc., 1759-91, 988.

opposed to the 'assimilating idea' in 1791 as he
had been in 1774. But he was not now in North's
Government, he was in Pitt's ; and it is a significant
symptom of the changed atmosphere, of the effects
of the Revolution, that he could no longer dismiss
the idea with a jibe, but, when Grenville asked his
opinion, he reproduced in serious form the argument with which he had amused the House seven-
teen years before. ' If political liberty,' he wrote,
' which is the governing principle of our constitution, be established in a colony, the sovereignty . . .
will also be established there . . . and consequently
independence.'[1] Again the logic was sound, but
Grenville did not flinch from it. And, secondly,
there is a sentence that springs from the debates
of 1791 with the same startling effect as Fox's
sentence from the debates of 1774. The speaker
was Dundas ; and Dundas was no doctrinaire
liberal, very much the contrary : nor was he ex-
hibiting the easy idealism of opposition ; he was
on the point of succeeding Grenville as Secretary
of State and was speaking therefore with some knowledge and responsibility ; and, if no one had been
more stubborn in contesting the claims of the American colonists, no one knew better how to trim his
sails to meet a change of wind. ' We will not
pretend,' said that hard-headed Scot, ' to give
Canada the same constitution as we ourselves live
under. All we can do is *to lay the foundation for*

[1] Thurlow to Grenville, 1, ix, 89. *Simcoe Papers*, i, 5.

the same constitution when increased population and time shall have made the Canadians ripe to receive it.' [1] The requisite ' progressive policy,' the doctrine of ' assimilation,' the second half of the lesson—it is all in those few plain words.

It is not surprising to find a new colonial policy emerging from the shadows of the Revolution. It would, indeed, be far more strange if Pitt and his colleagues, in that decade of new imperial ideas, had learned nothing from the Revolution in that one field of the Empire in which it had occurred. None the less, we must not exaggerate the significance of what was said in 1791. We may take it for granted that neither Dundas not Pitt nor Grenville had any conception of the method by which the Canadians were in due time to acquire ' the same constitution ' as Englishmen at home. Like most politicians, they were content to meet the needs of their own day ; and we can only claim that they did regard the system of colonial government, however vaguely, as dynamic, as progressive. Nor, again, must we misconceive their actual application of the ' assimilating idea.' We must not think of the British constitution of Pitt's day in terms of 1929 or even of 1832. The ' blessings ' of British liberty which the Loyalists asked for and Parliament conceded in 1791 were eighteenth-century ' blessings.' They had nothing whatever to do with Democracy—a word which still and for years to come conveyed

[1] *Parl. Hist.*, xxix, 428.

to conservative public opinion in Britain almost as sinister a meaning as Bolshevism to-day. The constitution which Burke worshipped and which Pitt felt it ' a glory and a happiness ' to live under was a mixed or balanced constitution in which the element of aristocracy was regarded as essential ; and the ' want of resemblance ' in the old colonial constitutions to the British model, in which Englishmen like Grenville detected the cause of the Revolution, seemed to them to lie mainly in their lack of the true British balance. An interesting memorandum, drafted in preparation for the Bill of 1791, almost certainly by a high permanent official in Downing Street, contains this passage : ' In the formation of those governments, while full scope and vigour were given to the principles of democracy by the establishment of a popular representation in their Houses of Assembly, no care was taken to preserve a due mixture of the monarchical and aristocratical parts of the British Constitution.' [1] And it was, as Grenville explicitly declared, in order to make good that lack of balance that the queer idea of converting the Legislative Council into a partly hereditary body was formulated.[2] The Canadian constitution of 1791 was, in fact, as far as the internal government of the provinces was concerned, a sincere copy of the British constitution of 1791—with this main difference, that the

[1] *Can. Con. Doc.*, 1759-91, 983.
[2] *Parl. Hist.*, xxix, 657. See Thurlow's comment, *Simcoe Papers*, i, 5.

Executive in Canada was not to be dependent on the support of the representative part of the Legislature. But on that point again we must be careful not to confuse our periods. There was more ' responsible government ' in Britain after 1782 than there had been in 1781, but not so much as after 1830. Between York Town and the Reform Bill the constitutional principle of ministerial responsibility to the House of Commons rather than to the King was in operation, but it was not yet fully or finally established. And the further step, the modern idea of popular sovereignty, was still inconceivable to all but a handful of Radicals. The Governments of 1782 to 1830 regarded themselves as the masters, not the servants, of the ' people ' ; and they tried to maintain their mastery not by free and open appeals to the electorate but by what was known as ' influence '—by the careful manipulation of interests and classes and individuals, by ' management,' by borough-mongering, by jobbery. When British Tories, therefore, strove to strengthen the Executive in the post-Revolution colonies—when Thurlow, reluctantly accepting the ' assimilating ' policy of 1791, urged that it should be so applied ' as to preserve the greatest degree of habitual influence possible in the executive branch of the government ' [1]—when Governor Milnes in 1800, deploring the growing ' spirit of democracy ' in Lower Canada and the ' independence ' and ' equality

[1] *Simcoe Papers*, i, 5.

of station ' among its inhabitants, suggested schemes for extending ' the influence of government ' [1]— none of these oligarchs was preaching for Canada anything that he did not practice at home. Such was the normal operation of government in Britain in 1791 and for nearly forty years thereafter. A strong Executive, resistance to Democracy—that is what real ' assimilation ' meant.

If, then, from our modern standpoint the colonial policy of 1791 was old-fashioned, it was not re-actionary. The measure of self-government con-ceded to the Canadians was not pushed back from the stage attained in Britain : it was meant to be ' as much as possible ' the same. But it was less, of course, than the more advanced American col-onies had acquired before the Revolution, less than the American Republic now enjoyed, and less than the small Radical minority of Englishmen desired England to enjoy. And Fox, for that reason, was as much ahead of Ministers in 1791 as he had been in 1774. His general doctrine was more whole-hearted. ' The only means of retaining distant colonies with advantage is to enable them to govern themselves.' ' Canada must be preserved to Great Britain by the choice of its inhabitants.' [2] And his particular proposals outran ' assimilation.' He was not now content to give Canada what Britain had.

[1] Milnes' long dispatch of 1 Nov., 1800 (*Can. Con. Doc.*, 1791-1818, 249-55), is as interesting for the light it throws on current political ideas in England as on the situation in Canada.
[2] *Parl. Hist.*, xxviii, 1379 ; xxix, 110.

He would anticipate. He would give Canada what he wanted Britain to have. In some respects, indeed, he was assimilating more to the American than to the British model. A larger assembly, annual or triennial parliaments, an elective second chamber—these were among the amendments he desired to the Bill. But Pitt and Grenville were convinced that the Loyalist settlers, for whom, as we have seen, they were primarily catering, did not desire any novelties from over the border. ' These men,' said Burke, ' have fled from the blessings of American government.' [1] What they wanted was the real British article, old-fashioned maybe but old like Britain, a commonplace thing but their own, a thing they had lost everything else to keep. And that is what they got. For Pitt and Grenville believed that the way to preserve what was left of the British Empire in North America, the way to prevent a second secession, was to meet the challenge of the new American ' liberty ' by boldly setting the old British ' liberty ' beside it.

Such, then, was the contribution of the post-Revolution decade to the solution of the political problem in the colonial field. In spirit, as we have seen, it was right ; but it could only succeed if that spirit were maintained. The young forces of democracy both in Britain and in Canada were stronger than those eighteenth-century statesmen imagined. They would presently break down

[1] *Parl. Hist.*, xxix, 365.

Burke's venerable barriers and upset the historic balance of the constitution. Then the testing-time would come. For Canadians would no longer be content with the ' liberty ' of 1791 when Englishmen had achieved the ' liberty ' of 1832. Colonies and mother-country must advance—at least in the domestic field—more or less in step. In other words, the only hope of the new policy lay in its preserving through the changing years ahead its vital doctrine of assimilation.

The third and last scene of the prelude was staged in Upper Canada and in London. It reached its climax when Governor Simcoe wrote a dispatch from Kingston on 21 December, 1794, and the Duke of Portland replied to it from Downing Street on 20 May, 1795.

John Graves Simcoe, first lieutenant-governor of Upper Canada, was a vigorous, efficient, single-minded soldier who had commanded a Loyalist regiment in the War. Elected to Parliament in 1790 he closely followed the discussions on the Bill of 1791, and as one who knew the Loyalists he was taken into consultation on the operation of the new policy by Grenville and Dundas. The first paragraph of a memorandum he submitted to the latter shows how fully he agreed with the Government's ideas.

' It appears to me [he wrote] that the Colony of Upper Canada in its original form should contain within itself an epitome of those establishments, civil and military, which must gradually but necessarily be extended hereafter as it shall increase in numbers, in political and commercial consequence, and become capable of supporting its own expences or contributing to those of the Empire, and that the utmost attention should be paid that British customs, manners, and principles in the most trivial as well as serious matters should be promoted and inculcated to obtain their due ascendancy to assimilate the colony with the parent state and to bear insensibly all their habitual influence in the support of that British Constitution which has been so wisely extended to that country.'[1]

Simcoe, indeed, had embraced the doctrine of assimilation with an almost naïve enthusiasm. In the interval between his appointment and his departure from England his mind was full of schemes for the detailed reproduction of English life in Canada. He wrote to Sir Joseph Banks pleading for assistance to establish ' the Arts and Sciences.'[2] He begged a grant from Grenville to buy books for the foundation of a public library. He contemplated ' a literary Society.'[3] He agreed with ministers as to establishing the Anglican Church, complete with bishop [4]—a factor in ' assimilation ' which was one day to lead to trouble. But it was in its politics above all else, in ' the infinite superiority of constitution,' that the new colony was to excel its American neighbours and rivals and so ' become the means of preserving all the transatlantic dominions of Great Britain by exemplifying the felicities of its laws and government.'[5]

[1] *Simcoe Papers*, i, 27.   [2] *Ibid.*, 18.   [3] *Ibid.*, 49.
[4] *Ibid.*, 252.   [5] *Ibid.*, 50.

When, therefore, he entered on his office and, in the autumn of 1792, addressed the little party of pioneers gathered in a log-built house near Niagara for the first meeting of the Representative Assembly of Upper Canada, it was on their new constitution that he laid most stress.   It was, he told them, ' the very image and transcript of the constitution of Great Britain '[1]—an exaggeration certainly, but no less certainly sincere ; and three weeks later from ' Navy Hall ' he wrote in sanguine terms to Dundas of ' the experiment that is now making whether the British Government cannot support itself by its own superiority in this distant part of the world.'[2] Wholly absorbed by this great ambition, gloriously confident of its achievement, he busied himself for the next two or three years in the multifarious tasks of creating a new society—in cutting roads and building bridges and laying out townships—with an unresting energy and a practical capacity that earned him the gratitude of the infant colony and a high place in the ranks of colonial founders.

Meanwhile a series of events in far-off Europe were coming to a climax which was to affect the life of the whole civilised world.   In the autumn of 1792 the French Revolution entered on its phase of active aggression, and at the beginning of 1793 France and Britain were at war.   So ended Pitt's great decade of peace, retrenchment, and reform.

[1] *Journal of Upper Canada Assembly*, 15 Oct., 1792.
[2] *Simcoe Papers*, i, 252.

All along the line of British politics reaction settled down for a generation.

Among other immediate results was the junction in 1794 of the moderate Whigs with the Tory majority under Pitt, and in the consequent re-shuffling of portfolios their leader, the Duke of Portland, succeeded Dundas as Secretary of State. It was to a new chief, therefore, that Simcoe wrote that winter to report the progress of his work, and he naturally took the opportunity of explaining the main idea of the policy he had been charged to carry out. 'A principle,' he began, ' on which I have considered this government as most wisely established and which I have never lost sight of in its administration has been to render the Province as nearly as may be a perfect image and transcript of the British government and constitution.' In pursuance of that aim, he reported, he had divided the Province into Counties and appointed Lieutenants over the more populous of them, with power to appoint or recommend magistrates and to nominate officers of the militia. By this means, as he had told Dundas, he hoped ' to promote an aristocracy,' essential to a true assimilation and unattainable by the method adopted in the Act of 1791. Further, he was now proposing to elevate the towns of Kingston and Niagara into cities, each with a mayor and corporation of six aldermen, justices of the peace *ex officio*, and ' a competent number of Common Council '—all on the English model. Again, we must not misconceive the position. Simcoe, of course, was quite untainted by liberal ideas. His policy was not a democratic policy. On the contrary, he saw in it ' the best method gradually to counteract and ultimately to destroy or to disarm the spirit of democratic subversion in the very country which gave it existence and growth.' And how ? ' By exemplifying a better practical system of internal government than the separate States of America can possibly demonstrate, and setting forth the superior advantages which a union with Great Britain presents to this Province.' [1] And so he closes with one more confession of the faith that is in him. ' I am happy to believe,' he says, ' that nothing but want of reasonable support and systematic arrangement will prevent a successful termination of *the great experiment*—whether the enjoyment of the principles and forms of the British Constitution internally and a common interest and union externally may not attach for ages this commanding Province to the side of Great Britain.' [2]

We may smile at Simcoe's simple and single mind. The almost meticulous assimilation he desired seems to us now as absurd as it was impossible.

[1] The concession of the British municipal system was doubtless intended to preclude the development in Canada of the more independent and equalitarian forms of local government which had grown up in the thirteen colonies. See D. McArthur, *American Historical Review*, xxi, 432, and C. Van Tyne, *Causes of the War of Independence*, 19-20.

[2] *Can. Con. Doc.*, 1791-1818, 196-204 (Kennedy, *Documents of the Canadian Constitution*, 234-6).

The Revolution may have bred a conservative temper in what was left of British North America; the Loyalists, especially, might be quite content with the constitution of 1791; they might tolerate, for many years, an irresponsible Executive; some of them might even have ' had enough of Assemblies ';[1] but nowhere in the New World could the structure of society be built up on the class-divisions and vested interests of the old. None the less, the core of Simcoe's policy was sound. The social oligarchy of eighteenth-century England, the dukes and squires and parsons, could no more be reproduced in Canada than their castles and manors and churches; but the essentials of the English political system, the roots of English liberty in parliamentary and local government, these could be transplanted into Canada, and, if allowed to grow as they had grown in their mother-soil, would enable the Canadians in due course to create their own social life in their own way to suit their own conditions. And though Simcoe might wish to entwine them with ' habitual influence ' and a new-born aristocracy, he did sincerely desire to transplant those roots of English liberty. That is what assimilation, first and foremost, meant to him.

He imagined, no doubt, when he wrote those confident sentences, that the Duke of Portland would as a matter of course accept the principle expressed in them as his predecessor had accepted it. The

[1] Chester Martin, *op. cit.*, 92.

full current of anti-Jacobin reaction had not yet reached him in his inland province far beyond the Atlantic. He was still thinking in terms of 1791— the ' blessings ' of British Liberty, ' the glory and happiness ' of the constitution. Not so the Duke of Portland. Like too many other Englishmen, he had been frightened by events in Paris into the belief that British liberty was not so blessed after all : there was too much of it. On receipt of Simcoe's dispatches, therefore, he at once administered a sharp rebuff. ' I should be wanting in the duty I owe to my station,' ran the ducal missive, ' if I were not unequivocally to state it as my opinion that neither the plan of creating Corporations nor that of establishing Lieutenants of Counties is at all eligible in the present situation of Canada.' And he went on to argue that, so far from ' filtering down his direct power ' by any devolution of self-government, ' every kind of authority that is not inconsistent with the constitution given to the Province, ought to be concentrated ' in the Governor's hands. As to ' Corporations and separate Jurisdictions of all sorts,' ' we permit ' such institutions ' to continue here '—in England !—' only because they already exist and are interwoven with other parts of the government.' They are ' means and instruments of independence.' After this angry onslaught on the local liberties of England, the source and mainstay of all her broader freedom, it is not surprising to find that the Duke makes short work

of the principle of assimilation in the colonies. ' I
have entered personally more at large into those
proposed measures,' he writes, ' because I observe
that your adoption of them arises from an idea that
by assimilating the modes of the government of the
Province to the modes of the government of England, you will obtain all the beneficial effects which
we receive from them : whereas to assimilate a
colony in all respects to its mother-country is not
possible, and, if possible, would not be prudent.' [1]
. . . The curtain falls. Our prelude is over, leaving
us where we were when it began. For Portland's
conception of British citizenship in 1795 at home or
overseas is not Pitt's or Grenville's in 1791. It is real
reaction this time. We are back in 1774. It might
be Thurlow speaking from his old place beside Lord
North. The principle of assimilation is once more
rejected, and as summarily and contemptuously as
if it were still a wild-cat idea of some Radical in
the opposition, as if Tory ministers had never even
looked at it, as if the American Revolution had
never happened.

That is why the colonial policy of 1791 must stand
by itself, in its own peculiar setting of the decade
between two Revolutions, a prelude to the story of
the Second British Empire, not its opening chapter.
In every field of British policy, indeed, the effects
of the American Revolution were countered in some
degree by the effects of the French Revolution,

[1] *Can. Con. Doc.*, 1791-1818, 204-5 (Kennedy, 237-8).

but in colonial policy they were practically cancelled out. What the statesmen of 1791 had learned from the tragedy of their own time and its aftermath seems to have been wiped from their memory; and their successors of the next generation, when the long hard years of the Napoleonic War were over and the frost of reaction had at last begun to break, had to face the colonial question quite afresh, to make another start, to learn for themselves anew what the American Revolution had to teach.[1]

The hope of maintaining a Second British Empire in North America may well have seemed fainter in the 'eighteen-thirties' than in 1791. The political problem was more difficult, the situation more dangerous. The difficulty and the danger were most acute in the mainly French province of Lower Canada with which, since the constitutional issue was there distorted and confused by race-antagonism, we will not now concern ourselves; but in the British provinces they were serious enough. The ardent 'loyalism' kindled by the American Revolution had had fifty years to cool in. If the second generation of Loyalists were still devoted to the imperial connexion, their devotion was now flavoured with a new ingredient of personal or party interest; and, if they still tolerated the eighteenth-century system

---

[1] As late as 1829, Sir G. Murray (Colonial Secretary, 1828-30) repudiated the 'assimilating idea.' 'I think,' he said in the House of Commons, 'that the analogy between this country and the Canadas must be given up.' *Parl. Hist.*, xxi, 1333.

of 1791, it was largely because it enabled them to retain a dominant position in their provincial politics, to appropriate the confidence of the Governor, to monopolise appointments on the Executive and Legislative Councils. They corresponded, in fact, to those Tories in Britain who were quite content with the unreformed Parliament and the system of ' habitual influence '; and until the Napoleonic Wars were over and the forces of progress began to move again on both sides of the Atlantic, the political position in Canada was still roughly ' assimilated ' to that in the mother-country. As long as the ' Family Compact ' maintained their majority in the Assembly, there was little to make Canadians in general feel politically inferior to Englishmen under those forty years of Tory Government in England.[1] But by 1830 the population had increased more than thirty-fold since 1791 ; many of the new immigrants were Americans from over the border, some of them were Radicals from England ; and a Reform party had grown up which had secured in 1824 a small, and in 1828 a great, majority at the polls. Just at the same time the party tide was turning at last in Britain. In 1830 the Whigs came back, and, consolidating their position by the Act of 1832, set themselves to put in operation their big

[1] The passage in the *Durham Report* on the ' Family Compact ' will be found in Lucas' edition (Oxford, 1912), ii, 148. The rejoinder by the Committee of the Legislative Council is printed in Kennedy, *Documents*, 470. For sound comment, see A. Dunham, *Political Unrest in Upper Canada*, 1815-36 (London, 1927), 34-5.

programme of long-overdue reforms. For Britain it was a new era. Industrial democracy was not yet in, but the landed oligarchy was out. In Canada, on the other hand, it seemed as if the eighteenth century was still alive. For, while at Westminster, Wellington and Eldon and the rest had retreated to the Opposition benches, the Tories were still glued to the Government benches at Toronto ; and, so far from introducing any programme of reform, the Government continued in its reactionary course in defiance of the electorate. The contrast was crudely clear. Where now was the promise of 1791 ? Could anyone say in 1835 that the Canadian Constitution was ' a perfect image and transcript ' of the British ? Was not the measure of self-government conceded to Canadians manifestly less, even in the field of their own local affairs, than that enjoyed by Englishmen ?

The Whig statesmen in Britain were no less convinced than their beloved and now almost ' canonised' leader had once been that the colonial problem could only be solved by an extension of self-government. Why, then, did not Lord John Russell revive Fox's ' assimilating idea ' ? Why did he not show at least as much faith in ' British liberty ' as Pitt or Grenville ? Because assimilation now meant more than it had in their day. There could now be no assimilation worth the name which did not add Responsible to Representative Government. And Russell, though worlds away in spirit from

Thurlow, shrank from this second stage of assimilation for precisely the same reasons as Thurlow had
shrunk from the first. Responsible Government
seemed to him ' incompatible with the relations
between the mother-country and the colony.' [1]   If
the Governor ' is to follow the advice of his Council,
he is no longer a subordinate officer but an independent sovereign.' [2]   ' Sovereignty,' ' independence,'
those were Thurlow's words, and to Russell as to
Thurlow—though with far more excuse, since
Russell was faced with an immediate practical
dilemma which Thurlow had only vaguely foreseen—the prospect to which they pointed seemed
' a grossness.' He stiffened his back. Responsible
Government was refused. The deadlock was complete. And since it was not to be expected that
nineteenth-century Canadians would long remain
content with the representative government enjoyed
by eighteenth-century Americans before the Revolution—since Russell's view of colonial status was
apparently the same static view as Burke's—the
Second British Empire began to drift fast towards
the same tragic ending as the First. In 1837, in
both Canadian provinces, the extremists broke out
in armed rebellion ; and, though those risings were
ill-organised, feebly supported, and easily suppressed, their significance was unmistakable. Quite
certainly, sooner or later, if British statesmen did

[1] In his speech on the Ten Resolutions in 1837 : *Parl. Hist.*,
xxxvii, 1249.
[2] Russell to Thomson, 14, x, 39 ; Kennedy, *Documents*, 522.

not change their policy, there would be another
Revolution in North America.

Russell, as we know, was right in his logic but
wrong in his interpretation of it. Assimilation was
the only method of keeping Canadians and Englishmen within one political society—whatever the end
to which it might logically lead. The might and
majesty of Britain could no longer determine the
political allegiance of Britons oversea. Force had
been tried in 1775 and would never be tried again.
The alternative was consent. And consent was unattainable except on a basis of equality. To refuse
equality, therefore, meant another schism. To concede it, as stage by stage it was required, would
doubtless lead to difficulties about ' sovereignty '
and ' independence,' but it might not necessarily
end in schism. No logical disputations on the
meaning of words, no text-books of political science,
no Austinian theory, could ever compel the Second
British Empire to break up unless it wanted to.

Durham had more faith than Russell in the power
of liberty to bind as well as to loose. The greatness
of the *Durham Report* lay not only in the clearness
with which it restated the doctrine of assimilation
but also in the courage with which it faced the
consequences of its application. ' Follow out con-
sistently the principles of the British Constitution.'
' Administer the government on those principles
which have been found perfectly efficacious in Great
Britain.' ' More of equality, of freedom, and of

local independence.' ' It is difficult to understand
how any English statesman could have imagined that
representative and irresponsible government could
be successfully combined [in a colony]. . . . To
suppose that such a system would work well there
implies a belief . . . that Englishmen renounce
every political opinion and feeling when they enter
a colony or that the spirit of Anglo-Saxon freedom
is utterly changed and weakened among those who
are transplanted across the Atlantic.'[1]   That language has an authentic, a familiar sound.   It might
almost be Burke's voice, breaking the silence of
sixty years to expound to another generation the
meaning of an Englishman's political inheritance.
But Durham was bolder in practice than Burke.
He was not content to assimilate the liberties of
Canada to those of Britain in the field of domestic
government alone.   Reviving Chatham's wisest contribution to the colonial problem of his day, he
recommended yet another step in assimilation—
national government as well as responsible government.   Learn from ' the experience of the two
Unions in the British Isles.'   Let the disjointed
colonies of British North America be united to
' form a great and powerful people, possessing the
means of securing good and responsible government
for itself.' ' Raise up for the North American
colonist some nationality of his own.'[2]   The imagination and the courage of these appeals leave Burke

[1] *Durham Report*, ii, 79-81, 277-8.   [2] *Ibid.*, 308-9, 311.

behind.   They are not expounding an old tradition, they are prophesying a new age.   Was Durham himself, indeed, aware how potent was the spirit he evoked, the spirit of nationality ?   Did he realise all that was implied by ' a great people ' able to secure the kind of government it wanted ?   Do not his actual proposals suggest that Durham's conception of colonial policy was static too ?   He would take a long step forward, but there he would stop —seemingly for ever.   Clinging to the shreds of Mercantilism, he would have the Imperial Parliament still control the colonies' external trade.   Beguiled by Gibbon Wakefield's attractive theories, he would keep their public lands also under imperial management.   And, as seemed more naturally a matter of course in his day, the colonies would leave their relations with foreign states entirely in the hands of the mother-country.   ' A perfect subordination on the part of the colony on these points is secured by the advantages which it finds in the continuance of its connexion with the Empire.'[1] Take these proposals out of their context of principles and aspirations : isolate Durham against a Canadian background ; and it might well appear that, in the circumstances of a later age, his imagination was almost as constricted as Burke's.   But re-read the whole Report, bearing in mind that its object was to recommend the immediate steps required at the time and to persuade British public opinion,

[1] *Report*, ii, 282.

whatever its party colour, to adopt them : remember that Burke's whole mind and temper were Conservative, and Durham's Radical : recall his career in British politics, and especially his part in framing the Reform Bill, and especially the fact that ' Radical Jack ' was the only statesman who refused to regard the Bill from the static viewpoint of ' Finality John ' ; and then it becomes very hard to believe that Durham was legislating for eternity, that he contemplated ' a great people ' fulfilling its national destiny inside the boundaries he marked out so precisely for his day, that he supposed that that old eighteenth-century word, ' subordination,' could be retained indefinitely in the vocabulary of the Second British Empire. And, in any case, these questions had no importance at the time. What mattered then was the unanswerable case which Durham made for giving the Canadians an equal power with Englishmen to fashion and control their own government. To concede the principle that *the people* should be masters of their own destiny—there lay the greatest contrast between the thought of 1839 and the thought of 1775 or 1791 : and by that concession —irrevocable, once made—the future of the Second British Empire was determined.[1]

As every one knows, the case for Responsible Government presented in the *Durham Report* did not convince Russell, still less his Tory successors.

[1] The question of ' finality ' is well discussed by C. W. New, *Lord Durham* (Oxford, 1929), 508-10—a biography at last worthy of its subject.

Only the second part of Durham's advice was implemented : the two Canadas were united as the first step to a wider combination. The more vital, the more immediately needed concession of Responsible Government had to wait till Durham's brother-in-law, Lord Grey, was at the Colonial Office, and the final confirmation of it in practice till Durham's son-in-law, Lord Elgin, was Governor of United Canada. And if, out of the little company of British and Canadian statesmen, to whom the success of the Second British Empire has been mainly due, one man may be selected to rank as high as Durham, and possibly even higher, that one must be Elgin.[1] It was not only his personality, his practical capacity for dealing with men and things, his unusual bravery. In his intellectual grasp of the colonial problem he went deeper and farther than anyone had gone before and as deep and far—in general theory at least—as anyone has gone since; and his contribution to its ultimate solution was the requisite sequel and complement of Durham's. If Durham had been right to look mainly at the present, Elgin was equally right to look mainly at the future. He brushed aside the limitations which Durham had set in his day, and which Grey was still setting, to the process of assimilation. Before they had had time to harden into a permanent code of inter-imperial relations

[1] For recent appreciations see J. L. Morison, *The Eighth Earl of Elgin* (London, 1928); Kennedy, *Lord Elgin* (London and Toronto, 1926); and Chester Martin, *op. cit.*, chap. v.

or to be sanctified by a tradition which might have
been as difficult to break as Burke's, he declared
outright that, till the process of assimilation reached
its end in the ' maturity and full development ' of
the colonies, their relationship with the mother-
country could never be static. He denied any
logical or lasting validity to the hypothesis that ' a
line of demarcation between the questions with
which the Local Parliaments can deal and those
which are reserved for the Imperial authority could
be drawn.' [1] He could even leap forward seventy
years and more and ' contemplate a time " when
it may be expedient to allow the Colonists to elect
their Governors," while Great Britain would be
" represented in the colony by an Agent. . . . If
your Agent were well chosen and had a good status
I am not sure but that the connexion might be kept
up under such an arrangement quite as well and
as profitably for England as under the present." ' [2]

[1] T. Walrond, *Letters and Journals of Elgin* (London, 1872),
114. Elgin, of course, was not denying that such a division
could not be roughly maintained in practice—as it has been till
our own day.

[2] Chester Martin, *op. cit.*, 318. Mr. Martin has done a service
to all students of the subject by printing this very significant
passage hitherto omitted from the published versions of the
dispatch of 23 March, 1850.—The Report of the Imperial Conference of 1926 on Inter-Imperial Relations declared that the
Governor-General in a Dominion was the representative of
the Crown and of the Crown alone, and was no longer ' the
representative or agent of His Majesty's Government in Great
Britain' (p. 16). It also suggested that, in view of this change
in the position of the Governor-General, the system of personal
inter-communication between the various Governments needed

The crucial point was that the colonies should never feel that there was anything in that connexion ' to check the development of healthy national life.' [1] ' You must renounce the habit of telling the Colonies that the Colonial is a provisional existence. You must allow them to believe that, without severing the bonds which unite them to Great Britain, they may attain *the degree of perfection and of social and political development to which organised communities of free men have a right to aspire.*' [2]

This faith in the future was something of a portent in 1850 ; but it was spreading fast in Canada, largely owing to the unmistakable sincerity with which Elgin preached it. The conversion of Britain was a slower business. Elgin carried all liberal opinion with him as regards the actual policy of the day—the unequivocal grant of full responsible government in local affairs—but most Englishmen still shook their heads over the future. The famous dispatch from which some quotations have just been made was written partly in reply to the speech which Lord John Russell, now Prime Minister, had recently delivered in the House of Commons. In that speech he declared that Responsible Government had been introduced in Canada and would be maintained. In the choice of his advisers the Governor ' will act

to be supplemented (p. 27). Among the steps taken to meet this need was the appointment in 1928 of Sir William Clark to act at Ottawa as Agent of the British Government with the title of ' High Commissioner.' See p. 142 above.

[1] Kennedy, *Documents*, 590.   [2] *Ibid.*, 584.

strictly according to the rule that has been adopted here.' But he did not confess himself converted from the views he had held a decade earlier when he was Colonial Secretary : he paid no tribute to Durham ; his nearest approach to an admission of surrender was his statement that a long conversation he had held with Mr. Baldwin, the Canadian protagonist of Responsible Government, had resulted in ' nearly entire agreement.' And at the very end of the speech he betrayed the fact that, despite all that had happened since the *Durham Report*, despite all Grey and Elgin had done, he was still obstinately clinging to the same stony, logical ground on which he had taken his stand before the Canadian Rebellions. The continued extension of self-government to the colonies, he very plainly hinted, would inevitably lead to the rupture of their links with Britain.[1]

The most encouraging retort to the academic pessimism of the British Prime Minister came from the man who was now, except that he shared his leadership with a French-Canadian colleague, virtually the first Prime Minister of Canada. ' Have you read the latter part of Lord John Russell's speech ? ' Baldwin asked Elgin. ' For myself, if the anticipations therein expressed prove to be well-founded, my interest in public affairs is gone for ever.'[2] But the new process of assimilation could never have been set so confidently and steadily on

---

[1] *Parl. Hist.*, cviii (1850), 551, 550, 567.
[2] Kennedy, *Documents*, 584.

its course if Englishmen had not shared Canadian hopes, if Elgin had not felt like Baldwin. As it was, for Elgin and for all those English friends and acquaintances for whom, as he put it, his faith proved ' catching ' because it was sincere, the biggest obstacle had been removed. Thurlow's bogey had been exorcised. Incantations about ' independence ' had lost their spell. The Great Experiment—it was Elgin's phrase as well as Simcoe's—could now suc- ceed because in Britain as in Canada there were men who realised that freedom and unity are, in their deepest meaning, two aspects of one political ideal, and that there can be no stronger communion than a ' free association ' of equals.

To return, for the last time, to our main theme— what was the influence of the American Revolution in shaping this decisive chapter in the story of the Second British Empire ?

It was, unquestionably, a great influence—at least as great half a century after the Revolution as on its morrow, as great in 1839 or 1849 as in 1791. No length of time, indeed, could weaken the most immediate and most certain effect of the American tragedy, namely the determination of all Englishmen that never again would they fight a civil war on the colonial issue. Dull-witted reactionaries might still talk about ' our colonies ' in the nineteenth century in much the same temper as that of 1774 ; but they no longer thought of combating colonial aspirations with penal laws and bayonets. Pessimistic Liberals of Russell's type did not dream of enforcing their static policy. 'We can give the colonies no more liberty,' they said in effect. 'If they must have more, we must separate and go our own ways: but we will never quarrel about it. "Since there's no help, come, let us kiss and part."' To the optimists, on the other hand, the ever-present memory of the schism of 1783 was a constant incentive to thought and deed. Inaction would be as fatal as wrong action. Only by thinking out their positive policy and whole-heartedly applying it could they hope to justify their faith.

Nor, secondly, was the Revolution only a salutary memory of the dead past. It was a living fact. It was permanently embodied in the American Republic. And the American Republic lay side by side with Canada, sharing the same continent with the 'fourteenth colony,' a perpetual example of successful revolt, a standing temptation to every Canadian malcontent. Almost of necessity, therefore—till Durham and Elgin had cleared the air and opened a new horizon—revolution lurked in the background of Canadian politics, suffusing a sense of instability and insecurity, exciting dangerous hopes and unscrupulous ambitions. The idea of force had been abandoned by the Englishmen who had lost the American War, but not by the colonists who lived next door to those who had won it. It may almost be said, indeed, that the rising of the Radicals of the Left in Upper Canada in 1837 could not have occurred in any other continent. Those new rebels against the British Crown were lured into their mad adventure not only by the example of the old rebels over the border but also by the hope of winning their sympathy and support. ' Disaffection exists in many other countries as well as here,' wrote Elgin, twelve years later, of less excusable sedition among Tories of the Right ; ' but this is the only country in the world where rebellion is the resource always present to the minds of place-hunters—where to threaten the *ultima ratio* is not considered an impudence even, far less a crime.' And he ascribed this ' peculiarity ' first and foremost to the contiguity of the United States.[1]

There was a still graver peril to the Second British Empire in the joint effects of North American history and geography. Only the hot-heads in Canada were thinking of an open rupture in those critical days of '37 or '49. But every Canadian, however sober and however ' loyal,' was being subjected, year after year, to a steady strain pulling at his reason if not at his heart, dragging his eyes reluctantly southwards, forcing him to think that the destiny of his country must lie outside the British Empire. This strain was the contrast between American progress and prosperity and Canadian backwardness and poverty. Presenting itself, as Durham said, ' in respect to every sign of

[1] J. L. Morison, *Eighth Earl of Elgin*, 108.

productive industry, increasing wealth, and progressive civilisation,' this mortifying contrast was one of the dominant refrains that ran through the *Report*. ' It is a singular and melancholy feature in the condition of these Provinces that the resources rendered of so little avail to the population of Great Britain are turned to better account by the inhabitants of the United States.' ' On the American side, all is activity and bustle. . . . On the British side of the line, with the exception of a few favoured spots where some approach to American prosperity is apparent, all seems waste and desolate.' Every one is bound to feel that there must be ' something wrong to have caused so striking a difference in progress and wealth between Upper Canada and the neighbouring states of the Union.' [1] Nor was the contrast economic only : it was political too. The United States had already made themselves a powerful, self-reliant, expanding nation, while British North America remained a string of disconnected provinces in which the mere thought of nationhood or a national destiny seemed hardly possible. And, of course, the contrast, economic or political, pointed straight back to the parting of the ways in 1783. Success had come to those who broke away from the Empire ; failure, it seemed, to ' what was left.' How long, then, could Canadians be expected to resist the pull ? How long could the Great Experiment endure ? Must not the very founda-

[1] *Report*, ii, 211, 201, 212, 185.

tion on which it rested, the love of British liberty, be steadily sapped and weakened ? Many Canadians, reported Durham, had been induced by that grievous contrast with conditions in the South, ' in despair of obtaining such benefits under their present institutions, to desire the adoption of a Republican constitution or even an incorporation with the American Union.'[1] By Elgin's time this danger had materialised. The introduction of Free Trade in Britain—reproducing, as we saw in our fifth lecture, in its effect on the colonies the converse of the old Mercantilism[2]—had spread ruin among Canadian corn-merchants ; and the policy of race-equality and conciliation, embodied in a Franco-British coalition ministry and favoured by Elgin, had aggravated the bitter discontent of the ' anti-Gallican ' minority in Lower Canada. In 1849 a manifesto was signed by several hundred leading British-Canadians at Montreal, advocating a friendly separation from the Empire as a preliminary to fusion with the United States.[3]

In such drastic fashion the success of the Republic drove the lesson of the Revolution home. It may be that Durham and Grey and Elgin would have interpreted the lesson aright if no British colonies had survived in North America, and if they had had to deal, say, with Australia alone. It may be that they would have recognised the supreme rightness

[1] *Report*, ii, 261.   [2] See p. 177 above.
[3] For the economic crisis, see Kennedy, *Lord Elgin*, chap. v ; Martin, *op. cit.*, 314-18 ; and Morison, *op. cit.*, chap. iv.

of the ' assimilating idea,' in principle, on its own merits. But would they have embraced it with such ardent conviction, would they have applied it so quickly and boldly, would Elgin, above all, have faced so frankly all its ultimate implications, if the Revolution had not fought and triumphed on adjacent soil and if the Republic had not presented just across the border its contrast, its invitation, its alternative ? It is more than doubtful. In 1849, as in 1791, British liberty was the only card which Britain could play against American liberty with any hope of winning the game ; but in 1791 she had played it guardedly, without looking far ahead, without considering all it meant, whereas in 1849 it was practically forced from her hand. And why this change ? Because in 1791 the United States was a young and weakly child, not expected by supercilious Englishmen to grow very big or indeed to live very long, while in 1849 it was an adult nation, fast advancing to a place among the great powers of the world. That, surely, was the main reason why Durham's language was more generous than Simcoe's, why the latter dreamed of a ' commanding province ' and the former of a great Canadian nation.

' No large community of free and intelligent men [runs a famous passage in the *Report*] will long feel contented with a political system which places them, because it places their country, in a position of inferiority to their neighbours. The colonist of Great Britain is linked, it is true, to a mighty Empire. . . . But the influence of the United States surrounds him on every side and is for ever present . . . the influence which a great nation exercises on the small communities which surround it. . . . If we wish to prevent the extension of this influence, it can only be done by raising up for the North American colonist some nationality of his own ; by elevating those small and unimportant communities into a society having some objects of a national importance ; and by thus giving their inhabitants a country which they will be unwilling to see absorbed even into one more powerful.'[1]

Surely, too, it was the contrast, the rivalry, of the United States, with the memory of the Revolution for its background, that, more than all else, inspired Durham's candour in demanding real assimilation in the *form* of government—apart from the question of its *scope*—and inspired Elgin's courage in applying it. Nor was there only a fuller understanding of the card that was played in 1849 ; the intrinsic value of it had, as it happened, been enhanced since 1791. The rival ' liberties ' no longer stood on the same ground of comparison. One had changed, the other had not. In Britain a great step forward had been taken. Not only was Representative Government more truly representative, more honest, and more popular. Still more important, Responsible Government, the key to the smooth working of the British Constitution because it harmonises legislature and executive, had now become clearly recognised and firmly established. The new American Constitutions, on the other hand, had passed through their experimental stage ; they

[1] *Report*, ii, 310-12.

had stiffened, as it were, in their mould. And since in the States that mould was virtually a copy of the old pre-Revolution system, and since the Federal Government had been deliberately framed on the old principle of separating the executive from the legislature, separate they remained at the risk, it seemed, of constant friction or even deadlock. It was possible, therefore, for the champions of British liberty in 1849 to take higher ground, to commend their candidate not merely because it was British, still less because it retained the ' influences ' and ' balances ' of the Old World, but because it was— in their eyes at any rate—a better political instrument and one, furthermore, which suited the New World at least as well as the Old because—so at least they could assert—it enabled public opinion to control the whole field of government more quickly, more smoothly, and more continuously than its rival. Elgin, as Durham before him, respected the American nation, and he liked, and was liked by, the American people ; and it was in no cavilling or jealous or resentful spirit that he proclaimed his belief in the superior merits of British constitutional practice in the nineteenth century. ' The fact is,' he wrote in 1850, ' that the American system is our old Colonial system with, in certain cases, the principle of popular election substituted for that of nomination by the Crown. . . . There is the same absence of effective responsibility in the conduct of legislation, the same want of concurrent action between the parts of the political machine. . . . Now I feel very strongly that, when a people have been once thoroughly accustomed to the working of such a Parliamentary system as ours, they never will consent to revert to this clumsy irresponsible mechanism.'[1] With as definite a purpose, then, as Simcoe's and with a partiality for British ways as strong as Pitt's or Burke's, but with longer vision and surer confidence than eighteenth-century statesmen could attain, Elgin preached and practised the creed that saved the Second British Empire. ' I have been possessed . . . with the idea that it is possible to maintain on this soil of North America, and in the face of Republican America, British connexion and British institutions, *if you give the latter freely and trustingly.*'[2]

It is manifest, then, that the course of the new colonial policy was largely determined by those two interwoven factors—the example of the American Revolution and the rivalry of the American Republic. To that extent the losing of the thirteen British colonies meant the saving of their successors. To that extent the Revolution prevented its own repetition.

We have now traversed all the fields of the First British Empire that survived the disaster of 1783, and we have observed in each of them a process of change, a birth of new ideas, an attempt at

[1] Kennedy, *Documents*, 586-7.
[2] Chester Martin, *op. cit.*, 321.   Italics not in the original.

reconstruction or readjustment, which, though in some cases their natural development or fuller understanding were obstructed and long delayed, were all in being within a few years from the end of the War of Independence. And the farewell thought that suggests itself at the end of the journey is this. Was there only an American Revolution? Was there not a revolution or something very like it in Britain, in Ireland, in India, in the Afro-Caribbean system—an Imperial Revolution which broke out at successive points between 1775 and 1793? It was not the American Colonies only that were ripe for it. In almost every limb the great ungainly creature which Mercantilism had born and bred was distempered and decaying because it could no longer live on Mercantilism alone. The inevitable convulsion came first in America. Coming first, it caught British statesmanship unprepared and gave it no time to throw off its inveterate habits of mind and think out a new philosophy for the colonial field. And so in America the requisite revolution could only be achieved by schism. But, coming first, the American Revolution enabled or rather compelled British statesmanship to ' examine what was left ' before it was too late, to discover and provide the new nourishment which the imperial system needed, to advance from the ideas of the eighteenth towards those of the nineteenth century, and thereby in all the other fields, and in a new colonial field as well, to achieve, sooner or later, a revolution without schism.

APPENDIX.

A NOTE ON THE QUEBEC ACT.

THE opinion that the Quebec Act of 1774 was a wise measure, stated in Lecture VII and at greater length in *The Quebec Act* (Oxford, 1925), has been sometimes questioned in Canada, but is held by most historians in England. Lecky speaks of the Act as marking 'an epoch in the history of religious liberty.'[1] 'It stands out,' says Sir G. O. Trevelyan, 'as the work of statesmen and not of policemen.'[2] Grant Robertson calls it 'a welcome contrast to this parody of statecraft,' and Carleton 'a true soldier and statesman.'[3] Egerton regards the Act as 'a wise measure' in its treatment of French-Canadian nationality.[4] Similar opinions are expressed by Lucas,[5] Basil Williams,[6] and G. M. Trevelyan.[7] Among American

---

[1] *History of England in the XVIIIth Century* (London, 1913 ed.), iv, 299.

[2] *American Revolution* (London, 1913), ii, 75-6.

[3] *England under the Hanoverians* (London, 1912), 259.

[4] *American Revolution* (Oxford, 1923), 118; *Short History of British Colonial Policy* (London, 1910), 243-6; *History of Canada* in 'Historical Geography of British Dominions' (Oxford, 1923), 10-16; *Cambridge Modern History*, ix, 743. Egerton condemns the annexation of the hinterland.

[5] *History of Canada*, 1763-1812 (Oxford, 1909), chap. ii.

[6] *Life of Chatham* (London, 1913), ii, 300.

[7] *British History in the Nineteenth Century* (London, 1922), 56.

historians the Act is defended by Van Tyne[1] and Alvord.[2]

Those who contest the wisdom of the Act, either in itself or in its application, regard it as having needlessly reversed ' the progress made towards a sane working arrangement ' between the two races, and so stiffened French-Canadian nationalism that it has never been able to fit itself as smoothly as might be wished into the life of Canada as a whole. In other words, there was a better alternative policy. What was it ?

(1) As to religion, it is generally agreed that complete toleration was wise and that the legalisation of tithes was a reasonable implementation of the pledge in the Treaty of Paris.

(2) As to law, no ' progress ' had been made in practice. The legal system of the province was in confusion.[3] It is not suggested that the whole of the French-Canadian Law ought to have been suppressed. Opinion as to whether Carleton was right or wrong in rejecting the concession in commercial law must depend on the view taken of the dangers of the war-period and of the purpose of the Act as a whole. But would concession on that one point have appeased the critics of the Act at the time or afterwards ?

(3) As to the constitution, it is agreed that a wholly Protestant Assembly was unthinkable ; and would not an Assembly, which, while admitting Roman Catholics, was so ' rigged ' as to put them in a minority (as recommended, for instance, by the Board of Trade in 1769) have inevitably

---

[1] *Causes of the War of Independence* (London, 1921), 401-7.

[2] *Mississippi Valley in British Politics* (Cleveland, 1917), ii, chap. viii.

[3] See W. P. M. Kennedy, *Constitution of Canada*, 48 ; W. S. Wallace, *Canadian Historical Review*, vi, 220.

intensified race-antagonism ? [1] French-Canadians would scarcely have accommodated themselves to ' British liberty ' on those terms. The only tolerable Assembly must surely have been ' representative,' i.e. predominantly Roman Catholic ; and this, though it had been permitted to the French of Grenada,[2] was not yet acceptable either to the British minority in the province or to public opinion in Britain. Even Fox refused to assert that an Assembly was ' expedient ' ; he was only ' inclined to think ' so.[3]

But there are wider considerations. When a weak or ' subject ' nationality exhibits a morbid self-consciousness, is it not mainly due to a fear that its freedom and perhaps ultimately its existence are in danger ? If that is so, is there any other cure than to convince the patient that his fears are groundless ? And can that be done otherwise than by giving him complete liberty and genuine equality, holding nothing back, imposing no compromises or concessions, but only hoping that, when assured of his freedom, he will freely choose to make them ? Such ideas, though they may not always be ' practical politics,' are widely held by those who have been impelled by recent events to study the history and problems of nationality and nationalism in Europe and

[1] In chap. iii of his *Empire and Commonwealth*, the most valuable contribution to Canadian History of recent years, Professor Chester Martin extols the Board's policy as a consistent attempt to apply to Quebec the system adopted in Nova Scotia. But was not the problem of nationality far less difficult in Nova Scotia than in Quebec, owing to the relative smallness of the French population, especially when it had been reduced by the expulsion from 8000 to 2000 ? Note that in May, 1768, Masères, writing from Quebec, opposed an Assembly ' which all fear here will increase the confusion,' quoted from Brit. Mus. Add. MSS. 35915, f. 280 ; by Alvord, *op. cit.*, ii, 228, note 420.

[2] C. C. S. Higham, *English Historical Review*, xli, 366.

[3] Egerton and Grant, *Canadian Constitutional Development*, 88.

elsewhere. If they are right, were not the authors of the Quebec Act building better than they knew ? May not Carleton and North, innocent as they were of modern ideals and only trying to enable the French-Canadians (in Murray's words) to ' get the better of every national antipathy to their conquerors,' have really laid the foundation on which alone an *ultimate* race-harmony could be established ? And, if the results (as is often said) have so far been disappointing, may it not have been due not so much to the Quebec Act as to a continuing fear that the freedom it gave was insecure ? There were some grounds for anxiety—memories of the attitude of the British minority after 1763, the transformation of that minority into a growing majority by the development of Upper Canada, and the various projects of ' anglicization ' on foot between 1791 and 1840. No one would wish to justify the perversities of the French-Canadian ' extremists ' ; but, if Papineau and his friends did harm to Canada, so in their way did men like Herman Ryland and Jonathan Sewell. If the purpose of the Quebec Act policy was an unequivocal and permanent toleration of French-Canadian nationality, it might almost be said that it did not really begin to operate till the period of Confederation, and that was not very long ago.

On the narrower questions—the motive of the Act and its immediate effect—further argument is, perhaps, redundant, in view of the inadequate evidence. There can be no question that the news of the ' Boston tea-party ' of 16 December, 1773, and the decision to take penal measures made Carleton's whole-hearted policy more attractive to the North Government. But it may be worth while to recapitulate the following points. (1) That the settlement of the question was delayed till 1774 may have been due, apart from its complex character and the mass of paper-work devoted to it, mainly to hesitation to override the

British commercial interests and their champions in the City. Note the ' loop-hole ' and the subsequent instructions to Carleton. (2) The evidence educed by Alvord [1] to prove that the principles of the Bill were decided on before the end of January, 1774, seems conclusive. (3) Between 1763 and 1774 the renewal of war by France and Spain as soon as it suited them was rightly regarded in England as certain. As it was, Choiseul's re-arming of France and his revival of French imperialist designs in America very nearly led to war in 1770. Intrigue in Canada was feared, and there was a rumour of a French conspiracy in 1768. An armed rebellion on the part of the American colonists, on the other hand, was not seriously or immediately expected, especially after the repeal of the Stamp Act, nor was it dreaded overmuch by the soldiers who habitually underrated the military capacity of the colonists. Whatever Carleton said *post eventum*, did he desire to conciliate the French Canadians from the outset only or principally in order to use them as a check on the ' independent notions ' of New England ? [2]

Lastly, as to the immediate effects of the Act—how much of its effect on the *habitants* was due to its actual provisions and how much to American misrepresentation of them ? And is it possible, after weighing all Coffin's evidence, to be certain as to what proportion of the *habitants* took any particular view ? The effect of the Act on the clergy and the *seigneurs*, on the other hand, is beyond doubt ; and there are surely strong reasons for believing that this loyalty was

[1] *Op. cit.*, ii, 235-6.
[2] The affirmative answer to this question is forcibly urged by Martin, *op. cit.*, 114, etc. In view of the sentence quoted by Martin (*op. cit.*, 109), from Knox's *Thoughts on the Late Act* (p. 28), the second footnote on p. 117 of the writer's *Quebec Act* should be corrected.

' the decisive factor '[1] in the retention of Canada within the Empire.

Quot homines, tot sententiae may be, as Professor Kennedy suggests,[2] all that historical science can achieve on the subject of the Quebec Act. And it is not, it need hardly be said, in any dogmatic spirit, still less for the sake of idle controversy, that the present student of the general history of the British Empire has defended his own *sententia*. If agreement is ever to be attained, it can only be through the contribution of all candid opinions to the common stock.

[1] W. P. M. Kennedy, *op. cit.*, 69.   [2] *Ibid.*, 70.

INDEX.